The Origin and Meaning of Courtly Love

To my father

Roger Boase

THE ORIGIN AND MEANING
OF COURTLY LOVE

A critical study of European scholarship

MANCHESTER UNIVERSITY PRESS

ROWMAN AND LITTLEFIELD

© Roger Boase 1977

Published by
Manchester University Press
Oxford Road, Manchester M13 9PL

UK ISBN 0 7190 0656 2

USA
Rowman and Littlefield
81 Adams Drive, Totowa, N.J. 07512

US ISBN 0 87471 950 x

Produced by offset lithography by
UNWIN BROTHERS LIMITED
The Gresham Press, Old Woking, Surrey, England
A member of the Staples Printing Group

Contents

List of plates

Foreword

The question of the nature and origin of medieval courtly love is not only a perennially fascinating problem of scholarship, but is also, or should be, a matter of wider sociological and cultural concern. It is true that some recent scholars have sought to prove that there is no problem at all—that the whole thing is a chimaera, the invention of later critics. But in that case what forces within Western European culture hatched that chimaera? I myself belong to a generation for whom such books as C. S. Lewis's *The Allegory of Love* and Denis de Rougemont's *L'Amour et l'Occident* were, when we were undergraduates, a stimulus and a revelation. One may no longer agree with their arguments, but surely they illuminated something that we otherwise might have missed. If they were right much of Western art and poetry, our conventions of courtesy and courtship, even our presuppositions as to the respective roles of the sexes in society, were the products of a specific cultural and historical experience. It was because we were still living within its shadow that the problem of defining its exact nature was so important and so difficult. Now, a quarter of a century later, we find these same conventions, and particularly the presuppositions about sexual roles, increasingly under challenge. This in itself highlights the problem, and gives it a renewed and yet more topical significance.

The reader in search of a compass bearing in a region where so many divergent charts have been offered him will find in Mr Boase's careful and always fair-minded scholarship what he most needs.

JOHN HEATH-STUBBS

Preface

This work grew out of a study of Courtly Love in fifteenth-century Spanish poetry; I felt it necessary to investigate the European background to the subject, but originally planned to do no more than write a brief review of scholarship. However, I soon realised that a chronological survey failed to do justice to the wealth of material, most of which had never been systematically studied. I therefore decided to attempt, as best I could, to classify and to assess the major trends in Courtly Love scholarship from the sixteenth century onwards. There are, almost certainly, some relevant critics whose names have inadvertently been omitted, and there are many critical works which might have been discussed in more detail. I hope, however, that this book will be useful to those working on courtly literature in any of the languages of medieval and Renaissance Europe, and that it will, by clarifying the issues involved, contribute to the debate on this important but perplexing element in European culture.

I should like to thank those individuals who have made this work possible. My supervisor, Professor A. D. Deyermond, first inspired me to undertake this research through his own interest in the subject. His teaching will remain an example to his students. He has always made himself available to answer my questions; his support and patient guidance have been a constant source of strength. Without his help and interest this work would not have been possible. Professor Sir E. H. Gombrich has shown me great kindness. His discussion introduced me to ideas that a lifetime of research would not have revealed. John Heath-Stubbs has given me much of his valuable time, and allowed me the privilege of listening to his encyclopaedic mind. He has had a profound influence on my work. I am grateful to Professor J. F. Burke, Dr A. J. Close, Dr L. Close, Dr B. Jeffery, Dr I. R. Short, Professor J. E. Varey and Professor K. Whinnom for their critical comments; to Dr R. M. Walker for his seminars, which I attended in the first year of my research; and to Dr J. H. M. Taylor for some useful suggestions. I am also grateful to Dr J. A. Abu-Haidar for correcting mistakes in the transliteration of Arabic words. I should like to thank the staff members of the British Library, Senate House Library, Westfield College Library and the Library of the Warburg Institute for having assisted me in obtaining the books which I required. I should also add that I am deeply indebted to A. S. Forster, J. M. N. Spencer, and R. H. Offord, whose sympathy and co-operation have made the publication of this book possible. Above all, I wish to thank my father for having communicated to me his love of poetry, and for giving me constant encouragement and advice. My real debt and gratitude to him and my supervisor can never be expressed.

I must emphasise that I alone am responsible for the conclusions reached in this work and for any faults in the argument. In no way do they reflect upon my friends and teachers.

List of Abbreviations

AESC	Annales. Économies—Sociétés—Civilisations
AKML	Abhandlungen zur Kunst.-, Musik- und Litteraturwissenschaft
AnFi	Anuario de Filología
AnMed	Annuale Mediaevale (Pittsburgh)
AnMus	Anuario Musical (Barcelona)
AMid	Annales du Midi
And	Al-Andalus (Madrid and Granada)
AR	Archivum Romanicum
Arab	Arabica, Revue d'études arabes (Leiden)
BARB	Bulletin de l'Académie Royale de Belgique (Classe de Lettres)
BCSS	Bollettino del Centro di Studi Filologici e Linguistici Siciliani
Bel	Belfagor (Messina and Florence)
BGPTM	Beiträge zur Geschichte der Philosophie und Theologie der Mittelalters (Munich)
BH	Bulletin Hispanique (Bordeaux)
BHS	Bulletin of Hispanic Studies
BJR	Bulletin des Jeunes Romanistes (Strasbourg)
BJRL	Bulletin of the John Rylands Library (Manchester)
BRAE	Boletín de la Real Academia Española
BYUS	Brigham Young University Studies (Provo, Utah)
BZRP	Beihefte zur Zeitschrift für romanische Philologie
CCMe	Cahiers de Civilisation Médiévale
CEC	Cahiers d'Études Cathares (Arques)
CFMA	Les Classiques Français du Moyen Âge
CH	Clásicos Hispánicos
CHR	Catholic Historical Review (Washington)
CL	Comparative Literature
CN	Cultura Neolatina
Crit	Critique. Revue générale des publications françaises et étrangères (Paris)
Criterion	The Criterion (London)
CS	Les Cahiers du Sud
CSSH	Comparative Studies in Society and History (The Hague)
CUP	Cambridge University Press
DA	Dissertation Abstracts
ELH	English Literary History (Baltimore)
EstRom	Estudis Ròmanics (Barcelona)
Fi	Filología (Buenos Aires)
FMLS	Forum for Modern Language Studies (St Andrews)
ForIt	Forum Italicum (Buffalo, N.Y.)
FR	French Review
FS	French Studies
GRM	Germanisch-Romanische Monatsschrift
Her	Hermaea: Germanistische Forschungen (Halle)
His	Hispania (Madrid)
HR	Hispanic Review (Philadelphia)

HSRL	Harvard Studies in Romance Languages
HUSNPL	Harvard University Studies and Notes in Philology and Literature
JA	*Journal Asiatique*
JAF	*Journal of American Folklore*
JAL	*Journal of Arabic Literature*
JNES	*Journal of Near Eastern Studies*
JS	*Journal des Savants*
LR	*Les Lettres Romanes* (Paris)
MA	*Le Moyen Âge*
MAe	*Medium Aevum*
MAeM	*Medium Aevum* Monographs
MedS	*Mediaeval Studies*
Mes	*Mesures* (Paris)
MH	*Medievalia et Humanistica*
MLN	*Modern Language Notes*
MLR	*Modern Language Review*
MP	*Modern Philology*
MRo	*Marche Romane* (Liège)
MUP	Manchester University Press
N	*Neophilologus*
NBL	Neue Beiträge zur Literaturwissenschaft
NMi	*Neuphilologische Mitteilungen*
NRFH	*Nueva Revista de Filología Hispánica* (Mexico City)
OUP	Oxford University Press
P	*Poétique* (Paris)
PMLA	*Publications of the Modern Language Association of America*
PQ	*Philological Quarterly*
PsR	*Psychoanalytic Review* (New York and Baltimore)
PRF	Publications Romanes et Françaises
PUF	Presses Universitaires de France
R	*Romania*
RABM	*Revista de Archivos, Bibliotecas y Museos* (Madrid)
RDM	*Revue des Deux Mondes*
RF	*Romanische Forschungen*
RFE	*Revista de Filología Española*
RGand	*Romanica Gandensia* (Ghent)
RIL	*Rendiconti dell'Istituto Lombardo, Classe di Lettere, Scienze Morali e Storiche* (Milan)
RJ	*Romanistisches Jahrbuch*
RKP	Routledge & Kegan Paul Ltd
RLit	*Revista de Literatura*
RLLO	*Revue de Langue et Littérature Occitane*
RLR	*Revue des Langues Romanes*
RMAL	*Revue du Moyen Âge Latin*
RML	*Revue du Monde Latin*
RO	*Revista de Occidente*
RoN	*Romance Notes*
RPFP	*Revue de Philologie Française et Provençale*
RPh	*Romance Philology*
RR	*Romanic Review*
RUB	*Revue de l'Université de Bruxelles*
S	*Symposium*
SCSML	Smith College Studies in Modern Languages, new series
SM	*Studi Medievali*

SP	*Studies in Philology*
Sp	*Speculum: a journal of mediaeval studies*
Th	*Thought* (Fordham University Quarterly)
TLS	*Times Literary Supplement*
TR	*La Table Ronde*
Trad	*Traditio*
UCPMP	University of California Publications in Modern Philology
UMPLL	University of Michigan Publications. Language and Literature
UMS	University of Missouri Studies
UNCSCL	University of North Carolina Studies in Comparative Literature
UNCSGLL	University of North Carolina Studies in the German Languages and Literatures
UNCSRLL	University of North Carolina Studies in Romance Languages and Literatures
UPPRLL	University of Pennsylvania. Publications in Romanic Languages and Literatures
YCGL	*Yearbook of Comparative and General Literature*
ZFSL	*Zeitschrift für französische Sprache und Literatur*
ZRP	*Zeitschrift für Romanische Philologie*

Ailas! tan cujava saber
d'amor, e tan petit en sai!
Bernart de Ventadorn

God cannot be seen apart from matter, and He is seen more perfectly in the human *materia* than in any other, and more perfectly in woman than in man.
Ibn Arabī

Introduction

The term *amour courtois* was coined by Gaston Paris in an article on 'Lancelot du Lac: Le Conte de la Charrette' in 1883.[1] Since then Courtly Love has been subjected to a bewildering variety of uses and definitions, and has even been dismissed as a fiction of nineteenth-century scholarship.[2] In the last decade the notion, ascribed to Charles Seignobos or to C. S. Lewis, that love, in the modern sense of the word, is 'une invention du douzième siècle'[3] has been repudiated as pre-posterous by a number of critics, including Peter Dronke. The 'courtly experience' is not, according to Dronke, confined to the courts of medieval Europe, but 'might occur at any time or place' (Dronke, 1965–66, p. xvii).

In view of the present uneasiness about the use of the term, three points should be made in its defence. First, medieval love poets con-sciously wrote within a literary tradition, inspired by a particular ideal of 'true love' which motivated their conduct: Provençal poets spoke of *verai'amors*, *bon'amors* and, above all, *fin'amors*, words which find their counterparts in other Romance languages.[4] Secondly, the study of this social and literary phenomenon was not initiated by Gaston Paris: Courtly Love became a subject for critics when, in the Renaissance, it was superseded by new modes of thought and expression. Many theories on the medieval love lyric are much older than is commonly supposed. Thirdly, most critics since the sixteenth century have shared the con-viction that modern European poetry begins in twelfth-century Provence, and that the concept of love implicit in troubadour poetry is utterly different from that which was expressed by the poets of ancient Rome:

In general, the Greeks and Romans, not unlike the Chinese, regarded love as a sickness, as soon as it overstepped the bounds of that sensual pleasure which was regarded as its natural expression. This attitude is still more inimical to passion than the almost pathological reprobation of sex which was that of patristic Christianity.[5]

Mario Equicola, writing at the very end of the fifteenth century, drew attention to the novelty of the sentiment propagated by the troubadours (Equicola, 1525, fols. 3–4). Thomas Rymer, the first English critic to recognise their importance, maintained, in 1693, that 'all our Modern

Poetry' comes from Provence (Rymer, 1693, p. 120). Since the troubadours did not appear to be constrained by the need to imitate classical models, they were to prove a useful weapon in the campaign against Neoclassicism: in the early years of the nineteenth century they were proclaimed the initiators of 'le goût moderne' and the harbingers of Romanticism. Allowing for the fact that every age has its own vision of the Middle Ages, it is evident that all these critics were discussing the same phenomenon.

The theories could have been arranged differently. They might, for example, have been divided into the 'traditionalist' school of thought, on the one hand, and the 'individualist' school of thought, on the other. Exponents of the former would tend to argue that Courtly Love was rooted in a popular and anonymous oral tradition, whereas exponents of the latter would take the view that it was elaborated by a group of literate and highly individual poets. This division of opinion has remained a feature of the study of the medieval vernacular lyric since the late eighteenth century, when German pre-Romantic scholars differentiated *Naturpoesie*, judged to be the authentic voice of the people, from *Kunstpoesie*, the artificial creation of a sophisticated élite.[6] The chief disadvantage of employing this system of classification as an organising principle is that it introduces aesthetic prejudices which are an impediment to the understanding of *amour courtois*. Furthermore, the majority of critics agree that Courtly Love was the product of a court environment, and that, especially in its initial stages, it was far from being a collective or uniform doctrine.

The controversy over the question of popular and learned (or literary) influences is linked with another polarising issue: the theory of Arabic origins. According to Menéndez Pidal, a representative of the 'traditionalist' school of thought, the strophic Arabic *zajal*, like the *cantica Gaditana* of Roman times, was an expression of the popular genius of Andalusia. He thus favours the theory that a Hispanised Arabic culture contributed to the formation, in southern France, of Courtly Love.[7] European scholars have, on the whole, been reluctant to concede the possibility that the troubadours might have been indebted to the lyrical tradition of the Arabs. Nationalism, a sentiment unknown to those who participated in the cosmopolitan culture of medieval Europe, and the belief that Western civilisation is the sole heir of Graeco-Roman culture, have made it difficult to view the problem dispassionately. Islamic scholarship is given credit for having served as a medium for the transmission of Hellenic philosophy, mathematics and science, but it is assumed not infrequently that Islamic society was a passive or dead transmitter and that, particularly in the sphere of poetry, the Arabic contribution to the West was negligible. The Hispano-Arabic thesis is, admittedly, only one of a number of theories on Courtly Love, but it seems to me to be of central importance.

After much deliberation it became clear that the best way of handling my material was to draw a distinction between theories of origin and theories of meaning. This distinction may be faulted for its artificiality, since it is almost impossible to discuss the problem of how Courtly Love originated without first defining what the term means. This system of classification is nonetheless justifiable on heuristic grounds. Theories of origin are divided, according to the conclusions reached, into seven sub-categories: (1) Hispano–Arabic, (2) Chivalric–Matriarchal, (3) Crypto–Cathar, (4) Neoplatonic, (5) Bernardine–Marianist, (6) Spring Folk Ritual, (7) Feudal–Sociological. Theories of meaning include the theories of those critics who are principally concerned with the critical analysis of Courtly Love or who question the validity of the concept. Theories in this category are divided into five sub-categories: (1) Collective Fantasy, (2) Play Phenomenon, (3) Courtly Experience, (4) Stylistic Convention, (5) Critical Fallacy.

In Chapter I scholarship on Courtly Love and the troubadour movement is studied chronologically from the sixteenth century to the present day. Strict chronology is broken at various points where an author's later works are discussed or where it has been found necessary to mention certain minor works related to a particular theory. In Chapters II and III the features of the theories are briefly listed, and the arguments for and against each are given as objectively as possible. The features express, in a condensed and abbreviated form, the main lines of argument in a given theory. This method of presentation inevitably introduces an element of distortion or simplification, but it is useful for purposes of argument. In a work of this kind it is impossible to arrive at any definitive conclusions. The reader who disagrees with the Conclusion is therefore invited to form his own on the basis of textual analysis and in the light of further research. Appendix I discusses the etymology of two words associated with Courtly Love: *trobar* and *amor hereos*; Appendix II draws attention to some parallels which can be established between Arabic and European literature in passages defining the paradoxical nature of love. The bibliography covers the major works to date on the subject, but it does not cover editions or critical works on individual poets.

NOTES

1   Paris, 1883: References in text and footnotes to works included in the Bibliography
    are normally confined to the author's name and short title or date of publication. It
    would perhaps be more accurate to say that Paris rediscovered or popularised the
    term *amour courtois*. The only medieval precursor of the term traced by Jean Frappier
    was *cortez'amors* in a poem by Peire d'Auvergne (*fl.* 1138–80), *CCMe*, II (1959), 137.
    Amor cortes occurs in the thirteenth-century *Roman de Flamenca*; see Martin, p. 1 n.
    Elizabeth S. Donno discovered three instances of the phrase *courtly love* in the poem
    'Orchestra' (1575) by Sir John Davies (sts 5 and 50); see Donaldson, 1970, p. 163 n.
2   Robertson, 1962, pp. 391–503; Robertson, in Newman, 1968, pp. 1–18; Donaldson,
    Ventures, V, 2 (1965), 16–23; Benton, in Newman, 1968, pp. 19–42. See below,
    pp. 47–8, 111–12.
3   Seignobos (1854–1942), possibly under the influence of Paget, 1884, claimed that
    amour courtois was 'a new sort of feeling' (Seignobos, 1939, p. 156). See Lewis, 1936,
    p. 4.
4   G. B. Gybbon-Monypenny, 'Lo que buen amor dize con rrazon te lo prueuo', *BHS*,
    XXXVIII (1961), 13–24; G. Sobejano, 'Escolios al *Buen Amor*', *Homenaje . . . Dámaso
    Alonso*, III (1963), pp. 431–58; F. Márquez Villanueva, 'El buen amor', *RO*, III (1965),
    269–91; Brian Dutton, '"Con Dios en Buen Amor"'. A semantic analysis of the title of
    the *Libro de buen amor*', *BHS*, XLIII (1966), 161–76, and '*Buen Amor*. Its meanings and
    uses in some medieval texts', in '*Libro de Buen Amor*' *Studies* (London: Tamesis, 1970),
    pp. 95–121; Jacques Joset, 'Le *bon amors* occitan et le *buen amor* de Juan Ruiz,
    Arcipreste de Hita. Refléxions sur le destin d'une expression *courtoise*', in *Actes du
    VIème Congrès International de Langue et Littérature d'Oc et d'Études Franco-Provençales*
    (Montpellier, 1971), II, pp. 349–68, and '*Buen amor* en las literaturas hispánicas
    posteriores a Juan Ruiz', a paper read at the fifth Congreso de la Asociación Inter-
    nacional de Hispanistas (Bordeaux, September 1974). Little research has been
    undertaken on *fin' amors* in other Romance languages. Pedro Manuel Ximénez de
    Urrea, one of the last of the Spanish troubadours, referred to *fino amor*: 'El amor
    qu'es fino amor / ningún galardón procura, / sino alegrar la tristura / con ser la causa
    mayor' (*Cancionero delas obras de dõ Pedro mãuel de Vrrea* [Logroño: Arnao Guillén de
    Brocar, 1513], fol. 40r).
5   Alan M. Boase, *The Poetry of France, 1400–1600* (London: Methuen, 1964), p. xx.
    'Romantic love or Courtly love are perhaps the usual expressions, though in the
    modern journalese which infects our speech these terms, no doubt, have today
    different associations, "courtly" evoking a quaint or even empty social etiquette, and
    "romantic" the tawdry bohemianism which Flaubert once satirized in his Emma
    Bovary. In a different guise, these ideas, that of a love which in terms of a special
    aristocratic code of rules becomes itself the principle of noble action, of *service* to the
    loved one—and in second place that of "the world well lost", of an all-absorbing
    passion which can know no rule but its own consummation—both are present in the
    chivalric world of the Troubadours'. (*Ibid.*, p. xx.)
6   Bertoni, 1939; Bec, 1969, 1310–15. The dividing line between popular and courtly
    is often hard to define, because courtly themes enter the popular lyric, whilst court
    poets incorporate popular material in their compositions. For the study of Courtly
    Love in the popular Spanish lyric see Aguirre, 1965.
7   Menéndez Pidal, 1941; see also Monroe, 1970, pp. 254–6.

Chronological survey of Courtly Love scholarship

1   1500–1800

In sixteenth-century Europe chivalric and sentimental romances were immensely popular amongst a growing book-reading public. Such devout persons as Teresa of Avila, Ignatius Loyola and Juan de Valdés confessed that in their youth they had spent many idle hours engrossed in this deliberately archaic literature. In court circles the traditions of the troubadour lyric persisted well into the sixteenth century, although they were modified by new aesthetic and sentimental ideals.[1] Scholars, on the other hand, tended to despise medieval literature as unworthy of serious consideration. Montaigne, for example, referred to *Lancelot du Lac*, *Amadis* and *Huon de Bordeaux* as a 'fatras de livres à quoy l'enfance s'amuse'.[2] It was unexpectedly in Italy, the least 'medieval' of countries, that scholars first took an academic interest in medieval vernacular literature. This research was motivated by an upsurge of interest in the history of the Romance languages, coinciding with the first publication of Dante's *De vulgari eloquentia* in 1529;[3] by the transference to Italian literary practice of the humanist principle of *imitatio*; and by an increasing awareness of the differences separating the literatures of different countries and historical periods.

Before the sixteenth century a considerable number of treatises were written which codified the art of love for the prospective *fin amant* or furnished the aspiring poet with lessons in grammar, style and versification. The interdependence of love and poetry is illustrated by the title of the largest of the Provençal 'grammars': *Las flors del gay saber, estier dichas las Leys d'amors*.[4] The earliest Provençal art of poetry was Raimon Vidal's *Las razos de trobar* (c. 1200). These works helped to make the troubadour lyric academically respectable. Already in 1210 Boncompagno, a professor at the University of Bologna, held Bernart de Ventadorn in high esteem: 'Quanti nominis quanteve fame sit Bernardus e Ventator, et quam gloriosas fecerit canciones et dulcisonas invenerit melodias, multe orbis provincie reconoscunt. Ipsum ergo magnificentie vestre duximos conmendandum'.[5]

Dante's unfinished *De vulgari eloquentia* (1303–04) was possibly the first critical work since Longinus' *On the Sublime* which was not confined to prescriptions.[6] In his promotion of love as a subject befitting the high or tragic style in poetry, Dante departed, as did the Provençal grammarians, from the precepts of the *trivium*. There were, in his opinion, three intrinsically worthy subjects for the poet writing in the 'illustrious vernacular': 'armorum probitas, amoris accensio, et directio voluntatis' (*De vulg. eloq.*, II, ii, p. 176). By adhering to the trinity of *Salus*, *Venus* and *Virtus* courtly poetry was expected to fulfil the needs of man's threefold constitution, a compound of vegetable, animal and spiritual substance. In the *Vita nuova* Dante suggested that poetry in the vernacular was inspired from the beginning by the desire to communicate with women, who found it difficult to understand Latin. This, he stated, was an argument against the choice of themes other than love: 'E questo è contra a coloro, che rimano sopra altra matera che amorosa; con ciò sia cosa che cotale modo di parlare fosse dal principio trovato per dire d'amore' (*Vita*, XXV, 6). Dante regarded himself as a participant in a poetic tradition which originated in Provence 150 years earlier. In *De vulgari* he awarded himself the prize for *Virtus* (II, ii, p. 179), and in the *Convivio* and in the *Divina Commedia* he was to move far beyond the sphere of Courtly Love.[7] It is nevertheless significant that he should select the word *amor* in order to demonstrate the underlying unity of the three branches of Romance, differentiated by the forms of the affirmative, *oïl*, *oc* and *sì*, and that he should prove the point by citing the poetry of Guiraut de Borneil, Thibaud, king of Navarre, and Guido Guinicelli (*De vulg. eloq.*, I, ix, p. 62).

The largest vernacular treatise on poetry and the first of its kind to be compiled in southern France for native speakers of Provençal was the anonymous *Leys d'Amors* (1328–37). This encyclopaedic work was commissioned by the Consistori dels Sept Trobadors, a poetic academy which was founded at Toulouse in 1323 in order to rejuvenate the spirit of troubadour poetry. The specific objectives of the treatise were to publish widely diffused material on grammar and versification; to clarify the art of composing poetry, which the early troubadours had veiled in secrecy; and to restrain the lover from succumbing to dishonest love (*Leys*, p. 4).[8] It is taken for granted that a poet cannot become technically proficient unless he displays integrity and self-discipline in his amatory conduct. It was not, however, the purpose of the *Leys* to interpret the conditions which gave rise to the *Gay Saber*, the art of troubadour poetry.

The study of Provençal poetry was promoted by Peter IV of Aragon (ruled 1336–87), who annexed Toulouse in 1344. His successor, John I, obtained permission from the king of France, Charles VI, to found a poetic academy, modelled on the Consistori at Toulouse, which took effect in 1390. King Martin the Humanist established a faculty of Limousin or Provençal at the University of Huesca in 1396, which has been described as the earliest faculty of the modern humanities in Europe.[9] In 1410 the death of King Martin, the last of the royal dynasty of Aragon and the House of Barcelona, brought the younger branch of the Trastámaras to the throne of Aragon, thus making a flourishing Aragonese culture easily accessible to Castile. Ferdinand of Antequera, elected by a commission which met at Caspe in 1412, became an enthusiastic patron of the Floral Games, a poetic competition organised by the Academy of the Gay Science, which was celebrated annually on 1 May.

Enrique de Villena (1384–1434), one of the *mantenedores* of the Aragonese poetic academy, wrote the earliest surviving treatise on poetry in Castilian. This fragmentary *Arte de trovar* appears to have been written with the express purpose of fostering a troubadour school in Castile, under the auspices of the Marquis of Santillana, to whom the work is addressed: 'vos informado por el dicho tratado seas originidat donde tomen lumbre, y dotrina todos los otros del Regno que se dizen trobadores, para que lo sean verdaderamente'.[10] The treatise contains an eye-witness account of the solemn procedure of electing a poet laureate, together with observations on phonetics, linguistics, pronunciation and spelling. Santillana, in his turn, summarised his views on poetry in a prefatory letter to his collected verse, which he sent to Dom Pedro, the Constable of Portugal, in 1449. In this epistle, known as the *Prohemio e carta*, the Gay Science was defined as a divinely inspired frenzy, to which noble and perspicacious minds are particularly susceptible:

un zelo çeleste, una affectión divina, un insaçiable çibo del ánimo; el qual, asý como la materia busca la forma e lo imperfecto la perfección, nunca esta sçiençia de la poesía e gaya sçiençia buscaron nin se fallaron, sinon en los ánimos gentiles, claros ingenios e elevados spíritus.[11]

This definition begs the question whether belief in the charismatic nature of poetic creation was a conventional element in Provençal poetics or an innovation introduced by Renaissance Neoplatonism.[12]

Spanish poets, whether they were writing in Catalan or in Castilian,[13] still endeavoured, in the fifteenth century, to adhere to the principles of early Provençal poetry. Alfonso the Magnanimous introduced Spanish poetry into Italy, after his triumphal entry into Naples in 1443. Alfonso's enthusiasm for antiquity is widely attested, but his taste in poetry remained curiously medieval, and the Spanish love lyric composed at the Neapolitan court was scarcely touched by Renaissance influences.[14] Spain was consequently able to play a part in the transmission and in the interpretation of troubadour texts. Angelo Colocci (1474–1549),[15] secretary to Pope Leo X, discussed Provençal studies with the Catalan poet Cariteo in Rome in the early years of the sixteenth century, and in 1515 he bought an anthology, known as the *Libro limosino*, from the poet's widow (Debenedetti, 1911, pp. 13–15). Cariteo (d. 1515), whose real name was Benedetto Gareth, was a friend of Sannazaro and a member of the Academy of Pontanus; in his poetry he was nevertheless a firm disciple of the troubadours. Onorato Drago, in the service of the Spanish nobleman Alfonso d'Ávalos, marquese del Vasto, wrote a treatise on Provençal phonetics and a dictionary (Debenedetti, p. 71).

In the late fifteenth century Spanish poets ceased to trace their literary descent to Provence, but looked to Italy for guidance. Encina stated in his *Arte de poesía castellana* (1496) that the word *trobar* derived from the Italian for *hallar*, to find,[16] and that the *poeta* surpassed the *trobador* in his theoretical understanding of poetry and in his critical abilities: 'Assí que quanta diferencia ay de señor a esclavo: de capitán a hombre de armas sugeto a su capitanía: tanto a mi ver ay de trobador a poeta' (*Arte*, p. 333). He believed that Spanish poetry, especially as regards purity of diction, had already passed its prime and faced the prospect of an imminent decline. This view was shared by Antonio de Nebrija (1442–1522), author of the earliest scientific grammar of a Romance language: *Gramática sobre la lengua castellana* (1492).

The study of Provençal literature was justified, in sixteenth-century Italy and elsewhere, by the debate on the kinship of the Romance languages, initiated by Dante. Dante believed that Latin was not the native idiom of Italy but a literary construct of the rhetoricians; he recognised that the *langue d'oc* was the first Romance language used by educated poets; and he wrote that all languages derived from a single idiom spoken before the confusion of Babel (*De vulg. eloq.*, I, vii, pp. 41–3). He did not, however, maintain that Provençal was the common ancestor of the Romance languages. This theory was conceived by Pietro Bembo (1470–1547) in *Notizione della lingua* (1500) and in *Rime . . . nelle quali si ragiona della volgar lingua* (1525). According to Bembo, the Latin or Romance languages derived from a single *lingua franca*, formed by the corruption of Latin and preserved faithfully in the poetry of the Provençal troubadours. 'Y quando Roma se enseñoreó de aquesta tierra,' wrote Encina, 'no sola mente recebimos sus leyes y constituciones, mas aún el romance, según su nombre da testimonio, que no es otra cosa nuestra lengua sino latín corrompido' (*Arte*, p. 330). This theory was accepted by most scholars in the seventeenth and eighteenth centuries.[17] It was repeated by Étienne Pasquier (1529–1615), Pierre-Daniel Huet (1630–1721), Thomas Rymer (1641–1713), Voltaire (1694–1778) and Marmontel (1723–99). The last scholar to champion the primacy of Provençal seriously was François Raynouard in his *Choix des poésies originales des troubadours* (1816–21). The myth of an archetypal Romance was finally exploded by Friedrich von Schlegel in *Observations sur la langue et la littérature provençale* (1818), and by Friedrich Diez (1794–1876), the founder of Romance philology.[18]

Another reason for studying medieval poetry was to discover the sources of Dante and Petrarch, both of whom had been accorded the status of *auctores*, which is to say that they had become authorities, or curriculum authors. This was especially true of Petrarch: 'Per il cinquecentista la conoscenza dei trovatori era sopratutto (o ci se illudeva) la chiave per penetrare più addentro nell'opera di Messer Francesco' (Debenedetti, 1911, p. 17). Tullia d'Aragona, a lady renowned for her beauty and her literary talents, is known to have presided over a colloquium on the Tuscan and Provençal poets to whom Petrarch was indebted.[19] Many annotated editions of the works of Dante and Petrarch were published during the course of the sixteenth century. Vernacular humanism had in fact transferred to Italian literary practice the basic principle of Latin humanism: the imitation of great models.[20]

Mario Equicola (1470–c. 1525),[21] a noted bibliophile, courtier and writer, was one of the few scholars of this period who took an interest in contemporary European poetry. In his *Libro de natura de amore* (1525), a work written in Latin between 1494 and 1496 and translated between 1509 and 1511, he combined theoretical considerations on the nature of love with a comparative study of the European love lyric. This treatise was disparaged for being eclectic and unacademic, but it was evidently widely read, to judge by the number of editions published. Moreover many authors pillaged material from it without acknowledging their debt.[22] The section entitled 'Como Latini et Greci Poeti, Ioculari Provenzali, Rimanti Francesi, Dicitori Thoscani, & trovatori Spagnoli habiano loro Amante lodato & le passioni di loro stessi descritto' (Equicola, fols. 187*v*–208*v*) is particularly relevant to students of Courtly Love, because it indicates what texts were available to the sixteenth-century scholar and offers an interesting panorama of lyrical themes and concepts.[23]

Equicola's critical procedure is rudimentary: he makes a few general remarks, which he then illustrates by paraphrasing selected passages from authors who usually remain nameless. As a firm Aristotelian he believed that there was an inevitable element of dissimulation in a love convention which claimed to be simultaneously chaste and erotic:

Provenzali gentilmente con dissimulatione nascondevano ogni lascivia de affecti: Et ne loro carte disio de honorare più che altro mostravano, dicendo Amor vol castità, & per castità bene ole, senza questa no è Amore, quando è senza lege & modo perde suo nome. [fol. 194r]

This statement was probably occasioned by the poetry of Guilhem de Montanhagol (*fl.* 1233–57), the first poet to assert that chastity is born of love.[24] The troubadours' attitude towards women was, adds Equicola, entirely novel: 'il modo de descrivere loro amore fu novo diverso de quel de antichi Latini, questi senza respecto, senza reverentia, senza timore de infamare sua donna apertamente scrivevano' (fol. 194r). The style of Provençal poetry is evoked, in words scarcely distinguishable from those employed by the Spanish love poet: love is returned as a favour, not as an obligation, and if it is honest and true it will endure for ever; love is a prison and a delightful malady; the lover, like the butterfly drawn towards the light, senses mortal danger in his lady's beauty; in her presence he is fearful, fear being a true sign of love,[25] but he gazes at her image when he is alone; love is a source of virtue and joy, uniting two hearts and two wills, but offering no solace; it is a profession which, above all, requires courtesy: 'Iusto & ragione è (dicel Provenzale) ch'io cante de Amore . . . che per amor cresce valor, senza valor non è honor, per amor virtù suo premio receve, & suo offitio exequisce cortesia' (fol. 195v).

According to Equicola, poetry in Provençal and in French was unfamiliar to Italian readers, whereas Spanish poetry was easily accessible and widely read (fol. 205r). Juan de Mena, the Spanish Petrarch, was reproved for his use of sacred hyperbole: 'Ioan de Mena homo singulare tra Spagnoli, qual tra noi Petrarcha (con bona pace sia decto) non me piace dove canta li difunti per molto sancti che se siano esser penati ne la gloria per non haver vista sua amica' (fol. 205v). The Spanish love poet wishes to die, because he has already ceased to live in the memory of the lady he loves; his love, a torment worse than death, burns him to ashes; he yearns to be killed by his mistress, in order to be liberated from his misfortune; without mercy he is condemned to perdition; his body lives without a soul as a result of his lady's absence.[26] He concluded that the Spanish lyric is passionate rather than lachrymose, involving frequent recourse to oxymora: 'Hor vediamo avanti de ingeniosi Spagnoli, non suspire, non lacrime, non querele, ma fochi, incendii, & morte: E lo amante Spagnolo ceco illuminato . . . remedio che da pena, & occidendo da vita' (fol. 206v). Death is a recurrent theme in Spanish literature: 'Così son piene de morti le carte spagnole, & esso Amadis de Gaula sotto'l nome del bel tenebroso canta, già che me si nega victoria, che de iusto me era devuta, lì dove more la gloria, è gloria morir la vita' (fol. 208v). Equicola did not propose any new theory on the origin of troubadour poetry; he repeated what Dante had said in his *Vita nuova*, and alluded to Juan del Encina's opinion that rhymed verse reached Spain from Italy: 'Gioan de Enzina confirma da Italia tal dire esser passato in Hispagna' (fol. 4r).

Giammaria Barbieri (1519–75) was the first scholar to advocate the theory that contact with Moorish Spain contributed to the rise of the troubadour lyric in the twelfth century. He believed, contrary to Encina, that the Arabs, in the sixth or seventh century, invented rhymed verse, and that Provence learnt the art from Spain.[27] The moment when this cultural transmission occurred was, he proposed, the year 1112, when Ramon Berenguer IV, Count of Barcelona, succeeded Gilbert, Count of Provence, thus bringing about the union of two linguistically unified territories:

Però è ben verisimile che gli Spagnuoli per la vicinanza e commercio d'una nazione all'altra fossero i primi da quella banda ad apprendere da gli Àrabe . . . con la lingua insieme la maniera di poetare. La quale è verisimile anchora, che da i medesimi Spagnuoli passasse alle altre vicine regioni, & specialmente nella Provenza. [Barbieri, 1790, p. 45]

Although Barbieri's treatise *Dell'origine della poesia rimata* was not published until 1790, his ideas were disseminated by his colleagues. Italian literary historians continued to mention the theory during the seventeenth and eighteenth centuries, and Robert Briffault still subscribed to it in *Les Troubadours et le sentiment romanesque* (1945).[28]

In 1575 Jean de Nostredame (1507–77), brother of Michel, the celebrated astrologer, published *Les Vies des plus célèbres et anciens poètes provençaux*. Many scholars have misguidedly used this biography as a book of reference. Joseph Anglade's introduction to Camille Chabaneau's edition of the work, published in 1913, gave a detailed account of the damage done by Nostredame to Provençal scholarship.[29] C. F. X. Millot, who arranged and edited the papers of the eighteenth-

century historian La Curne de Sainte Palaye, criticised Nostredame for
having referred to non-existent poets and historians, and for having
initiated the myth that the troubadours wrote theatrical works (Sainte
Palaye, 1774, p. xvi). Despite Millot's warning, Stendhal, Sismondi,
Raynouard and other nineteenth-century writers continued to rely on
Nostredame, which explains, in particular, their belief that the
Provençal courts of love were actual legislative bodies.

The Provençal poets were virtually unknown in France during the
sixteenth century, although links were increasingly established between
French and Italian medievalists in the latter half of the century.[30] 'Je ne
pense point avoir veu livre en limosin', wrote Claude Fauchet to Jacopo
Corbinelli. 'Il me souvient en avoir veu un escrit à Bésiers (le Breviari?),
mais je ne sçai si c'est en provençal ou catalan' (Nostredame, introd.
Anglade, p. 147). Fauchet assembled one of the earliest collections of
medieval French poetry: *Recueil de l'origine de la langue et poésie française*
(1581). The first part is an inquiry into the origin of the French language;
the second part lists the names of 127 poets writing before 1300, and
includes some biographical anecdotes and a summary of certain works.
This work has a strong nationalistic bias, evident in the title of chapter
seven: 'Quand la Ryme, telle que nous l'avons, commença: & que les
Espagnols & Italiens l'ont prise des François'. Fauchet argued that
rhyme was not a Provençal invention but developed soon after the fall
of the Roman Empire, and was certainly practised during the reign of
Charlemagne (p. 64). He dated the troubadour era from the First
Crusade in 1096, and suggested that by the reign of Saint Louis the
term *jongleor* had become debased (p. 75).

In 1647 Jean Chapelain (1595–1674) wrote a dialogue, *La Lecture des
vieux romans*, published posthumously in 1728,[31] in which Gilles
Ménage, Jean-François Sarrasin and the author discuss the philological,
ethical and literary qualities of *Lancelot du Lac*. Ménage, author of a
Dictionnaire étymologique des origines de la langue française (1650), is openly
hostile to the work. Sarrasin, author of a dialogue on *Perceforest*,[32] has a
high regard for the medieval ideal of courtesy and for the chivalric code
of honour, and shares the author's opinion that *Lancelot* is 'une repré-
sentation naïve, et une histoire certaine et exacte des moeurs qui
régnaient dans les Cours d'alors' (Huet, ed. Gégou, p. 177). Chapelain
maintained that Lancelot's passion for Guenevere, proved through
danger and military exploit, surpassed the superficial desire to please
characteristic of the polite society in which he lived: Lancelot 'ne joue
pas l'amoureux, il l'est véritablement' (p. 197).

Pierre de Caseneuve's investigation into the origin of the Floral

Games, *L'Origine des Ieux Floraux* (1659), marked a renewed interest in this ancient institution.[33] According to Caseneuve, the poetic academy of Toulouse was an offshoot of the courts of love held by the Emperor Frederick II (1194–1250), by Thibaut (1201–53), King of Navarre and Count of Champagne, and by Ermengarde of Narbonne. He quoted from a letter addressed by Melchior Goldast to Jean Schelenburg: 'Viri Principes & Equestres nonnunquam etiam Imperatores, Reges, certamina instituere poetica; in quibus nobili familia Virgines offerebant victoriam cantus; non secus ac in hostiludiis, contentio de praemis erat, ab Imperatore propositis, aut quodam Principum magnate' (p. 50). Frederick II and his son Henry elected the wife of a poet and a lady of great virtue to act as an umpire and a prize-giver at these poetic contests (p. 51). The prizes at the Floral Games were distributed by a lady, personifying Love (p. 88). Caseneuve stressed the spiritual aspect of troubadour love by associating it with the heavenly Venus, the daughter of Uranus: 'les Poètes Provençaux avoient banny de leurs exercices ce fol amour, que Platon dit estre fils de Vénus *Pandimie*, c'est à dire publique et prostituée, & n'y recevoient que celuy qu'il appelle fils de Vénus *Uranie*, c'est à dire Céleste' (p. 36).

In *De l'origine des romans*, first published as a preface to Regnauld de Segrais' *Zayde, histoire espagnole* in 1671, Pierre-Daniel Huet briefly mentioned the poetic competitions held annually at Fez to mark the Prophet Muhammad's birthday (Huet, 1671, p. 51), but he did not compare these festivities to the Floral Games or other similar institutions in Europe.[34] Huet's thesis was that the prose romance or novel was a genre invented by Egyptians, Arabs, Persians, Syrians and other oriental peoples (p. 10). The French, he argued, excelled other nations in the composition of this genre because in France women did not lead a cloistered existence, as they did in Italy, Spain and other countries, and therefore men were obliged to develop a sophisticated art of gallantry and courtship:

Mais en France les Dames vivant sur leur bonne foy, & n'ayant point d'autres défences que leur propre coeur, elles s'en sont fait un rampart plus fort & plus seur que toutes les clefs, que toutes les grilles, & que toute la vigilance des Doüegnes. Les hommes ont donc esté obligés d'assiéger ce rampart par les formes, & ont employé tant de soin & d'adresse pour le réduire, qu'ils s'en sont fait un art presque inconnu aux autres peuples. C'est cet art qui distingue les Romans François des autres Romans. [p. 63]

Huet's essay was extremely popular in France, Italy and England, and his ideas were more fully elaborated by Thomas Warton.[35]

The troubadour lyric was virtually unknown in seventeenth-century England prior to Thomas Rymer's *A Short View of Tragedy* (1693). Rymer (1641–1713), better known for his disparaging comments on the plays of Shakespeare, affirmed in this work that modern poetry originated in Provence, and that '*Provencial* was the first of the modern languages, that yielded and chim'd in with the musick and sweetness of ryme' (p. 126). He believed that Chaucer had improved the English language by borrowing Provençal words, and it was under his influence that Pope and Gray planned to begin their histories with the 'school of Provence'.[36] The poets of Provence were similarly credited by Warton with having laid the foundations of polite literature (Warton, 1775–81, I, diss. p. 148), and the same view was taken in the twentieth century by T. Earle Welby.[37] However, no textbook was available in English until Sainte Palaye's *Histoire littéraire des troubadours* was translated in 1779.

La Curne de Sainte Palaye (1697–1781) was the prime example of an eighteenth-century scholar who placed his antiquarian curiosity at the service of Enlightenment. Like Montesquieu, he was chiefly concerned with establishing general laws of human behaviour and social organisation. He was, for this reason, less interested in the customs, beliefs and institutions that made medieval culture unique. Chivalry was, in his opinion, an institution in no way peculiar to the Middle Ages, and was one which might, with certain modifications, be made part of a modern reformed monarchy.[38] Despite these drawbacks, Sainte Palaye's *Mémoires sur l'ancienne chevalerie* (1753) were a landmark in the history of medievalist scholarship.

In the late seventeenth century chivalry was very much in vogue. Already in 1683 Claude-François Ménestrier could write, with reference to it, 'il n'y a guère de sujet dont on ait autant écrit que de celuy-ci'.[39] In the eighteenth century nostalgia for the medieval past produced, in literature, the *genre troubadour*.[40] Sainte Palaye's editor, Millot, was, however, under no illusions about 'le bon vieux tems': 'Nous regrettons le tems passé: les troubadours regrettoient le tems passé, aux douzième & treizième siècles, & l'histoire ne connoît rien de plus affreux que les deux siècles antérieurs à cette époque' (Sainte Palaye, 1774, pp. lxi–lxii). This archaising tendency in medieval courtly literature has been noted by a number of critics, including Simonde de Sismondi and Johan Huizinga.[41]

Millot touched on the problem of troubadour origins. He suspected that the earliest troubadour whose poetry is extant, Guilhem IX of Aquitaine, could not have inaugurated the new genre: 'les grâces de

son style supposent un art déjà cultivé' (Sainte Palaye, 1774, p. xxii). [42]
He suggested that the First Crusade and dissension between Papacy and
Empire provoked new sensations and opened up new horizons; religious
fanaticism was, paradoxically, a stimulus to the fine arts and to the
triumph of the Muses (pp. xxiv–xxv). Nordic veneration for women
was, in his opinion, the basis of 'cette galanterie fameuse qui devint un
des principaux mobiles de la société' (p. xxxii). Amongst Celtic,
Germanic and Scandinavian peoples, women, despite their servile status,
were respected for the supernatural gifts with which they were
believed to be endowed. This attitude strengthened the dominion of
beauty: 'Pour mériter la beauté qu'il idolâtroit, le guerrier bravoit les
fatigues, les blessures & la mort' (p. xxxiv). The idea had been
expressed by Simon Pelloutier in his *Histoire des Celtes* (1750). [43]

The 'spirit of chivalry' was the key phrase in Thomas Warton's
dissertation 'On the origin of romantic fiction into Europe', which he
prefixed to his *History of English Poetry* (1775–81). Warton's thesis,
clearly modelled on Millot's 'Discours préliminaire', was as follows:
the Provençal concept of love and modern manners in general were
dictated by the 'spirit of chivalry' which evolved amongst the Gothic
or Germanic barbarians soon after the fall of the Roman Empire, when
the female character assumed 'an unusual importance and authority . . .
in all the governments established by the northern conquerors' (diss.,
p. 65). Unlike Millot, Warton believed that in the early Middle Ages
women were comparatively emancipated. He maintained, on the
authority of Tacitus, [44] that they fulfilled a prominent role in Germanic
society, both as prophetesses and as administrators: they conferred
with the Romans, negotiated peace treaties, and commanded respect
and submission from the male warriors who competed in arms to gain
their favours (pp. 66–7). At a later date the ethics of chivalry were
consecrated to religion, and women of noble birth acquired a further
aura of sanctity as a consequence of the feudal constitution which
placed them in seemingly impregnable castles (pp. 70–1).

Warton was one of the first to oppose the terms 'romantic' and
'classical': he spoke of Dante's 'wonderful compound of classical and
romantic fancy' (*History*, III, p. 241). The word 'romantic', from the
kind of literature written in the vernacular or *lingua Romanica*, had
already, in the late seventeenth century, acquired the connotations
'false as a fairy-tale' or 'strange and dream-like as a fairy-tale'. [45] It was
only at the very end of the eighteenth century that the term became
one of total approbation. Before the rise of Romanticism the troubadours were regarded as half-civilised rather than anti-classical: 'on ne

doit considérer les Troubadours que comme peintres des moeurs d'une nation qui, sans être encore civilisée, cessoit pourtant d'être barbare'.[46]

In spite of his theories on chivalrous love, Warton did not hold that romantic fiction was indigenous to Europe. Following Huet, he declared that prose romances, in particular the *matière de Bretagne*, reached Europe, from the eighth century onwards, from Arab-occupied Spain through wars and commercial intercourse (Warton, I, pp. 2–3). As regards the Gay Science, the poetical art of the troubadours, he also subscribed to the Hispano-Arabic thesis, which, with the decline of Neoclassicism and the growth of literary historiography, was in the ascendant.

Juan Andrés, a Spaniard whom the king of Naples had appointed as his librarian, ambitiously embarked on a history of world literature: *Dell'origine, progressi e stato attuale d'ogni letteratura* (1782–1822). A German, Friedrich Bouterwek, undertook a similar project, with far greater scholarship, in *Geschichte der Poesie und Beredsamkeit* (1801–50).[47] Both were of the opinion that the cultural importance of the Arabs had been minimised. These early literary historians drew extensively from Miguel Casiri's *Bibliotheca Arabico-Hispana Escurialensis*, published in two volumes in the years 1760–70. This catalogue of the Arabic manuscripts in the Escorial library, commissioned by Ferdinand VI in 1749, contained numerous excerpts from Arabic works, accompanied by translations into Latin (Monroe, 1970, pp. 32–3).

Andrés (1740–1817) is usually regarded as the first eighteenth-century scholar to advance the theory of Arabic origins. In fact, however, many of his ideas had been stated in a work by a Catalan scholar, Xavier Lampillas (1731–1810): *Saggio storico-apologetico della letteratura spagnola* (1778–81). Lampillas, like Andrés, was a Jesuit who had been exiled from Spain by the mandate of Charles III in 1767. Like Andrés, he was anxious to refute the adverse criticism of Spain by Italian literary historians, such as Saverio Bettinelli, Girolamo Tiraboschi and Ludovico Antonio Muratori. The thesis of his work was that Spain should be accorded 'the honour and distinction of having contributed to the development of both the modern Italian language and its poetry, through Provençal' (Gibson, 1962, p. 222). Lampillas sought to substantiate this claim by repeating a theory expounded by the Catalan philologist Antonio Bastero in *La crusca provenzale* (1724): Catalan and Provençal were once identical languages; Catalan, introduced into southern France from the ninth century onwards by the Counts of Barcelona, became the literary idiom of Provence.[48] Italian scholars were criticised for having failed to mention Spain in their discussion of

Provençal poetry (Lampillas, 1778–81, I, p. 172). Lampillas was none theless able to discover Italians who supported his argument: ' "Gli Spagnuoli," dice Fontanini,[49] "l'arte di Romanzare non apparrono da' Provenzali, ma piutòsto i Provenzali dagli Spagnuoli all' Impero de' quali soggiacquero lungo tempo" ' (I, p. 188). According to another Italian literary historian, Quadrio, Provençal poets imitated and emulated the Moorish poets of Spain. Lampillas concluded that 'un sincero ricercatore della storia poetica, trovarebbe che la volgar Poesia Europea ebbe l'origine sua nella Spagna' (III, p. 39).

Andrés discussed the scientific and literary achievements of Hispano-Arabic culture, and arrived at the same conclusion regarding the origin of Provençal poetry: 'Figlia parimente dell'arabica poesia può in qualche modo dirsi la provenzale' (Andrés, 1782–1822, II, p. 48). He argued that Provençal genres corresponded to those in use amongst the Arabs, and that poetic academies in Italy, France and Spain were modelled on similar Arabic institutions (I, p. 254). He referred, on the authority of the English orientalist Edward Pococke, to the annual poetry festival at 'Okaz (I, p. 313). He noted Arabic pre-eminence in musicology,[50] and observed that many of the Spanish names for musical instruments were Arabic in origin. He claimed that, together with their poetry, the Arabs bequeathed to Europe the principles of modern music (I, p. 291), a theory taken up more recently by Julián Ribera y Tarragó in *La música de las Cantigas* (1922) and *La música andaluza medieval* (1923). Spain was not only the cradle of troubadour poetry but the place where it sought refuge in adversity: 'La poesia provenzale ebbe d'uopo di cercare onorato asilo nella Catalogna, ove, come abbiam detto altrove, è assai probabile, che abbia avuta la culla' (II, p. 53).

At this auspicious moment Tiraboschi, who was engaged in the composition of his *Storia della letteratura italiana* (1782–98), found time to publish a hitherto unpublished work: Barbieri's *Dell'origine della poesia rimata*. This work evoked a critical response in Stefano Arteaga's *Della influenza degli Arabi sull'origine della poesia moderna* (1791). Arteaga, the only Arabist to enter into this polemic, refuted the theory that Arabic prosody could have given rise to the accented verse of Romance poetry.[51] He pointed out that Arabic verse is based on quantity, not on stress. Tiraboschi felt impelled to moderate his views, and to concede, in later volumes of his *Storia*, that any nation might have invented rhyme (Gibson, 1962, p. 42). It appears, however, that Arteaga was ignorant of popular Arabic poetry. Consequently his argument is 'less valid than the less technical though more intuitively historical ideas of Barbieri, Juan Andrés and their Italian partisans' (Monroe, 1970, p. 43). Since the cult of the Orient was to become one of the features of the Romantic movement, the Hispano-Arabic thesis continued to be advocated, in one form or another, until the middle of the nineteenth century, to be revived once again in the twentieth.

To recapitulate, troubadour scholarship has its beginnings in sixteenth-century Italy as part of the debate on the kinship of the Romance languages. It was in Italy during this period that the Hispano-Arabic theory was first formulated. The seventeenth and eighteenth centuries witnessed a growing interest in the institution of chivalry, in medieval prose romances, and in the social implications of the troubadour lyric. By the late eighteenth century the troubadours were regarded by many as the originators of modern European literature, and they were accordingly assigned a prominent place in the history of Western civilisation. The Hispano-Arabic controversy flared up in Italy, where the theory had been conceived. However, it was commonly believed that chivalrous sentiments, in particular veneration for women, were native to northern Europe, and that these sentiments were refined by the troubadours of southern France into 'le système galant de la chevalerie' (Sainte Palaye, 1774, p. liii).

2   1800–1900

It has been claimed that the nineteenth-century predilection for the Middle Ages among scholars, artists and creative writers was the consequence of a genuine rediscovery, comparable in some ways to the rediscovery of classical antiquity by the humanists of the Renaissance (Dawson, 1935, p. 125). Yet, as in the Renaissance, this new vision of the past was shaped by the political, imaginative and emotional requirements of the time. During the course of the century the Middle Ages were exploited as a slogan of contempt or approbation by different literary and political factions for purposes which were often mutually exclusive. The Middle Ages were variously associated with feudal oppression, religious intolerance, the origins of Romanticism, the spirit of anti-papalism and insurrection, the virtues of traditional Roman Catholicism, and the world of the Gothic and the macabre.[52] The most important of these conflicting visions for the future of Courtly Love scholarship, and one which continued to exert an influence throughout the century, was that of Romanticism.

At the time of the French Revolution the pro-monarchist *genre troubadour* declined, and the image of the medieval nobleman as patron and dilettante was replaced by that of the wandering minstrel. Despite the undemocratic basis of chivalry, opposition to Neoclassicism made Madame de Staël (1766–1817) an ardent propagandist for 'la littérature romantique ou chevaleresque'. In 1800 she published *De la littérature considérée dans ses rapports avec les institutions sociales*. Here one would expect to find some reference to the social milieu in which Courtly Love flourished, but in this respect the title is misleading. Unlike some of her contemporaries, she did not attempt, in this work, to reconcile Gothic chivalry with the Hispano-Arabic theory of origins. Oriental melancholy, occasioned by the instability of fortune and the memory of lost happiness, was contrasted with 'la mélancolie des peuples du nord', caused by metaphysical *Angst*: 'le vide que la sensibilité fait trouver dans l'existence, et la rêverie, qui promène sans cesse la pensée, de la fatigue de la vie à l'inconnu de la mort' (*De la lit.*, I, pp. 177–8). She believed that Arab chivalry and Moorish attitudes to women were influenced by the example of Spain, and not vice versa (I, p. 166). Furthermore she claimed that Christianity did not diminish the status of women. On the contrary, it guaranteed more freedom to them, demanding the consent of both partners in the marriage contract, and according equal rewards and punishments to both sexes in the after-life (I, pp. 139–40). Madame de Staël was thus able, in *De l'Allemagne* (1810), to give the following definition of the term *romantique*: 'Le nom *romantique* a été introduit nouvellement en Allemagne pour désigner la poésie dont les chants des troubadours ont été l'origine, celle qui est née de la chevalerie et du christianisme' (*De l'All.*, II, p. 11). To the early poets of the Romantic movement, who took this work as their manifesto, the Germanic north symbolised the romantic legacy of the Middle Ages.

Madame de Staël's ideas are remarkably similar to those expressed by François-René de Chateaubriand (1768–1848) in *Génie du Christianisme* (1802). This work contained a chapter entitled 'Du vague des passions' which analysed the Romantic malaise:

On est détrompé sans avoir joui; il reste encore des désirs, et l'on n'a plus d'illusions. L'imagination est riche, abondante et merveilleuse; l'existence pauvre, sèche et désenchantée . . . Les anciens ont peu connu cette inquiétude secrète.[53]

The modern sensibility, prone to this precocious world-weariness, is, according to Chateaubriand, essentially Christian. Love, in the modern sense, was unknown to the ancient world: 'Ce que nous appelons proprement amour parmi nous, est un sentiment dont la haute antiquité a ignoré jusqu'au nom' (I, Bk. 3, ch. 2, p. 120).

J. C. L. Simonde de Sismondi (1773–1842), a friend of Madame de Staël and a member of the 'groupe de Coppet', was an enthusiastic exponent of the Hispano-Arabic thesis. Admitting his debt to Andrés and Bouterwek, he wrote his *Histoire de la littérature du Midi de l'Europe* (1813). The Arabian tales were the source of 'that tenderness and delicacy of sentiment, and that reverential awe of women, by turns slaves and divinities, which have operated so powerfully on our chivalrous feelings' (Sismondi, trans. Roscoe, 1823, I, p. 65). Chivalry, 'the soul of the new literature', was an Arab importation, initially unconnected with the feudal system: 'Raymond Berenger and his successors introduced into Provence the spirit both of liberty and chivalry, and a taste for elegance and the arts, with all the sciences of the Arabians' (I, pp. 86–7). Women were served and protected as if they were 'representatives of the divinity upon earth' (I, p. 90). Sismondi nevertheless conceded that, in reality, they remained dependants and inferiors. It was this obvious discrepancy between theory and practice which made it necessary to antedate the age of chivalry 'at least three or four centuries before any period of authentic history' (I, p. 92).[54]

August Wilhelm von Schlegel (1767–1845), who also belonged to Mme de Staël's circle of friends and admirers, attempted to disprove the theory that Provençal poetry was influenced by the Arabs in his *Observations sur la langue et la littérature provençale* (1818). He argued that poetry based on the worship of women could not have been inspired by a hostile people who kept their women in a state of subjection (Schlegel, 1818, p. 67). This was not, however, the opinion of the majority of his contemporaries.

In *De l'amour* (1822) Stendhal (1783–1842) cited and discussed some excerpts from two Arabic works: *Le Divan de l'amour*, compiled by Ebn Abi Hadglat,[55] and an anonymous *Histoire des Arabes qui sont morts d'amour*. Although he did not make an explicit analogy between the *amour-passion* of the Arabs and that of the Provençal troubadours, it seems to be implied by the juxtaposition of the section entitled 'De l'amour en Provence jusqu'à la conquête de Toulouse, en 1328, par les barbares du nord' (Beyle, 1926, II, pp. 41–9) with the section on 'L'Arabie' (II, pp. 61–6). In the latter he writes:

On voit que c'est nous qui fûmes les barbares à l'égard de l'Orient, quand nous allâmes le troubler par nos croisades. Aussi devons-nous ce qu'il y a de noble dans nos mœurs à ces croisades et aux Maures d'Espagne. [II, p. 62]

Claude Fauriel (1772–1844), the scholar from whom Stendhal gleaned most of his information by correspondence, stated in his *Histoire de la poésie provençale* (1846) that 'rien ne contribua tant à éveiller l'instinct poétique des populations du Midi que leurs guerres et leurs relations avec les Arabes d'Espagne' (Fauriel, 1846, p. 7).

Stendhal's *De l'amour* has an appendix on the courts of love, together with a 'Notice sur André le Chaplain' (II, pp. 233–48). Critics have long been misled into believing that Andrew the Chaplain's *De amore* can be taken as the bible of Courtly Love.[56] Stendhal believed, on the basis of Andreas and Nostredame, that the *cours d'amour* actually existed as legislative tribunals: 'Il y avait une législation établie pour les rapports des deux sexes en amour, aussi sévère et aussi exactement suivie que peuvent l'être aujourd'hui les lois du *point d'honneur*' (II, p. 41).

E. J. Delécluze contended, in *Dante Alighieri, ou la poésie amoureuse* (1846, p. 66), that the cult of Woman as a symbol of the divine was not bequeathed to the Arabs by the crusaders but was, on the contrary, present in the Islamic world from the beginning, and he cited an article on 'Eschk Allah' in Herbelot's *Bibliothèque orientale*.[57]

The Arab origins of European chivalry were the subject of an article by J. von Hammer-Pürgstall in 1849. In 1865 Adolf Friedrich Schack published his *Poesie und Kunst der Araber in Spanien und Sicilien*. He accepted the view that certain aspects of European chivalry were derived from the Arabs, and he observed that ninth-century Arabic poetry written in Al-Andalus manifests the quasi-religious veneration for women which was to become a characteristic feature of Christian chivalry and troubadour poetry (Schack, trans. Valera, 1867–71, I, pp. 76 and 95). However, he did not maintain, as Hammer-Pürgstall and some earlier scholars of the Romantic era had done, that chivalry originated in the orient, nor did he share Huet's opinions on the origin of romantic fiction.

The ideas of Sismondi, Fauriel, Raynouard and others were re-capitulated by Eugène Baret in *Espagne et Provence. Études sur la littérature du Midi de l'Europe* (1857). Meanwhile another school of thought was gathering momentum. Gabriele Rossetti, the patriot exile and father of the Pre-Raphaelite painter,[58] was the first to maintain, contrary to the mainstream of scholarship, that Courtly Love was the vehicle of religious dissent, and that the troubadours were members of a secret fraternity, opposed to the dogmas and the sacraments of the Roman Catholic Church. In *Sullo spirito antipapale che produsse la riforma . . . Disquisizioni* (1832) he cited some passages from Petrarch's letters, in which Avignon, the seat of the Papal court, was compared to the Whore of Babylon, and concluded that a secret bond must have existed between the Italian poet and the English theologian Wyclif (*Disquisitions*, 1834, I, pp. 8–13). Dante, Petrarch and Boccaccio were, he wrote, all members of a 'Love Sect' which exploited the language of profane love for the propagation of Catharist beliefs. This secret language was taught through the 'Grammar of the Gay Science' (I, pp. 200–1). This esoteric approach to Courtly Love was further elaborated by Rossetti in *Il misterio dell'amor platonico del medio evo derivato da'Misteri Antichi* (1840). The *Roman de la Rose* was interpreted as a spiritual allegory, in which the rose, the flower sacred to the Rosicrucians, is an emblem of Christ (*Il misterio*, I, p. 202). The courts of love were similar to masonic lodges (I, p. 215); the troubadours were called minstrels (*ministrelli*) because they were ministers (*ministri*) of a secret religion (I, p. 222). According to Rossetti, the Albigensian heretics wished to abolish the worship of images, prayers for the dead, indulgences, and the celebration of holy communion (I, p. 16). The troubadours were thus regarded as the harbingers of the Reformation.[59]

Rossetti's ideas were developed by Eugène Aroux, from a Roman Catholic position, in a work with a startling title: *Dante hérétique, révolutionnaire et socialiste* (1854). Dante and the troubadours who preceded him were described as 'les auxiliaires et dévoués de l'hérésie albigeoise' (*Dante*, p. 15). Dante's opposition to a theocratic political system was seen as part of a vast 'protestant' conspiracy to overthrow the established order.[60] In *Les Mystères de la chevalerie et de l'amour platonique au Moyen Âge* (1858) Aroux, imitating Rossetti's example, turned his attention to European love poetry and prose romances: 'La chevalerie, que nous appellerons amoureuse . . . dérive de l'Évangile par l'albigéisme, et elle eut pour pères les troubadours . . . Exclus des chaires doctorales, ils se firent professeurs de la *Gaie Science* et enseignèrent *l'art d'amour*, c'est à dire à suivre les lois de l'Évangile' (*Les Mystères*, pp. 71–2). The troubadours celebrated, under a veil of allegory intelligible only to the initiated, the trials and achievements of their missionaries, otherwise known as Goodmen or Perfects. The lady addressed by these poets symbolised the parish which they sought to woo to their persuasion; 'union by love', as opposed to orthodox 'union by marriage', signified the relationship which existed between an Albigensian congregation and a Perfect knight (pp. 74–6). The Crypto-Cathar theory was repeated by Antony Méray in *Les Libres Prêcheurs devanciers de Luther et de Rabelais* (1860) and in *La Vie au temps des Cours d'Amour* (1876). The troubadours were linked with Freemasonry by Joseph Péladan in *Le Secret des troubadours* (1906). Denis de Rougemont, the best-known exponent of the Crypto-Cathar theory, was later to adopt some of these ideas in *L'Amour et l'Occident* (1939).[61]

Towards the end of the nineteenth century medievalists became more aware of the problems of textual criticism. Reacting against Romantic scholarship, they attempted to be more detached and scientific in their judgements. These circumstances favoured the study of the Latin Middle Ages. Paul Meyer, who collaborated with Gaston Paris in the foundation of the *Revue Critique* in 1866 and of *Romania* in 1872, sought to explain Courtly Love in terms of the continuity of the Latin tradition in 'De l'influence des troubadours sur la poésie des peuples romans' (1876). W. Schrötter discussed the influence of Ovid's *Ars amatoria* in *Ovid und die Troubadours* (1905). Ovid was so widely read during the eleventh and twelfth centuries that Ludwig Traub called this period the Ovidian age of cultural history.[62] H. J. Chaytor referred to the troubadours as the literary descendants of the *scurrae*, *thymelici* and *joculatores* whom the Romans brought with them when they settled in Gaul (Chaytor, 1912, p. 7). However, Gaston Paris, Alfred Jeanroy, Menéndez Pidal, Eduard Wechssler and other medievalists of the late nineteenth century were not convinced by these medieval Latin and classical Ovidian theories, and other explanations were sought for in the religion, the folk-lore and the social environment of twelfth-century Europe.

John Addington Symonds (1840–93) compared the '*joy* of the medieval amorists' to the *mania* of *Phaedrus*, observing a resemblance between the philosophical ideal of *paiderastia* and 'chivalrous love', in *A Problem of Greek Ethics* (1883). Both, in theory at least, excluded the sensual appetites and aspired to an image of the divine in human flesh. According to Symonds, 'the mythology of Mary gave religious sanction to the chivalrous enthusiasm' (p. 96). The relationship between Marianism and Courtly Love was much debated in the early years of the twentieth century.

In this same year, 1883, there appeared an article by Gaston Paris on 'Lancelot du Lac: Le Conte de la Charrette'', containing what is reputedly the first instance of the use of the term *amour courtois* in modern criticism.[63] His definition of *amour courtois* may be briefly summarised: it is illicit, furtive and extra-conjugal; the lover continually fears lest he should, by some misfortune, displease his mistress or cease to be worthy of her; the lover's position is one of inferiority; even the hardened warrior trembles in his lady's presence; she, on her part, makes her suitor acutely aware of his insecurity by deliberately acting in a capricious and haughty manner; love is a source of courage and refinement; the lady's apparent cruelty serves to test her lover's valour; finally, love, like chivalry and *courtoisie*, is an art with its own code of rules (Paris, 1883, 518). According to Paris (1839–1903), this species of love first made its appearance in northern French literature in *Le Conte de la Charette*. The idea of treating love as an art with codifiable rules derived from Ovid's *Ars amatoria*, a work familiar to clerics and one which Chrétien had himself translated.[64] Other aspects of Courtly Love were clearly not Ovidian.

A collection of essays by Violet Paget (1856–1935), entitled *Euphorion* (1884), contained an imaginative and strikingly original account of the social reality which produced what she calls 'mediaeval love', an account to which both Jeanroy and C. S. Lewis were to give their approbation.[65] Interest in the social reality underlying the medieval lyric may owe something to the rise of Marxism and ideas about female emancipation. However, apart from an awareness of class differences as a factor determining the character of literature,[66] there is nothing specifically Marxist about *Euphorion*. Paget's definition of 'mediaeval love' was heavily charged with Romanticism: 'the feudal Middle Ages gave to mankind a more refined and spiritual love, a love all chivalry, fidelity, and adoration, but a love steeped in the poison of adultery' (Paget, 1884, p. 126). The chief characteristics of this 'new manner of loving', which culminated in Dante's love for Beatrice, can be arranged under three heads: first, love was inspired by the belief in the 'moral, aesthetical, and social superiority of a woman', a belief which sometimes reached 'the point of actual worship' (p. 128); second, love was the perfect vocation and 'an indispensable part of the noble life' (p. 128); third, there is no progress in love: the knight and his lady are always at the same distance from each other, and 'their passion burns on (at least theoretically) to all eternity' (p. 129). This definition was intended to comprise a wide range of moods, from the popular *alba* to the chivalric romance. It was within the confines of the feudal castle that such a love must have evolved:

there is an enormous preponderance of men over women; for only chiefs in command, the overlord, and perhaps one or two of his kinsmen or adjutants, are permitted the luxury of a wife; and the rest of the gentlemen are subalterns, younger sons without means, youths sent to learn their military duty and the ways of the world: a whole pack of men without wives, without homes, and usually without fortune. High above this deferential male crowd moves the lady of the castle: highborn, proud, having brought her husband a dower of fiefs. [pp. 136–7]

To the men appointed to defend and to entertain her the *châtelaine* seemed almost a goddess: she represented the feudal superiority which commanded respect, the social perfection to which young knights aspired, and 'a rare example of womankind' (p. 138). The adulterous character of 'mediaeval love' was a consequence of class distinctions and the shortage of females (p. 139).[67] This love nevertheless possessed a 'morality within immorality', based on 'a reciprocity of fidelity' which would have been unthinkable in classical times (p. 156). When, in the thirteenth century, 'mediaeval love' reached the Italian burghs from Provence and Sicily it became 'considerably more platonic and saturated with metaphysics' (p. 182), because the Italians would not tolerate adultery. Paget thus returned, once again, to contemplate the pure chaste passion of the *Vita nuova*.

In 1890 Alfred Jeanroy published *Les Origines de la poésie lyrique en France au Moyen Âge*. This work was almost exclusively devoted to the popular lyric. Paris, in a long review article on this work, published in the *Journal des Savants* in 1891–92, proposed a new theory on the origin of the courtly lyric:

Je voudrais . . . rendre vraisemblable cette thèse que la poésie des troubadours proprement dite, imitée dans le nord à partir du milieu du XIIᵉ siècle, et qui est essentiellement la poésie courtoise, a son point de départ dans les chansons de danses et notamment de danses printanières. [Paris, 1892, 424]

This folkloric theory of origins was criticised by Joseph Bédier (1864–1938) in 'Les Fêtes de mai et les commencemens de la poésie lyrique au Moyen Âge' (1896). His chief objection was that the May festivities could not account for the belief in love's ennobling effects. His definition of Courtly Love as 'un culte qui s'adresse à un objet excellent et se fonde, comme l'amour chrétien, sur l'infinie disproportion du mérite au désir' is remarkably succinct, and was quoted with approval by Peter Dronke in *Medieval Latin and the Rise of European Love-Lyric* (1965–66, I, p. 4). It was, wrote Bédier, 'une école nécessaire d'honneur, qui fait *valoir* l'amant et transforme les vilains en courtois . . . un servage volontaire qui recèle un pouvoir ennoblissant, et fait consister dans la souffrance la dignité et la beauté de la passion' (Bédier, 1892, p. 172).

Before the close of the nineteenth century the problem of the 'play element' in medieval courtly society, which was to become a central theme in Johan Huizinga's portrait of the Middle Ages,[68] had already been raised by William Allan Neilson in *The Origins and Sources of the*

Court of Love (1899). The latter dismissed, once and for all, the idea that the courts of love were legislative assemblies, and insisted that their ludic character in no way diminished their relevance as an influence on knightly conduct (Neilson, p. 250). Thus at the turn of the century a large number of alternative or complementary theories on Courtly Love were formulated simultaneously, and the term had entered the vocabulary of medieval studies.

To recapitulate, in the early nineteenth century the medieval past was substituted for classical antiquity as a source of literary inspiration. Liberal Romantics, who deplored the oppressive tyranny of feudalism, looked back nostalgically to the 'age of chivalry' and succumbed to the spell of Jean de Nostredame. The Hispano-Arabic theory of origins at first gained currency amongst literary historians, but in the latter half of the century it was no longer advocated. Some scholars believed that troubadour poetry was the vehicle for Catharist doctrines. In the late nineteenth century, with the rise of modern medievalist scholarship, a number of new theories on Courtly Love, based on the study of folk-lore, medieval Christianity and feudal society, were first conceived.

3   1900–75 (*see table*)

During the twentieth century the methods and insights of several intellectual disciplines have been applied to the Courtly Love phenomenon: sociology, anthropology, psychology, comparative literature, the history of ideas, linguistics, and textual criticism. In the first four decades of the century there were some scholars who believed that Courtly Love was a chaste and mystical doctrine which emerged, quite suddenly, in twelfth-century Languedoc; there were others who argued that it was not a novel sentiment but a mere cover for sensuality; meanwhile, a third group, midway between these extremes, saw it as the coexistence of spiritual aspiration and concupiscence in a world of play, illusion and make-believe.[69] In recent decades the anti-Romantic or anti-Platonic interpretation has prevailed, and most of the features of Courtly Love which were once regarded as essential have been proved non-essential. By some Courtly Love has been proclaimed a universal phenomenon; by others it has been rejected as a fiction of nineteenth-century scholarship. Attempts have been made to salvage the term, but modern critics have, on the whole, been distrustful of broad generalising hypotheses and period concepts. The problem of origins has thus been largely replaced by the problem of whether or not the term is worth redefining.

Chronological table of theories, by name of theory and author, 1880–1975

Theories	1880–90	1890–1900	1900–10	1910–20	1920–30	1930–40	1940–50	1950–60	1960–70	1970–75
CRITICAL FALLACY								Robertson	Benton Donaldson	Kelly
STYLISTIC CONVENTION								Sutherland	Dragonetti Guiette Zumthor Steadman	Topsfield Paterson
COURTLY EXPERIENCE							Frings?		Dronke	
PLAY PHENOMENON		Neilson			Huizinga?		Huizinga			
COLLECTIVE FANTASY								Taylor	Moller Cleugh Askew Howard Koenigsberg	
FEUDAL–SOCIOLOGICAL	Paget		Anglade	Chaytor		Lewis? Jeanroy?		Jackson Moller Valency	Köhler Heer Duby Howard	
SPRING FOLK RITUAL	Jeanroy	Paris	Anglade	Chaytor		C. B. Lewis				
BERNARDINE–MARIANIST			Wechssler	Adams	Lot-Borodine		Bezzola			
NEOPLATONIC	Symonds						Denomy		Lazar	
CRYPTO-CATHAR			Péladan			Rougemont		*Table Ronde* ('56)	Nelli?	
CHIVALRIC-MATRIARCHAL					Crane Briffault Vossler				Acworth	
HISPANO-ARABIC				Ribera Burdach Singer	Millás	Ecker Dawson Pérès M.-Pidal Nykl	Dermengham Denomy Lévi-Provençal		Nelli Lemay Dutton	Hussein Burckhardt Chejne Daniel

Joseph Anglade, in *Les Troubadours* (1908), and H. J. Chaytor, in *The Troubadours* (1912), both agreed that Courtly Love was constituted on the analogy of feudal vassalage; that love was an art restricted, like poetry, by formal rules; and that secrecy and patience were duties incumbent upon a lover. They moreover concurred in adhering to Gaston Paris's thesis that, whatever the influence exercised by Latin or Arabic poetry, the troubadour lyric was rooted in *albas*, *ballatas* and *pastourelles* and in the popular dance songs in honour of spring (Anglade, p. 9; Chaytor, pp. 8–9). Chaytor also emphasised the role of chivalry, as modified by 'the influence of mariolatry' (p. 15), a theory widely accepted by his contemporaries.

Eduard Wechssler advanced the theory, in *Das Kulturproblem des Minnesang* (1909), that the mysticism of St Bernard was an important influence on Courtly Love, since the latter was, in his opinion, a distorted image of Christianity. He contended that, through the infiltration of Platonic doctrines and a consequent deformation of Christian mysticism, *caritas* was transposed to a profane level. He also attributed the appearance of a 'pagan spirit' in a profoundly Christian country to an awakening of individualism by the First Crusade.

Marianism was the subject of *Mont-Saint-Michel and Chartres* (1913) by Henry Brooks Adams (1838–1918). In this eloquent introduction to the French cathedrals of the thirteenth century Adams studied the extraordinary expenditure of energy and resources on buildings which were almost invariably dedicated to the Virgin Mary. He linked Marianism with the activity of St Bernard, whom Dante selected as his intercessor with the Queen of Heaven (Adams, 1950, pp. 90–1). The literature of 'courteous love', sponsored by Eleanor of Aquitaine and by Marie de Champagne, was seen as an aristocratic counterpart to the growing cult of Mary.

The Bernardine–Marianist theory was advocated by Myrrha Lot-Borodine in an article, 'Sur les origines et les fins du *service d'amour*', in *Mélanges . . . offerts à M. Alfred Jeanroy* (1928). She argued that the courtly lover employed the language of mysticism (arrows, wounds, pierced hearts, etc), experienced the same fluctuating moods (hope, desire, humility, joy and torment), and was disinterested in his devotion (pp. 233–4). The lover purged his desire by interposing obstacles to its fruition: 'l'âme, endolorie, se prend comme à un piège, à ce jeu subtil qui est l'art d'aimer par excellence' (p. 229). Gaston Paris was criticised by Lot-Borodine for mingling primary and secondary features in his definition of Courtly Love. She listed three primary features: *l'amour vertu*, love as a school of virtue; *l'amour qui est sa propre fin*, disinterestedness; and *la suprématie de la dame*, the superiority of the love object (pp. 222–3). These ideas were the basis of a later work by the same author: *De l'amour profane à l'amour sacré* (1961). The Bernardine–Marianist theory was nevertheless seriously challenged by Étienne Gilson in an appendix to *La Théologie mystique de Saint Bernard* (1934).[70]

The research of a Spanish scholar, Julián Ribera y Tarragó (1858–1934), was meanwhile instrumental in bringing about a revival of the Hispano-Arabic thesis. In his study of Ibn Quzmān's *Dīwān*, *El cancionero de Abencuzmán* (1912),[71] Ribera claimed to have discovered in the Arabic *zajal* the key to the strophic forms of the troubadours, and invoked Juan Andrés as his witness. At the same time he argued that the themes and stress measures of popular Arabic-Andalusian poetry were inspired by a Romance lyric which had been imported into Andalusia from Galicia. This opinion was based on the prominent place occupied by Galicians amongst the slaves and soldiers of Cordova, and on the importance of the Galician lyric in the thirteenth and fourteenth centuries. In *La música de las Cantigas* (1922) and *La música andaluza medieval en las canciones de trovadores, troveros, y minnesinger* (1923) Ribera maintained that the principles of troubadour music were learnt from the Arabs. His attempt to infer the nature of medieval Arabic music from the *Cantigas de Santa Maria* by Alfonso el Sabio and from Arabic treatises on music provoked a controversy which has still not been resolved.[72] The theory that Hispano-Arabic poetry served as a model for that of Provence was opposed by Menéndez y Pelayo and Amador de los Ríos, but it gained recognition from Burdach in Germany, Massignon in France, Carolina Michaëlis in Portugal, and Menéndez Pidal in Spain. According to Konrad Burdach, 'troubadour poetry and courtly love were such out-of-the-way phenomena in the development of Western culture that it was necessary to suppose that they had been borrowed from somewhere, and Arabic poetry seemed a likely source' (Stern, 1974, pp. 215–16). Courtly Love was not reflected in popular European literature, nor was it implicit in the new ideals of chivalry; the feminine ideal of this cult contravened the Church's ideal of virginity; no antecedents in Greek or Roman literature could have served as its psychological basis. This was the argument advanced by Burdach in 'Über den Ursprung des mittelalterlichen Minnesangs, Liebesromans und Frauendienstes' (1918). In the same year Samuel Singer gave a paper in which he studied connections between epics and chivalrous romances in East and West: 'Arabische und europäische Poesie im Mittelalter' (1918). The story of Tristan and Iseult, the German *Rolandslied*, the Old French romance of *Floire et Blancheflour*, and the tale of *Aucassin et Nicolette* were among the works discussed.[73] Resemblances between the metric of the early popular poetry of Italy, as represented by the *Laudi* of Jacopone da Todi and the carnival songs, were studied in relation to the popular poetry of Al-Andalus by J. M. Millás Vallicrosa in 'Influencia de la poesía popular hispano-musulmana en la poesía italiana' (1920–21).

An entirely novel approach to the study of medieval culture, which had a special bearing on Courtly Love, was inaugurated by Johan Huizinga (1872–1945) in *The Waning of the Middle Ages* (1924). It was one of Huizinga's firm convictions that ideals, even if they are delusory and anachronistic, can have a civilising influence on the life, thought and art of a given epoch. Courtly Love, a refined and specialised off-shoot of chivalry, was, in his opinion, just such an ideal. Despite his antipathy to Freudian interpretations, Huizinga attributed the vitality of heroic and bucolic themes to their erotic character, and regarded cultural ideals as palliatives or illusions, veiling reality in a vision of harmonious beauty. His tripartite schema of religious, social and poetical flights from reality corresponded almost exactly with that which Freud proposed in *Civilization and its Discontents* (1929), where voluntary loneliness (the way of renunciation), collaborative effort (the way of social reform), and the use of intoxicants, whether of a chemical or a cultural nature (the way of the dream), were respectively corre-lated, as panaceas, to three sources of suffering and anxiety: man's relations with his fellow men, the external world, and the human organism.[74] The idea of the perfectibility of society was alien to medieval thought, because life on earth was considered a preparation for the hereafter and 'terrestrial beauty bore the stain of sin' (*Waning*, p. 38). Therefore, in the Middle Ages, the only real choice lay between the religious solution of renunciation and the poetical solution of illusion. The fundamentally un-Christian 'way of the dream' was not, however, a mere substitute for action, because courtly and chivalric ideals motivated the conduct of the aristocracy and governed cere-monial occasions. Courtly Love was thus far more than 'a question of literature' (p. 54).

Huizinga noted that the visionary ideals of the late Middle Ages were grounded in pessimism and were invariably retrospective: the late Middle Ages shared with the Renaissance the desire to make life conform as closely as possible to an ideal image of the past. He disting-uished two predominant themes: the heroic and the bucolic. The former, inspired by the imitation of an ideal hero, was the basis of chivalry; the latter, inspired by an illusion of natural harmony, gave rise to the pastoral genre (p. 37). Chivalry, which entailed the observance of elaborate precepts and formalities, served to cloak aristocratic life in 'the heroism and probity of a past age' (p. 39), whereas the arcadian fantasy was, in a sense, a flight from culture, offering a temporary relief from the ceremony and over-sophistication of life at court (*Men and Ideas*, p. 86). Chivalry claimed, even at its outset in the twelfth century, to be a revival of a romantic era, associated with Charlemagne and with the Knights of the Round Table (*Men and Ideas*, p. 85), and in the fifteenth century it still provided chroniclers with a 'magic key, by the aid of which they explained to themselves the motives of politics and history' (*Waning*, p. 66). Huizinga admitted that chivalry was responsible for a number of tragic political errors, but insisted that it was 'a noble game with edifying and heroic rules' (p. 66). He detected a primitive erotic asceticism of pagan origin in the initiation rites of knighthood and in the voluntary acceptance of privation as a spur to the keeping of a troth. Sensuality was 'transformed into the craving for self-sacrifice, into the desire of the male to show his courage, to incur danger, to be strong, to suffer and to bleed before his lady-love' (p. 76). The Church sought to consecrate this latent idealism to its own ends: the knight's vocation was to protect the oppressed, to swear fealty to his ruler, and to serve Christendom by waging war against the infidel. However, the 'new poetic ideal' expressed by twelfth-century troubadours 'was capable of embracing all kinds of ethical aspirations' (p. 104), and the standards of conduct enshrined in courtly literature enabled the aristocracy to feel 'less dependent upon religious admonition' (p. 105). These were the standards of polite society, but they bore no relation to the material considerations upon which a marriage was generally based (pp. 122–3). The anti-courtly bucolic dream was unable to supplant chivalry as a model of social life, and was moreover no less artificial than the conventions against which it revolted: courtiers played shepherd and shepherdess, just as they had previously played Lancelot and Guenevere; the shepherd replaced the knight as the ideal social type, and Courtly Love was 'transposed into another key' (p. 130). The inherent falsity of the bucolic genre was unmasked by Villon in *Les contrediz Franc Gontier* (p. 133).

In the Middle Ages literature, music and the arts in general were, to a greater or a lesser extent, associated with festivities (p. 240), while tourneys and jousts satisfied 'romantic needs too strong for mere literature to satisfy' (p. 54). Aristocratic culture was imbued with the spirit of contest, courtship, make-believe and ostentatious display.

Huizinga thus came to regard the heroic and bucolic themes as manifestations of the instinct of play, the subject of a later work, entitled *Homo Ludens* (1949).

Certain of Huizinga's contemporaries still believed that Courtly Love was formed by the ancient Germanic veneration for women, in conjunction with Christianity, and that it actually improved the social status of women. This view had been expressed by Thomas Frederick Crane in *Italian Social Customs in the Sixteenth Century* (1920). Crane traced the origins of polite society to twelfth-century Provence, a region which had long had contacts with Greece and Rome. He also mentioned the 'remarkable revival of Provençal forms of thought and expression' in fifteenth-century Castile, which could be ascribed 'either to the curious Provençal renaissance which resulted in the Floral Games of Toulouse and Barcelona, or to the influence of Portugal'.[75] Karl Vossler (1872–1949) suggested, in *Mediaeval Culture* (1929), that Courtly Love was the expression of the Gothic spirit of chivalry, transplanted to Provence. It was in Provence that knights first 'espoused the cause of the fair sex', or, to put it another way, it was here that women succeeded in domesticating the northern warriors: 'Woman, whose mouth the mediaeval Church had closed, became the aristocratic lady who set her claims against those of the Church. The service of woman took its place beside religious worship; woman's code of morals rivalled that of the Church' (Vossler, 1929, I, p. 299). This ethical code placed nobility of soul above nobility of birth, and brought with it a considerable refinement of manners (I, p. 300).

Robert Briffault did not accept the theory that Courtly Love was a 'new manner of loving' or a 'genuine act of moral creation'.[76] In *The Mothers* (1927), a three-volume treatise on social anthropology which proposed the thesis that matriarchy universally precedes patriarchy, he wrote that Courtly Love was a subterfuge whereby the European aristocracy sought to ensure the survival of pre-Christian sexual *mores* amid the ascetic ideals of a Christian era:

The reason why this refinement of analysis appeared in a society which had scarcely emerged from rudest barbarism is that these conventions expressed the desire to give the sanction of cultivated taste to customary sex relations. Thus the application of Christian standards was eluded. [III, p. 424]

Initially, courtly and chivalric theories were, as he was to repeat in *Les Troubadours et le sentiment romanesque* (1945), 'a manner of apologetics serving to shield the time-honored way of life to which the ruling class was accustomed' (*The Troubadours*, pp. 96–7). Troubadour poetry was a public entertainment, based on 'stage-conventions' which were the more seductive for being fictitious. Anticipating Étienne Gilson, Moshé Lazar, Keith Whinnom and others, Briffault maintained that in troubadour poetry love was, despite the appeal to lofty principles and the use of a deliberately enigmatic vocabulary, no less frankly sensual (*Mothers*, III, p. 477; *The Troubadours*, p. 125). After the start of the Albigensian Crusade in 1209, during a period of dissolution and dissemination, Courtly Love underwent a process of disincarnation, dictated by the asceticism of orthodox Christianity and by the fear of ecclesiastical censorship. The idea that love should be a chaste, platonic and ennobling sentiment was a development which did not occur until the middle of the thirteenth century:

The conventions of *amour courtois*, which had . . . arisen out of the rude usages of warlike matriarchal societies, had, in their original form, no reference whatever to ideals of chastity; no sentiments could have been more radically opposed to the ascetic conceptions of Christianity. [*Mothers*, III, p. 496]

Provençal poetry became moral only when it had lost 'every literary quality' (*The Troubadours*, p. 128). In the early days of 'chivalry' a lady was bound in honour to reward a knight for his faithful services on her behalf, and she would be 'dishonoured' if she failed to do so, but in a later age the dictates of honour were reversed. Thus Sordello di Goito, with a show of altruism that astounded his contemporaries, implored his mistress not to be moved by compassion to grant him favours which would compromise her honour (*Mothers*, III, p. 485). Sordello was, in reality, a notorious libertine, and this discrepancy between words and action was regarded by Briffault as symptomatic of the decadence of Provençal poetry. The love poet now repudiated the happiness which he had once demanded as his right, declaring himself content with a smile. 'I deem myself richly rewarded,' wrote Guiraut Riquier, 'by the inspiration I owe to the love I bear my lady, and I ask no love in return . . . Had she ever granted me her favours, both she and I would have been defiled by the act' (*The Troubadours*, pp. 151–2). Guilhem de Montanhagol, who invented the phrase *dolce stil nuovo*, was the first poet to state that true love is chaste.[77] Matfré Ermengaud's *Lo breviari d'amor*, containing chapters 'On the baseness of sin' and 'On the vileness of the flesh', represented an effort to rehabilitate Courtly Love when the Inquisition, established by St Louis, had reached its height (*Mothers*, III, pp. 489–90). Chiaro Davanzati, Guido Guinicelli, Guittone d'Arezzo and finally Dante extolled a love purged of the sin for which man had been expelled from Eden (III, pp. 494–5). Marianism, which thrived in the thirteenth century, was interpreted as the re-establishment of a Mother Goddess cult which had prevailed in pre-Christian Europe (*Mothers*, III, p. 499; *Troubadours*, p. 154).[78]

In *Les Troubadours* (1945) Briffault adjusted his ideas to accommodate certain aspects of the Hispano-Arabic theory of origins, which was in the ascendant. The sudden growth of amatory lyricism in southern France was ascribed to the exceptional prosperity of the region, to its relative immunity from the wars which plagued the rest of Europe, and above all to its proximity to Moorish Spain. However, Briffault did not take the view that the impact of Arab culture radically altered relations between the sexes. He believed that, by appropriating Ṣūfī terminology, troubadour poetry lent itself to 'a misinterpretation which in part it invited, since it appeared to flaunt an idealism which was in fact foreign to it' (p. 98). In his opinion Arab influence was largely confined to formal elements such as music and methods of versification.

John Wilcox, in an article 'Defining Courtly Love' (1930), and C. S. Lewis, in his classic work on the subject, *The Allegory of Love* (1936), both remained within the French tradition of scholarship set by Jeanroy and Paris. Wilcox argued that the 'doctrine' was fully developed in northern France under the patronage of Marie de Champagne, when she came to reside at Troyes in 1165 or thereabouts. It was exemplified in the later romances of Chrétien, and was solemnly codified by Andreas Capellanus. According to his definition, Courtly Love has three essential elements: the worship of woman, doctrinaire free love, and sublimation through chivalric activity. The second of these features is the most original to Wilcox: 'love is free in the sense that it is the spontaneous expression of mutual desire, unaffected by social, religious, or economic pressure' (Wilcox, 1930, p. 322); furtiveness was a necessary expedient in a hostile social order. This idea of love as a commitment, contrary to the established order, was later emphasised by Jean Frappier in 'Sur un procès fait à l'amour courtois' (1972). Wilcox dismissed as incidental the need for secrecy and the traditional pathological symptoms of love. The chaste restraint of the lady had also, in his opinion, been exaggerated: the lady's aloofness was principally a means of testing her lover's sincerity. Equating the terms courtly and chivalric, love was seen primarily as a source of heroic action. With regard to the problem of origins, Courtly Love must have begun as 'an idealization of grosser social facts' (p. 323). Marie de Champagne had decreed that 'Love cannot extend her laws over husband and wife' because, wrote Wilcox, love had become 'too sub-servient to economic and social ends for love in marriage to be more than a mere accident' (p. 324). Ovid was the chief literary influence mentioned: Christian asceticism was counterbalanced by the revival of pagan classical works.

In *The Allegory of Love* (1936) C. S. Lewis proposed the formula 'Ovid misunderstood' as a means of interpreting medieval love poetry (Lewis, 1936, p. 7). The medieval lover wilfully overlooked the irony of Ovid's lessons in 'love service' because he found nothing inherently ridiculous in the idea of running errands for a lady. However, it was not the *Ars amatoria* but the feudal relationship between vassal and overlord which provided the lover with a model for his humble and servile conduct. The ritual of *domnei* was, in Wechssler's phrase, 'a feudalisation of love' (p. 2). Paget's theory of origins was more plausible than most: a meiny of knights, squires and pages thronged round the chief lady and her damsels, eager to be schooled in courtesy and refinement. Thus even before she was loved the lady of the castle was, as a result of her feudal position, an 'arbitress of manners' and 'the scourge of "villany"'. Since, however, such conditions were not peculiar to Provence, Lewis admitted that 'part of the mystery remains inviolate' (p. 12). With regard to the meaning of Courtly Love, he could assert, with a self-confidence absent from recent critical works: 'Every one has heard of courtly love, and every one knows that it appears quite suddenly at the end of the eleventh century in Languedoc' (p. 2). He declared that the revolutionary effects of this 'invention' were such that the Renaissance was, by comparison, 'a mere ripple on the surface of literature'; it transformed European ethics, aesthetics and social customs, erecting 'impassable barriers between us and the classical past or the Oriental present'.[79] Antiquity knew love only as a 'merry sensuality' or as a 'tragic madness', and these attitudes still prevailed in Europe before the twelfth century. The advent of Christianity did not bring about any idealisation of human love: the medieval Church did not encourage reverence for women, nor did it consider that sexual passion, however refined, could ever become a 'noble emotion' (p. 8). Within the bonds of holy matrimony medieval Christianity found room for innocent sexuality, but ardent love, conjugal or extra-conjugal, was regarded as wicked and morally repre-hensible: 'omnis ardentior amator propriae uxoris adulter est'.[80] The Church denied to passion the indulgence which it reluctantly accorded to appetite, whereas in romantic love poetry, a category which seems to include the medieval courtly love lyric, 'it is precisely passion which purifies' (p. 17). Yet, according to Lewis, it was the Christian attitude to passionate love which, together with the utilitarian character of medieval marriages, prevented love from being connected with the married state. The status of the medieval wife was not an enviable one: 'The same woman who was the lady and "the dearest dread" of her vassals was often little better than a piece of property to her husband' (p. 13). Lewis also observed that the courtly lover played truant from religion by deliberately emphasising the antagonism of amatory and religious ideals. 'Humility, Courtesy, Adultery, and the Religion of Love' (p. 2) were, in short, the four marks of Courtly Love.

Immediately prior to the publication of *The Allegory of Love* Christopher Dawson had advanced the Hispano-Arabic thesis on a general historical and philosophical level in an essay on 'The origins of the Romantic tradition' (1935). He maintained that the moral standards of twelfth-century Provençal society were not those of Christianity, and that the patriotic epics of the north did not betray the imprint of the new ideals of chivalry and courtesy until these had been transmitted from the south. Vossler's theory, namely that the secular culture of Provence represented 'the natural flowering of the northern chivalrous spirit' (Dawson, 1935, pp. 128–9), was thus untenable. Ramón Menéndez Pidal, without denying the influence of popular vernacular and medieval Latin poetry, drew attention to a number of formal and thematic analogies between Arabic and European love poetry in 'Poesía árabe y poesía europea' (1938).[81] He suggested that the bilingual *zajal*, a poetic form which he identified with the *muwashshah*, was a product of the fusion of Romance and Arabic culture in the Iberian Peninsula, and that this strophic form passed to the Christians of northern Spain and was diffused throughout many parts of Europe, serving as a medium for the transmission of Arabic themes.[82] In this article Menéndez Pidal relied on a concordance of motifs which had been compiled by Lawrence Ecker: *Arabischer, provenzalischer und deutscher Minnesang: eine motivgeschichtliche Untersuchung* (1934).[83] These themes and motifs were mentioned by A. R. Nykl[84] in 'L'influence arabe-andalouse sur les troubadours' (1939) and in *Hispano-Arabic Poetry and its Relations with the Old Provençal Troubadours* (1946). They were also conveniently listed by Pierre Belperron in *La Joie d'amour* (1948). The masculine form of address, the concealed identity of the beloved and the roles of the guardian and slanderer were briefly discussed by Henri Pérès in *La Poésie andalouse en arabe classique au XIe siècle* (1937). The distinctive feature of love in Arab-Andalusian poetry was, according to Pérès, 'sa vertu ennoblissante'. Commenting on a passage by Ibn 'Ammar, he wrote, 'N'est-ce pas dire par des antithèses frappantes que la douleur et l'humilité ennoblissent l'homme qui aime et ne serait-on pas tenté de voir là une conception chrétienne?' (p. 427). Pérès was also the author of an article on 'La poésie arabe d'Andalousie et ses relations possibles avec la poésie des troubadours' (1947). E. Lévi-Provençal, the author of *La Civilisation arabe en Espagne*,[85] considered Hispano-Arabic poetry to be 'a mere philological exercise artificially practised by a people for whom classical Arabic was not a mother tongue' (Monroe, 1970, p. 208). He offered an exposition of most of the arguments in favour of the Hispano-Arabic thesis in 'Poésie arabe d'Espagne et poésie d'Europe mediévale' in *Islam d'Occident* (1948).

In *L'Amour et l'Occident* (1939) Denis de Rougemont took it for granted that the French troubadours had been inspired by Arabic poetry:

> To try to establish Andalusian influence upon the courtly poems is no longer needful. And I could fill pages with passages from Arabs and Provençals about which our great specialists of 'the abyss which separates' would possibly fail to guess whether they were penned north or south of the Pyrenees. The matter is settled. [*Passion*, pp. 106–7]

This was not, however, de Rougemont's main thesis. Resurrecting the ideas of Rossetti, Aroux and Péladan, he sought to establish a psychological affinity between Courtly Love and the Cathar heresy by identifying Eros with the highly controversial theory of Thanatos, the Freudian death instinct.[86] The Arabic and European love lyric had a common source: the former adopted the rhetoric of Ṣūfī mystics, which was influenced by Iranian Manichaeism and Neoplatonism, whilst the latter was likewise Manichaean in origin. Orthodox Islam and Roman Catholicism were equally hostile to those who aspired to personal union with the Godhead. De Rougemont argued furthermore that the three words 'passion', 'revolution' and 'nation' possess a special aura of sanctity because they are coloured by a self-destructive impulse.[87] Since, in his opinion, the dualist heresy shaped the course of European literature, politics, mysticism and social conduct, he was able to cover such diverse topics as Arthurian romance, Petrarch, Spanish mysticism, Don Juan, Wagner, the rise of Nazism and the 'breakdown of marriage', to take but a random sample. He consequently assigned an even greater significance and scope to Courtly Love than C. S. Lewis.

De Rougemont shared with Briffault the postulate that Courtly Love began as a reaction to Christianity, in particular to its doctrine of marriage, by an aristocracy whose spirit was still pagan (*Passion*, p. 74). Yet de Rougemont and Briffault differed radically in their understanding of key words such as 'pagan', 'passion' and 'erotic'. For Briffault the word 'pagan' had licentious, hedonistic and matriarchal connotations, whereas for de Rougemont it evoked the mystery religions that 'deify Desire' (p. 312) and was therefore entirely consonant with the asceticism of the Cathars. Briffault's thesis rested on the assumption that the sexual *mores* of modern Europe are rooted not in Courtly Love but in the misogynistic ideals of the early Church fathers, who vilified sexuality and frowned on marriage (*The Mothers*, III, p. 505). De Rougemont, however, pointed out that 'the condemnation of the flesh, which is now viewed by some as characteristically Christian, is in fact of Manichaean and "heretical" origin' (*Passion*, p. 82). According to orthodox Christianity, the state of matrimony hallows human love by directing sexuality towards the perpetuation of the species; adultery, whether in thought or deed, is considered a mortal sin. The point had already been made by C. S. Lewis. De Rougemont argued that Christian attitudes to passion and marriage were totally reversed by the Cathars or Manichees: they condoned, even encouraged, idealised adulterous love, but condemned marriage as *jurata fornicatio* (p. 85), because it was, in their eyes, an attempt to vindicate the procreative function of sexuality, which guaranteed the continuance of the work of the evil demiurge, the author of created matter. The Cathars were compelled, after the Albigensian Crusade, to conceal their beliefs in lyrics and prose romances, where they could be expressed indirectly in myths and symbols. The troubadours' *domna* was the Cathar Lady of Thoughts, the Church of Love (*Amor* as opposed to *Roma*), the Sophia Maria of the Gnostics (p. 90); she was an ambiguous symbol, mingling sexual attraction and eternal desire.

De Rougemont's thesis was based on the assumption that Courtly Love was chaste, extra-conjugal and perpetually unsatisfied. He frequently referred to it as a myth, or even a 'sacred myth' (p. 238), because he tended to equate the troubadour concept of love with the fatal passion of Tristan and Iseult. This story of adulterous love, of Celtic provenance, was for de Rougemont the supreme myth of passion, expressing in an exemplary form a love progressively vulgarised in European literature, but a love which remained essentially the same (p. 137). Everything he understood by the word 'passion' is contained in this legend: it is illicit, irresistible, narcissistic and mutually unhappy. It is in the very nature of passion to create obstructions in order to intensify desire and to evade the possibility of fulfilment, as he was to explain more fully in *Les Mythes de l'amour* (1961).[88] This process of *askesis* (Greek for exercise) is illustrated by Tristan's decision to place a drawn sword between himself and Iseult, a deed of prowess which is 'to his own cost' (*Passion*, p. 44). The tragedy of Tristan is precipitated by 'a secret but unerring *wish* on the part of the two mystic lovers' (p. 129); the love potion is a Freudian cover for the 'unmentionable fact that passion is linked with death' (p. 21). Death, in short, is the final obstruction to which passion irrevocably leads; in Manichaean terms it is 'the *ultimate* good, whereby the sin of birth is redeemed and human souls return into the One of luminous indistinction' (p. 66). Mutual affiliations existed between the Cathar heresy and the ancient Celtic mysteries; the passion of Tristan was thus the product of a confluence of heresies, involving a transference of Courtly Love 'from song to narrative' (p. 123). The myth 'actually became in the twelfth century . . . a religion in the full sense of the word, and in particular a Christian heresy historically determined' (p. 137).

In the 1956 edition of *Passion and Society* de Rougemont disowned the extreme view which he had once appeared to champion, namely that all troubadours were practising Cathars, but his basic thesis remained unchanged:

The troubadours . . . made up their lays about a kind of love which happened to correspond (and to respond) to a very difficult moral situation, the situation that had been produced both by the religious condemnation of sexuality by the Perfect and by a natural revolt against the orthodox conception of marriage which had recently been affirmed afresh in the Gregorian reform. [p. 95]

The book was widely read, but it attracted few supporters.[89] De Rougemont's polarity between a self-effacing Eros and a self-centred Agape was debated as a theological principle in Father M. C. D'Arcy's *The Mind and Heart of Love* (1945). D'Arcy summarised de Rougemont's thesis without subscribing to it himself.

In 1944 there appeared the first of a series of articles by Alexander J. Denomy, 'An inquiry into the origins of Courtly Love'. Father Denomy was convinced, like Dawson, de Rougemont and others, that the mentality of the troubadour lyric was non-Christian, despite the fact that it flourished in a Christian environment. According to him, the fundamental tenets of Courtly Love were the superiority of the lady, the insatiability of desire, and the ennobling power of love. He moreover asserted, on the authority of Andreas Capellanus, that it was characterised by insecurity, jealousy and inequality. The possibility of a mutual affinity between Courtly Love and Christian mysticism was dismissed for reasons already adduced by Gilson, the most important being that if the Christian mystic suffers it is not because his love is unrequited but because he is unable to repay God sufficiently for the love gratuitously bestowed upon him. 'In charity love must descend to us from the Beloved before we are able to love God; in Courtly Love there is no descent of love from the beloved prior to the birth of love in the lover' (Denomy, 1944, p. 191). After a long preamble, he concluded that the intellectual background to troubadour poetry was Neoplatonic.

Denomy's thesis was reinforced in 1945 by the publication of a translation of Avicenna's *Risāla fi-'l-'Ishq* (*MedS*, VII, 117–26), containing a chapter 'On the love of those who are noble-minded and young for external beauty'. This work, deeply influenced by the Neoplatonism of Plotinus, was proclaimed a 'possible source' for Courtly Love (Denomy, 1945). The significance of this treatise, wrote Denomy, 'lies in this, that Avicenna assigns to human love, the love of the sexes, a positive and contributory part in the ascent of the soul to divine love and union with the divine' (p. 202). The fact that Andreas Capellanus' *De amore* was amongst the list of books appended to the 218 propositions condemned by Stephen Tempier, Bishop of Paris, in 1277 was adduced as further evidence that the courtly ethic was divorced from Christianity and linked instead to Arab philosophy (Denomy, 1946). This condemnation was specifically directed against Latin Averroism, which upheld the view that natural reason was capable of arriving at its own conclusions without the guidance of faith. Denomy suggested that Andreas' exposition of Courtly Love in the first two books of *De amore* and his vehement retraction in the third could be interpreted in terms of the Averroist doctrine of 'double truth'.[90] Theodore Silverstein, in a review article on recent books concerning 'Andreas, Plato and the Arabs' (Silverstein, 1949–50), noted that certain traits of *fin'amors* are absent from Avicenna's doctrine of 'pure' love, and he discussed the problem of establishing evidence that Avicenna's works were available to the early troubadours. This was the subject of a later article by Denomy: 'Concerning the accessibility of Arabic influences to the earliest Provençal troubadours' (1953).

Samuel M. Stern's discovery of Mozarabic *kharjas* in 1948[91] seriously eroded the credibility of the theory that Provençal poetic forms were borrowed from the Arabs, and demolished the traditional theory, held by most scholars since Dante, that all lyric poetry in the Romance languages derived from Provençal. These *kharjas* were short poems, written in the dialect of Spanish spoken in those regions under Arab dominion, which were incorporated into Classical Arabic or Hebrew *muwashshaḥāt*, and which appear to have determined the metrical form of the latter.[92] Since, in the *kharjas*, the Arab poet repeated or imitated the songs of the women of Al-Andalus, Stern believed that the *zajal* was also modelled on a pre-existing Romance rhyme scheme. He did not accept the theory that Muslim Spain played a decisive role in the propagation of the *zajal* form, since in his view it might have arisen spontaneously in different countries. Furthermore he argued that 'similarities between the troubadour concept of love and certain ideas expressed in Arabic literature' (Stern, 1974, p. 216)[93] did not necessarily presuppose that they were linked by a genetic relationship. The troubadours of southern France could not, in his opinion, have had any direct contact with Arabic poetry, because 'they did not know, and could not have known, enough to understand it' (pp. 216–17). Certain poetic motifs might, he conceded, have been borrowed through intermediaries, but, he concluded, 'there is reason to doubt whether even a single element in the poetry of the troubadours is due to the influence of Arabic poetry' (p. 220).

Stern's findings were reviewed and interpreted by a number of scholars. In 'Cancioncillas ''de amigo'' mozárabes' (1949) Dámaso Alonso compared the newly discovered *kharjas* to Galician–Portuguese *cantigas de amigo*. He pointed out that there were no longer any grounds for affirming that the lyric was a genre alien to the native genius of Castile.[94] This article was followed by 'La lírica hispanoárabe y la aparición de la lírica románica' (1956), in which Alonso observed that the *kharjas* confirmed Ribera's intuition of a Romance lyrical poetry prior to the *zajal*.[95] In 1949 the philologist Theodor Frings gave a lecture to the German Academy, entitled 'Minnesang und Troubadours', which studied *Frauenlied* in diverse countries, ranging from Portugal to China and from Scandinavia to Egypt. In 1952 Leo Spitzer wrote an article on 'The Mozarabic lyric and Theodor Frings' theories'. The *kharjas* were here described as vestiges of a primeval lyric associated with the rites of spring. These same poems provided Paul Zumthor with a clue to the origins of the European courtly lyric in 'Au berceau du lyrisme européen' (1954). His argument was as follows: in the geographical region which experienced the ninth-century Carolingian renaissance the growth of vernacular literature was hampered by the traditions of classical rhetoric, but in Spain the distinction between learned and popular genres remained more fluid; the southern French troubadours, when they travelled to Spain, rediscovered in the Mozarabic *kharjas* the European Romance lyric which was in fact their own literary heritage.

Two works were published in 1949 which placed the love poetry of late medieval Spain within the European tradition of Courtly Love. Pierre Le Gentil studied the themes and poetic forms of this poetry in *La Poésie lyrique espagnole et portugaise à la fin du Moyen Âge* (1949–53). Transplanted from Provence to northern France, love service was divorced from the feudal reality upon which it had once been based, and developed into a polite game (I, pp. 91–2). Northern French love poetry betrayed a predilection for negative themes, such as the *dame sans merci* and *l'amant martyr*, and this latent pessimism became more marked in the poetry of Spain and Portugal. The distinctive feature of fifteenth-century Spanish poetry was its *préciosité*: 'la préciosité prend très naturellement la forme d'un authentique *conceptisme*, lequel ne se confond ni avec le *secentisme* italien, ni avec les jeux allégoriques d'un Charles d'Orléans' (p. 595). Otis H. Green, in 'Courtly Love in the Spanish *Cancioneros*' (1949), arranged a large number of quotations of verse under headings borrowed, for the most part, from C. S. Lewis: the religion of love; courtesy; humility; the *galardón*; adultery, truancy and recantation; courtly love and monogamy; beauty; and reason. He concluded that *amor-gentileza*, the name which he gives to *cancionero* love, coincides in its major aspects with the Provençal concept of *fin'amors*. Green was later to demonstrate the persistence of this phenomenon in the Spanish Golden Age: *Courtly Love in Quevedo* (1952).

During this period a number of sociological and psychological theories on Courtly Love were formulated. W. T. H. Jackson published an article on 'The *De amore* of Andreas Capellanus and the practice of love at court' (1958). He maintained that Andreas' work was neither a treatise on love nor a critique of courtly manners but a practical manual offering instruction in a social art. He added that the work has a feminist bias, since the woman in each dialogue fails to capitulate to the persuasive techniques of her male interlocutor. In *The Literature oj the Middle Ages* (1960) Jackson stated that the role of educated patronesses such as Marie de Champagne was the most important single causative factor in the development of Courtly Love; the difference in social rank between a poet and his patroness explains the distance which, in love poetry, separates lover and beloved (p. 240).

Maurice Valency, in a book which was intended as an introduction to the love poetry of the Renaissance, entitled *In Praise of Love* (1958), distinguished between heroic love and romantic passion: 'The heroic lover pleases himself; the romantic strives to please his beloved' (Valency, 1958, p. 15). The former is symbolised by the figure of Don Juan, whereas the latter is caricatured by Don Quixote. Courtly Love, which was predominantly romantic, was linked with the decline of feudalism, and was sponsored by the very classes whose basis it undermined (p. 84). The troubadours emerged from the ranks of the petty nobility, a chivalric class which was created in the early eleventh century, when *ministeriales* of the manor were dignified with knighthood and fiefs of land. This class, which had neither wealth nor traditional prestige, sought to justify its position by 'less tangible assets' such as honour, prowess and personal merit (p. 42). Countering the idea that nobility of character is an inherited predisposition, the southern troubadours introduced an 'aristocracy of the gentle heart' (p. 35), and 'founded their entire system on the social mobility of the individual, the perfectibility of man through his own efforts' (p. 46). However, Valency did not claim that these social factors were sufficient to explain the origins of the troubadour lyric.[96]

Social mobility, mentioned briefly by Valency, was central to Herbert Moller's 'The social causation of Courtly Love' (1958–59). Moller, like a number of his contemporaries, was opposed to the widespread tendency amongst medievalists to confine their research to the 'philology of influences' as though imitation were 'the sole motive force in history' (p. 138). Whilst admitting that Hispano-Arabic poetry, Platonism, Ovidian material, Christian liturgy and autochthonous folk traditions all played their part in the formation of the troubadour lyric, he argued, as many cultural historians have done, that the diffusion of cultural traits is a selective process determined by certain social and psychological factors. On the basis of obvious analogies between Provençal and Hispano-Arabic poetry he made a preliminary investigation of the class structure and sex composition of Moorish Spain, from which he deduced that there was a correlation between the incidence of amorous poetry and the extent to which females were outnumbered by males: love poetry prospered after 974, when an influx of Berber mercenaries and captives of war employed as slave labour accentuated the disproportion between males and females in the unattached population, a discrepancy already considerable owing to sex-selective immigration and the practice of keeping harems (pp. 141–2). The same phenomenon was detected in southern France: the apogee of Provençal poetry between 1150 and 1250 was ascribed to the relative ease with which persons of the lower nobility and bourgeoisie gained promotion to the ranks of the aristocracy (p. 147). Troubadour songs and *Minne-sang* flourished in precisely those regions of Europe which witnessed a spectacular growth of the upper classes, namely in Provence, Aquitaine, Alsace, Swabia, Austria and parts of Bavaria. In these regions the *ministeriales* developed into a separate juridical class, comprising judges, trained mercenaries, castle guards, novice knights and court enter-tainers. In northern France, where the nobility had become a closed class by the eleventh century, the term *ministeriales* (whence the word 'minstrel' derives) retained its original sense, denoting 'servile agents of feudal lords or court officers' (p. 150). The promotion of *mini-steriales* created a shortage of women in the upper classes, and made it difficult to obtain a suitable wife. The situation was further aggravated by the imperative for a knight to marry above his station. Every knight was anxious 'to avoid a misalliance, lest he jeopardize his status or his chances of promotion and the status and inheritance of his children' (p. 155). In the south of France, where the law of primogeniture had not as yet been established, and where daughters of the nobility could inherit property, the pursuit of heiresses became 'a fantasy subject for indigent knights' (p. 156). The troubadour generally belonged to the 'lower echelons of the military and administrative class' (p. 160). The lady to whom he addressed his verses was portrayed as a figure of authority, capable of judging his worth, raising his self-esteem and banishing his fear of detractors. If she seemed cruel and aloof it was because she could afford to be capricious. Even nobles of ancient lineage were obliged as a result of these social changes to redefine their position in society, and to admit, grudgingly, that wealth and noble birth are in themselves no guarantee of moral worth.

In 1960 Moller, in 'The meaning of Courtly Love', concentrated on the psychological origin and function of the complex of sentiments and modes of behaviour implicit in the troubadour lyric. Courtly Love was, he argued, the fantasy of a whole class: 'a projection of unconscious emotions, which in cooperation with a responding public crystallized into a collective fantasy' (p. 41). According to Moller and later psychological theorists, this fantasy was caused by a fixation on a mother image of infantile origin, analogous to an aberration described by Freud in an essay entitled 'The most prevalent form of degradation of erotic life'.[97] The theory appears to have been first conceived by Gordon Rattray Taylor, who attempted, in *Sex in History* (1953), to replace Briffault's discredited theory of evolution from matriarchy to patriarchy by a theory of matristic and patristic attitudes. Several Provençal poets referred to the lady to whom they addressed their songs as the person who reared and educated them, and in some cases fear of her anger seems to have aroused childhood memories of a punishing mother. 'She will not make me ashamed,' wrote Bertran de Born at the age of fifty, 'if she puts other children in my cradle.'[98] In view of the absence of a threatening father figure Moller suggested that this fantasy was a reversion to the rivalry of siblings for a mother's favour. It was the woman, after all, who was simultaneously a threat and a source of protection. This argument was also consistent with the theory of a 'high sex ratio', discussed above, a point which might have been made more explicit. That this rivalry was a source of moral refinement is attested by the numerous textbooks on etiquette written during the thirteenth century:

Courtly Love became an educational institution of the knightly class, and its crowning achievement was *joy* in the assurance of personal excellence—individually, by being singled out and favored over others, and socially, by being accepted as a member of a superior social class. [p.47]

Henri Davenson [H.-I. Marrou] reviewed some of the theories on Courtly Love in *Les Troubadours* (1961). He took it for granted that *amour courtois* was 'une invention du XIIe siècle', but he emphasised that it was not chaste. The *immoderata cogitatione* of Andreas is, in biblical terms, synonymous with adultery (Davenson, 1961, p. 151). He nonetheless shared Wechssler's view that Courtly Love was an inversion of Christian mysticism (p. 169), based on 'une véritable surestimation métaphysique de la femme' (p. 157). Maurice Bowra briefly surveyed the problem in *Mediaeval Love-Song* (1961). The unique quality of twelfth-century poetry in the *langue d'oc* is that 'it expects the most capricious of passions to conform to a strict type' (p. 7). It is characterised by eternal fidelity; by the idea that the lady is an embodiment of perfection, both physical and moral; by the desire to please her, to be worthy of her, and to win her favour; by the pleasure derived from a smile or word of recognition; by the emphasis on secrecy; and by the fact that the lady is not the lover's wife (p. 7). Bowra noted affinities between Courtly Love and the chivalrous love expressed in Persian and Georgian romances, in particular *The Knight in the Panther's Skin*.[99] Arab poetry was more idealised than the troubadour lyric, since it was customary for the Arab poet to refuse his mistress's favours (p. 9).

In the years 1944–63 Reto R. Bezzola published a monumental work on European courtly literature: *Les Origines et la formation de la littérature courtoise en Occident*.[100] In Part II (1960) he expressed the conventional opinion that at the courts of Poitou and Aquitaine during the twelfth century there developed 'une nouvelle conception de l'homme' and 'une image absolument nouvelle de la femme' (p. 242). This new ideology undermined the two pillars of medieval society: 'la séparation des classes' and 'l'institution sacrée du mariage' (p. 385). Yet, in his opinion, it was a native product of the feudal Christian environment. In Part I (1944) Venantius Fortunatus (530?–610?) had been described as a precursor of the troubadours: 'À l'idéal féminin des élégiaques latins est substitué d'abord celui de la *domina*, femme d'un grand seigneur, puis celui de la Vièrge, combiné à des éléments d'une mystique amoureuse' (p. 74). Radegonde, who inspired the *Vita Sanctae Radegundis*, was the first woman of the new ruling class to act as a patroness, and she was, moreover, a poetess herself. In an article on 'Provençal literature' which he contributed to *Cassell's Encyclopaedia of World Literature* Bezzola conceded the possible influence of Arab literature which he had previously denied, but he continued to regard the concept of love evolved by Guilhem IX (1071–1127) as 'a secularization of the mystic's veneration of Mary'.[101]

In *Music and Poetry in the Early Tudor Court* (1961) John Stevens studied the courtly love lyric *sub specie ludi*, as Huizinga had done. It was the symptom of a social activity, which can best be described as a '*game*, a good Middle English term with a wealth of association: fun; a diversion; amorous play; a contest, an intrigue; the chase; the quarry'. The ritual or game of courtly living must, he claimed, be reconstructed in the imagination 'if we are to understand the courtly lyric which it nourished and which adorned it' (p. 151). Some aspects of the game were mentioned by Stevens: commoning or *luf-talkyng*, which included devising riddles and love problems, starting a debate, or communicating through *double-entendre*; reading aloud to a small gathering of courtiers and court ladies; performing pageants and masks; listening to musical recitals; or participating in seasonal revels, such as those which occurred at Christmas, St Valentine's Day, and the May festival (pp. 158–216). In *Medieval Romance* (1973) Stevens discussed the relationship between courtly and romantic love. In a chapter entitled 'Man and woman: idealisms of love' he insisted that Courtly Love was not a fixed doctrine; Andreas' *De amore*, which gave currency to this opinion, was an early document in *luf-talkyng*, and should therefore not be taken too seriously (p. 33). The principal motifs of romantic love in subsequent ages were already present in medieval prose romances:

love derives from sudden illumination; it is essentially private, and must be kept a secret from the world; it is intensified by frustration and difficulty; it lifts the lovers on to a new level of being. [p. 34]

The striking paradox of love, as idealised in medieval romance, is that 'an intensely private experience is made the ground of social well-being' (p. 48).

In 'The court of Champagne as a literary center' (1961) John F. Benton interpreted Andreas' *De amore* as a humorous and ironic condemnation of concupiscence, and rejected the theory that the court of Champagne acted as a point of literary interchange between the north and the south of France. In 'Clio and Venus: an historical view of medieval love' (1968) Benton examined chronicles, law codes, court cases, medical treatises and other historical sources in order to find evidence for the existence of Courtly Love. The severe punishments which were meted out to those found guilty of adultery made it seem highly unlikely that the early troubadours could have openly celebrated adultery. Furthermore the Victorian idea that 'decent women did not enjoy sexual relations' (Benton in Newman, 1968, p. 32) did not accord with prevailing medical doctrines on the sexual needs of women. No medieval reader would have been deceived into believing that *amor purus*, as defined by Andreas, was chaste (pp. 31–2). Benton shared the opinion of D. W. Robertson, that love in the Middle Ages (and presumably in all ages) was either concupiscent or charitable, and that a medieval audience would not have made the mistake of confusing them:

It seems to me that medieval authors and their audiences enjoyed ambiguities in literature, not because they felt it reflected a basic ambiguity in the universe or the heart of man, but because their natural tendency was to think in very rigid categories. As the *Chanson de Roland* puts it (l. 1015), 'Pagans are wrong and Christians are right.' [p. 31][102]

The idea that Courtly Love should be abandoned as a critical fallacy was forcefully stated by D. W. Robertson in a chapter on 'Some medieval doctrines of love' in his *Preface to Chaucer* (1962). He accepted Benton's conclusions that 'there is no evidence whatsoever for the existence of troubadours at Marie's court, and little likelihood that Marie would have been seriously interested in what is now called *courtly love*' (*Preface*, p. 392). Taking Andreas Capellanus as an acknowledged authority on the subject, he maintained that the *De amore* was seriously moralistic, not only in the last section but throughout (p. 395).

Sentimentality was, he believed, alien to the Middle Ages: the interlo-
cutors in Andreas' dialogues appeal to logic, not to sentiment. Medieval
literature was, he wrote, 'rigorously non-psychological' (p. 34). He
contributed a paper to *The Meaning of Courtly Love* (1968) entitled 'The
concept of Courtly Love as an impediment to the understanding of
medieval texts'. Andreas' *De amore*, the *Lancelot* of Chrétien de Troyes,
the *Roman de la Rose* and Chaucer's *Troilus and Criseyde* were all interpreted as satirical or gently ironic attacks on idolatrous passion, 'a
chronic human weakness' (Robertson in Newman, 1968, pp. 3–4).
'The study of courtly love,' he concluded, 'if it belongs anywhere,
should be conducted only as the subject is an aspect of nineteenth and
twentieth century cultural history' (p. 17).

The methods of structuralism or semiology[103] were applied to
medieval court poetry by Paul Zumthor in *Langue et techniques poétiques
à l'époque romane* (1963) and in *Essai de poétique médiévale* (1972).
According to Zumthor, the medieval poet's scope for inventiveness was
largely confined to the formal rearrangement of traditional elements:
'La variation individuelle se situe dans l'agencement d'éléments
expressifs hérités, beaucoup plus que dans la signification originale qu'on
leur conférerait' (*Langue*, pp. 126–7). The themes, motifs and formulas
of medieval court poetry can therefore be analysed as constituents of a
semi-autonomous universe. Every literary topic comprises certain
themes or registers, which can be subdivided into a number of motifs.
Hope, fear, desire, service and prayer are motifs belonging to the
'registre de la requête courtoise' (p. 128). Each motif is associated with
certain key words and formulas, and the presence of a key word in a
given context is generally sufficient to evoke a specific motif. The words
merci, *pitié*, *essaucier* or *proier* would, for example, immediately call to
mind the motif of courtly prayer or entreaty (p. 129). The vocabulary
used by the court poet might thus be compared to the stops of an organ,
designed to play an infinite number of variations on a limited number of
set themes.

In a major work on troubadour love, *L'Érotique des troubadours* (1963),
René Nelli distinguished between two divergent but complementary
tendencies: 'amour chevaleresque' and 'amour courtois'. The former
was a love based on fidelity and reciprocity, which inspired the knight
with courage in the tournament or the battlefield; the latter was a love,
for ever unappeased, between a humble suitor and a lady of noble birth.
'Amour chevaleresque' implied comradeship between equals, whereas
'amour courtois' was proved by a reversal of the normal sex rôles:
'l'érotique chevaleresque ne tendait qu'à développer les qualités

viriles du héros pour le rendre digne de l'amour, alors que l'érotique
courtoise se proposait de faire naître cette passion d'une épreuve
sentimentale purificatrice' (p. 74). Nelli argued that a moral and
chronological progression could be traced from the primitive belief in
a magical communion of souls, which assured the warrior of protection
from harm, as in the ritual of blood-brotherhood, to the sentimental
heroism of the *asag*, a ceremony of chaste cohabitation described in
Flamenca. He attempted to study these phases of Provençal love from an
ethnographic or anthropological point of view, stressing the multi-
plicity of the origins of European romanticism but assigning a prominent
place to Arab sources.

In *Amour courtois et 'fin'amors' dans la littérature du XIIe siècle* (1964)
Moshé Lazar, a pupil of Jean Frappier, observed that critics had
hitherto failed to differentiate between *courtoisie*, *amour courtois* and
fin'amors (pp. 21–3; 253–4). This oversight was, in his view, responsible
for much of the confusion about the meaning of Courtly Love. *Fin'amors*
was the technical term for the amatory ideal of the early troubadours,
an ideal which was incompatible with Christian charity, and which was,
from the Church's point of view, devoid of morality (p. 82). *Cortezia*,
mezura and *jovens* were the three cardinal virtues of *fin'amors*. *Cortezia*
was not synonymous with *courtoisie*: it denoted the sum total of the
virtues expected of the *fin amant* or an attitude of politeness and
moderation, whereas the *courtoisie* of northern France referred to the
Christian chivalrous ethic (p. 44). *Mezura* denoted the inner discipline
of the lover, based on the harmonious co-operation of heart and head
(pp. 30–2). *Jovens*, a term used in poetry in a moralistic vein, denoted
youth, generosity and moral integrity. The semantic field of *jovens* was
probably contaminated by the connotations of the Arabic *fata*, as
Denomy has suggested (p. 42).[104] The ideal of *fin'amors* involved
privation and hardship, but it was, according to Lazar, adulterous and
sexual in intent: 'Le coeur de la Dame peut appartenir au troubadour,
puisque le mari n'a des droits que sur le corps. Mais le troubadour ne
désire pas seulement le coeur de l'amante, comme on l'a trop souvent
dit, il désire aussi ardemment son corps' (p. 61). This sensuality was
concealed by 'l'hermétisme aristocratique' (p. 135). The term *amour
courtois* was one which Lazar avoided using, except as a possible designa-
tion for the more idealised and conventional lyric which was written
after the twelfth century. He did not believe that the troubadours were
greatly indebted to Ovid or to medieval Latin literature. He himself did
not enter into the problem of origins, but he warned other researchers
not to seek a single origin for the diverse constituents of this poetry.

'La question des origines est à réviser. Il faut rechercher les origines de la *courtoisie*, de la *fin'amors*, de la poésie provençale, séparément' (p. 13).

In *Poetic Love* (1964) John B. Broadbent wrote that, between 1000 and 1300, there was 'a tendency to institutionalize, codify, and honour, motives of dedication' and that the 'exclusion of the pleasures of sex as in all circumstances profane, just when other motives were being idealized, made it inevitable that a special sanctity should be invented for them, outside marriage and outside the Church'. 'This,' he claimed, 'was the point of courtly love' (p. 18). He discerned in the poetry of the troubadours a tension between love and passion or mind and matter, which was his criterion of poetic excellence: 'Metaphysical poetry was the culmination of an associative effort which began with the trobadors and ended in Milton' (p. 2).

In 'Observations historiques et sociologiques sur la poésie des troubadours' (1964) Erich Köhler,[105] following Moller's lead, focused his attention on changes in the structure of the upper classes in twelfth-century France. After the disintegration of the Carolingian empire the *vassi dominici* and *vicarii* were obliged to raise their own private armies for purposes of self-defence. In an age of anarchy it was essential to devise a personal bond as a guarantee of allegiance. The practice of distributing land on the basis of an exchange of protection for military service created a new social class during the tenth and eleventh centuries. However, the sense of military obligation, which had once been inseparable from the concept of land tenure, lapsed as fiefs tended to become hereditary. The prince and overlord continued to secure loyalty by educating the sons of his more distinguished subjects in his own household. The courtly ethic answered the needs of these court officials and petty noblemen who sought integration into the ranks of the aristocracy. Princes and monarchs encouraged 'l'idéal courtois' because it neutralised 'l'état de tension permanente entre la basse noblesse et la haute féodalité dans leur vie commune à la cour' (p. 28).

Georges Duby, in the same year, published another study of the sociological background to the aristocratic culture of twelfth-century France: 'Dans la France au Nord-Ouest, au XIIe siècle: les *jeunes* dans la société aristocratique' (1964). The *juvenes* were young men, recently dubbed or aspiring to knighthood, who were either bachelors or married men without children; many of these men were rootless, being younger sons without lands or the hope of a legacy. Duby believed that this dynamic aggressive constituent of feudal society, with its taste for adventure and its quest for fame, determined the character of courtly and chivalric literature. The Provençal term *jovens* was the ideal which animated this group, as it attempted to replace the trio of husband, wife and married lover by that of husband, married lady and young suitor.[106]

Melvin W. Askew, in 'Courtly Love: neurosis as institution' (1965), referred to Courtly Love as 'a codification and institutionalization of neurotic and negative values', but denied that this statement implied a negative value judgement on individual works composed within this tradition.[107] He discerned an ambivalent attitude to women in the structure of Andreas Capellanus' *De amore* which, he concluded, was characteristic of Courtly Love. Richard A. Koenigsberg published a more sophisticated Freudian study of the problem: 'Culture and unconscious fantasy: observations on Courtly Love' (1967). He noted the sadism with which the women in the dialogues of Andreas' *De amore* humiliate their male suitors, and suggested that masochistic submission to the lady's will was an essential feature of Courtly Love. Love, according to Andreas, is a state of mind maintained by the cultivation of desire. The basic rules for increasing desire are twofold: one cannot love one's wife; one must be jealous.[108] Koenigsberg compared this concept of love to the syndrome discussed by Freud in his 'First contribution to the psychology of love':[109] the woman acquires her full value when there is some occasion for jealousy; the love object is overvalued, and preoccupies the lover to the exclusion of all other interests; and, finally, the man desires to 'rescue' the woman. A love complying with these conditions must, according to Freud, derive from a mother fixation of infantile origin. The desire to rescue the beloved (which was, incidentally, a common theme in chivalric romance) was transformed into 'the fantasy of being rescued by the beloved' (p. 43). The denial of heredity as the basis of nobility was interpreted as an expression of the unconscious wish to be father of oneself. Andreas wrote that a scolding lecture from parents 'gives a perfect reason for beginning a love affair which has not yet started' (*De amore*, trans. Parry, p. 154), from which Koenigsberg inferred that the courtly lover was motivated by the unconscious desire to take revenge on the father. He concluded that Courtly Love was 'an institutionalized response to the Oedipus complex' which justified the need for affection and tenderness. In this respect it was saner than the homosexual ideal of the ancient Greeks and the asceticism of early Christianity, both of which resolved the Oedipus complex by a 'ritualistic devaluation of women' (pp. 46–9).

Meanwhile E. Talbot Donaldson, following the example of Robertson, had published an article entitled 'The myth of Courtly Love' (1965). Courtly Love was, in his opinion, a fantasy of modern criticism, not a fantasy of twelfth-century Europe; even if it never existed 'scholars would have found it convenient to construct it—which, as a matter of fact, they have, at least partially, done' (Donaldson, 1970, p. 155). Andreas Capellanus, 'the real villain behind Lewis's definition', rewrote Ovid's *Art of Love* and his *Remedies of Love* as a *jeu d'esprit*; the third book, wrote Donaldson, is no more serious than the first two, and ends with an 'antifeminist tirade in which Andreas strives to out-Hieronymo St Jerome' (p. 161). Adultery was a comparatively rare theme in medieval literature, and was never elevated into a cult. The only generalisation that can be made about the troubadours was that they sublimated their love (p. 157).

Donald R. Howard paraphrased the ideas of Denomy, Jackson, Paget, Moller and others in *The Three Temptations* (1966), and attempted to reconcile the 'game theory' with the sociological and psychological approaches: Courtly Love was 'a gamelike revolt against traditional morality' (p. 102) and 'a ritualized expression of anxieties about social class and sexuality' (p. 97). He accepted Moller's thesis that Courtly Love was the fantasy of a particular milieu 'in which polyandrous relationships were desired (and *needed*, because of the high sex ratio), but forbidden' (p. 101). By the thirteenth century the courtly ideals and motifs had become fashionable in northern France, where the conditions which had been responsible for their development did not exist.

Peter Dronke called for a complete reorientation of Courtly Love scholarship in *Medieval Latin and the Rise of European Love Lyric* (1965–66). He did not denounce the term as an illusion of criticism, but on the contrary believed that Marrou had been correct when he referred to *amour courtois* as 'un secteur du coeur, un de ses aspects éternels de l'homme' (Marrou, 1947, p. 89). It was his belief in the universality of the 'courtly experience' that caused him to part company with traditional critics. *Amour courtois* is, he wrote, 'at least as old as Egypt of the second millennium B.C. and might occur at any time or place'. Moreover this experience 'is not confined to courtly or chivalric society, but is reflected in the earliest recorded verse of Europe'. Research into European courtly poetry should therefore be concerned with the learned development of themes, not with their specific origins (p. ix). Dronke also argued that the 'courtly experience' was based on the feeling 'that finite human love can, at its best, have something more than human about it', and that 'divinity hedges the beloved and can be experienced through her' (pp. 4–5).

To recapitulate, this century has witnessed the re-emergence of two early theories on Courtly Love: the Hispano-Arabic and the Crypto-

Cathar. At the beginning of the century scholars were chiefly interested in ideas which had already been developed, in an embryonic form, in the late nineteenth century: Bernardine mysticism; Marianism; feudal concepts; May Day ritual; and the study of Ovid. Sociological and psychological theories were formulated by later theorists. In recent years dialectical reasoning and generalising hypotheses have been replaced by a concern with semantics and close textual readings and by a respect for the integrity of individual works. Scepticism about the validity of the term Courtly Love has come from several quarters.

NOTES

[1] These include Renaissance Neoplatonism and the principle of decorum.

[2] *Les Essais de Michel de Montaigne*, ed. Pierre Villey (Paris: PUF, 1965), I, xxvi, p. 175. Montaigne disapproved of Spanish and Petrarchan poetry: 'je voy que les bons et anciens Poètes ont évité l'affectation et la recherche, non seulement des fantastiques élévations Espagnoles et Petrarchistes, mais des pointes mesmes plus douces et plus retenues, qui sont l'ornement de tous les ouvrages Poétiques des siècles suyvans' (II, x, p. 412).

[3] This was in an Italian translation by Gian Giorgio Trissino. The Latin text was first published by Jacopo Corbinelli, Paris, 1577.

[4] Ed. A-F. Gatien-Arnoult, with a French translation by Aguilar and d'Escouloubre (3 vols, Toulouse: J-R. Paya, 1841–43). Joseph Anglade published a Catalan reworking of this version, *Las flors del gay saber* (Barcelona: Institució d'Estudis Catalans, 1926). The second Toulousain version *Las leys* was also published by Anglade, as *Las leys d'amor* (4 vols, Toulouse, 1919–20). The *Doctrina de compondre dictats*, attributed to Jofre de Foixà, states that a song must treat of love: 'E primerament deus saber que canço deu parlar d'amor plazenment, / e potz metre en ton parlar eximpli d'altra rayso, e ses maldir e ses lauzor de re sino d'amor' (ed. J. H. Marshall, *The 'Razos de Trobar' of Raimon Vidal and associated texts* [London: OUP, 1972], ll. 7–9, p. 95). A useful work of reference is Warner F. Patterson, *Three Centuries of French Poetic Theory. A critical history of the chief arts of poetry in France (1328–1630)*, UMPLL, 14 and 15 (2 vols, Ann Arbor, Mich., 1935).

[5] *Antiqua rhetorica* (1215), in Debenedetti, p. 2.

[6] See Peter Dronke, 'Mediaeval rhetoric', in *The Mediaeval World*, ed. D. Daiches and A. Thorlby (London: Aldus, 1973), p. 339. Dante's originality as a critic is appraised by George Saintsbury, *A History of Criticism and Literary Taste in Europe* (Edinburgh: W. Blackwood, 1900), I, pp. 417–45.

[7] See Bibliography, Charles S. Singleton.

[8] This programme resembles that of Juan Ruiz in his prologue to the *Libro de Buen Amor*, ed. Manuel Criado de Val and E. W. Taylor (Madrid: CH, 1965), pp. 3–7.

[9] This point was made by W. J. Entwistle in the revised edition of Hastings Rashdall, *The Universities of Europe in the Middle Ages* (London: OUP, 1936), II, p. 100. See Ricardo del Arco y Garay, *Memorias de la universidad* in *Collección de documentos para la historia de Aragón*, VIII (Saragossa, 1912), Part 2, p. 3. The school of Limousin studies was a complementary institution to the poetic academy. Limousin was held to be the purest poetic dialect: 'Primerament deus saber que totz homs qui vol entendre en trobar deu saber que nenguna parladura no es tan natural ne tan dreta a trobar del nostre lengatge com aquella francesa de Lemosi [...] de totas aquellas terras qui entorn li estan o son lur vesinas' (Raimon Vidal in *The 'Razos del trobar'*, ed.

J. H. Marshall, ll. 61–4, p. 5). Jerónimo de Zurita recounts, in his *Indices rerum ab Aragoniae regibus gestarum* (Saragossa: D. a Portonariis de Ursinis, 1578), that in 1388 ambassadors were sent to the king of France 'ut vernaculae linguae celebres poëtae in Hispaniam ex Narbonensis provinciae scholis traducerentur: & studia poëtices, quam Gaiam scientiam vocabant, instituerentur. His vero, quorum ingenium in eo artificio elucere videbatur, magna praemia, industriae, & honoris insignia, monumentaque laudis esse constituta' (fol. 363r). It is possible that a Provençal school existed at Vicenza, chaired by Tuisio, in the early fourteenth century, but the evidence is not conclusive. See Debenedetti, p. 4.

[10] *Villena, Lebrija, Encina*, ed. I. Bullock (Cambridge: CUP, 1926), p. 2.

[11] *Letter of the Marquis of Santillana to Don Peter, Constable of Portugal*, ed. Antonio R. Pastor and Edgar Prestage (Oxford: Clarendon, 1927), p. 70.

[12] An illuminist or charismatic theory of poetry was shared by certain Spanish poets in the late fourteenth and early fifteenth centuries. See Charles F. Fraker, *Studies in the 'Cancionero de Baena'*, UNCSRLL, 61 (Chapel Hill, N.C., 1966), pp. 69–90. The miraculous properties of the Gay Science were expounded in a document issued by John I of Aragon in 1393: 'purissimo, honesto et curiali nitens eloquio, rudes erudit, inertes excitat, ebetes mollit, doctos allicit . . . occulta elicit, obscura lucidat, cor laetificat, excitat mentem, sensum clarificat atque purgat . . .'(Archivo de la Corona de Aragón, Reg. 1924, fols 149–50).

[13] In Castile Galician, the traditional language of lyrical poetry, was gradually replaced by Castilian in the late fourteenth century. The decay of Portuguese poetry after the death of King Dinis in 1325 and, more important still, the absence of close cultural contacts between Castile and Portugal after the accession of the bastard Trastámara dynasty in 1369, accompanied by a growing nationalist sentiment, induced poets at the Castilian court to forge a language and style of their own.

[14] Poetry written by Spaniards at Naples is scarcely distinguishable from poetry written by Spaniards who never left Spain. A. D. Deyermond writes: 'The poets of Alfonso V's Court . . . adhere closely to the traditional Spanish forms: *canciones* of courtly love, in which the lover suffering without hope of reward makes a frequent appearance, and in which the only discernible foreign influence is French' (*A Literary History of Spain: the Middle Ages* [London: Ernest Benn, 1971], p. 194).

[15] See Vincenti (1963), pp. xxvi–xxxii, and Axhausen (1937), pp. 5–6.

[16] Juan Carlos Temprano, '*El Arte de poesía castellana* de Juan del Encina (edición y notas)', *BRAE*, LIII (1973), 321–50, at pp. 326–7.

[17] 'Ce langage Romain estoit celuy que les Romains introduisirent dans les Gaules après les avoir conquises, & qui s'estant corrompu avec le temps par le mélange du langage Gaulois qui l'avoit précédé, & du Franc ou Tudesque qui l'avoit suivi, n'estoit ni Latin, ny Gaulois, ny France, mais quelque chose de mixte' (Huet, 1671, p. 48).

[18] The meaning of Romance is explained in Ernst R. Curtius, *European Literature and the Latin Middle Ages*, trans. W. R. Trask (London: RKP, 1953), pp. 30–5. The first English philologist to criticise Raynouard's theories was George Cornewall Lewis, in *An Essay on the Origin and Formation of the Romance Languages* (London: John Murray, 1893).

[19] Lodovico Domenichi, *Facetie, motti et burle* (Venice: Giovanni Griffio, 1581), p. 362. Gesualdo mentioned the troubadours in his edition of Petrarch: *Il Petrarcha colla spositione di Misser Giovanni Andrea Gesualdo* (Venice, Antonio di Nicolini, 1533). Alessandro Tassoni ransacked the poetry of the Provençal troubadours in search of passages which Petrarch had imitated in *Considerazioni sopra le rime di Petrarca* (Modena: Giulian Cassiani, 1609).

[20] Curtius, *European Literature*, p. 264.

[21] He was secretary to Isabella d'Este, a patroness of vernacular humanism. He accompanied her on a tour of Provence in 1517, and visited the archives at Aix. See

Domenico Santoro, *Della vita a delle opere di Mario Equicola* (Chieti, 1906), pp. 167 ff., and Alessandro Luzio and Rodolfo Renier, *Cultura e relazioni d'Isabella d'Este Gonzaga* (Turin: L. Roux, 1893).

22 Among those who do acknowledge their debts are Agostino Nifo, *De pulchro et amore* (Leiden: Davidis López de Haro, 1641), fol. 169r, and Giuseppe Betussi, *Dialogo amoroso* (Venice: Al segno del pozzo, 1543), fol. 18v. 'It was poor Equicola's fate to be shamelessly pillaged by his fellow authors, and in the century after his death to be hounded from Parnassus by the irrepressible Boccalini' (Nesca A. Robb, *Neoplatonism of the Italian Renaissance* [London: Allen & Unwin, 1956], p. 189). He was also cited in Spain by Lope de Vega; his name rubbed shoulders with León Hebreo and Ovid in *El maestro de danzar*, II, 5.

23 See Camillo P. Merlino, *The French Studies of Mario Equicola*, UCPMP, vol. 14, No. 1 (Berkeley, Cal., 1929).

24 'Ben devon li amador / de bon cor servir amor / . . . e d'amor mou castitatz, / qar qi.n amor ben s'enten / non pot far qe pueis mal renh' (R. T. Hill and T. G. Bergin, *Anthology of the Provençal Poets* [New Haven and London: Yale University Press, 1973], I, p. 231). According to Briffault, these lines were dictated by the need to conform to ecclesiastical requirements (*The Mothers*, III, p. 489).

25 Equicola wrote, 'che chi non teme non ama' (fol. 198r). This was one of the thirty-one rules pronounced by the King of Love in Andreas Capellanus' *De amore* (trans. J. J. Parry, p. 185). It is in fact a commonplace, traceable in Ovid, *Heroides*, I, 12: 'Res est solliciti plena timoris amor'. See R. Bossuat, *Drouart la Vache, traducteur d'André-le-Chapelain (1290)* (Paris: H. Champion, 1926), p. 75.

26 Equicola appears to have been using one of the Neapolitan *cancioneros*. María Rosa Lida de Malkiel discussed Equicola's criticism of Mena in *Juan de Mena, poeta del prerenacimiento*, Publicaciones de la NRFH, 1 (Mexico City, 1950), pp. 334–5. Mena's style was contrary to Renaissance canons of taste.

27 'Barbieri was not himself an Arabist, and his information was second-hand. Therefore he made some technical mistakes (i.e. classical Arabic poetry is based on *quantity*, though *stress* does appear in popular poetry—which he did not know. Furthermore, in late Latin poetry, such as that of St Augustine, stress does occur, as well as a rudimentary form of rhyme)' (Monroe, 1970, p. 40). See Giulio Bertoni, *Giovanni Maria Barbieri e gli studi romanzi nel secolo XVI* (Modena: G. T. Vincenzi, 1905).

28 Crescimbeni (1698), p. 6; Abbé Massieu, *Histoire de la poésie française* (Paris: Prault Fils, 1739), p. 103; Andrés (1782–1822), I, pp. 306–7; Sismondi (1823), I, pp. 101–3; Briffault, *The Troubadours*, p. 33: 'It was the Arabs who introduced rhyme into Europe'. Encina states in his *Arte de poesia*, BRAE, LIII (1973), 330, that rhyme was employed, chiefly as a mnemonic device, by the early composers of Christian hymns.

29 Anglade accepted Girolamo Tiraboschi's verdict that Hugues de Saint-Cyrc and Michel de la Tour were the only genuine historians of the troubadours cited by Nostredame (Nostredame, p. 160). Crescimbeni claimed to have seen a MS in the Vatican library by the Monaco dell' Isole d'Oro (d. 1408), containing poems in Italian, Spanish, Gascon, French and other languages, 'tra' quali s'annovera spezialmente il Re Alfonso d'Aragona, che di tal favella, e Poesia molto si dilettò' (*Istoria*, revised edn. [6 vols, Venice: Lorenzo Basegio, 1730–31], I, pp. 91–2). Yet Chabaneau argued, in *Le Moine des Isles d'Or* [Extrait des *Annales du Midi*, année 1907] (Toulouse: E. Privat, 1907), that the Monk of the Golden Isles is a fictitious person, whose name is an anagram of Reimond de Soliés (Jules-Raymond de Soliers), the author of an unpublished *Chronographia Provincia*. The monk's character was based on that of Soliers, who did indeed compile a list of Provençal poets. Since this list includes the name Monachus Insularum aurearum, Chabaneau concluded that Soliers, who refers his readers to Nostredame's work, acted as the latter's accomplice. It was merely to flatter his friend Scipion Cibo that Nostredame chose to make his monk a

member of this Genoese family. Chabaneau added in a footnote; 'Il va sans dire qu'avec le Moine des Isles d'Or doivent aussi disparaître de l'histoire littéraire et dom Hermentaire, dont il est censé avoir transcrit le recueil, et dom Hilaire des Martins, son prétendu biographe' (p. 13 n.).

[30] See Rita Calderini De-Marchi, *Jacopo Corbinelli et les érudits d'après la correspondance inédite Corbinelli-Pinelli (1566–87)* (Milan: U. Hoepli, 1914).

[31] It was published in 1728 by Desmolets in the journal *Continuation des Mémoires de Littérature et d'Histoire* (Paris: Simart), VI, Part II, pp. 281–342; by Alphonse Feillet (Paris: Aubry, 1870); by Alfred C. Hunter in *Opuscules critiques* (Paris: Droz, 1937), and by Fabienne Gégou. See Huet in Bibliography.

[32] *S'il faut qu'un jeune homme soit amoureux*; see Bibliography.

[33] In 1694, during the reign of Louis XIV, new rules were drawn up, and in 1725 Louis XV increased the number of academicians to forty. Similar poetic contests must have been held in twelfth-century Europe. The Wartburg song contest, added by Wagner to the Tannhäuser story, is based on a thirteenth-century poem. For references and a discussion of the problem see Neilson (1899), pp. 240–56. See also Chabaneau (1885).

[34] An annual poetry festival had been held in 'Okāz since *c.* 500 B.C. (Sismondi, 1823, I, p. 53).

[35] In France it was published at least eight times in the seventeenth, ten times in the eighteenth, and eight times in the nineteenth centuries. It was finally suppressed in the 1882 edition of the *Oeuvres de Mme de la Fayette*. See Huet, ed. Gégou, pp. 201–3. Huet ignores one of the chief precursors of the modern novel, the Spanish sentimental romance, a genre diffused throughout Europe in the sixteenth century. These romances were strongly influenced by the courtly love lyric. See Ruiz de Conde (1948); Barbara Matulka, *The Novels of Juan de Flores and their European Diffusion* (New York: Institute of French Studies, 1931); and Whinnom, ed., *Obras completas de Diego de San Pedro*, in Bibliography. For Warton see below, pp. 15–16.

[36] *The Critical Works of Thomas Rymer*, ed. Curt A. Zimansky (New Haven: Yale University Press, 1956), pp. 120 and 250.

[37] *A Popular History of English Poetry* (London: Methuen, 1933), pp. 3–4.

[38] Lionel Gossman, *Medievalism and the Ideologies of the Enlightenment. The world and work of La Curne de Sainte Palaye* (Baltimore, Md.: Johns Hopkins University Press, 1968), p. 352. Chivalry was regarded by nineteenth-century scholars as the very quintessence of the Middle Ages, not a detachable component. This illustrates a fundamental change in man's attitude to the past.

[39] *De la chevalerie ancienne et moderne, avec la manière d'en faire les preuves, pour tous les ordres de chevalerie* (Paris: R. J. B. de la Caille, 1683), p. 1. Ménestrier was, incidentally, the author of one of the earliest books on pageantry and ballet: *Des Ballets anciens et modernes selon les règles du théâtre* (Paris: René Guignard, 1682).

[40] F. Baldensperger, 'Le genre troubadour' in *Études d'histoire littéraire* (première série, Paris: Hachette, 1907), and Henri Jacoubet, *Le Compte de Tressan et les origines du genre troubadour* (Paris: PUF, 1923).

[41] Huizinga, 'Historical ideals of life', *Men and Ideas*, p. 86. For Sismondi see below, pp. 15–16.

[42] The same point was made by Dronke, *RF*, LXXIII (1961), 327–38.

[43] *Histoire des Celtes, et particulièrement des Gaulois et des Germains, depuis les tems fabuleux jusqu'à la prise de Rome par les Gaulois* (2 vols, The Hague: I. Beauregard, 1750). Pelloutier identified the Gauls with the Celts.

[44] 'They even suppose somewhat of sanctity and prescience to be inherent in the female sex; and therefore neither despise their counsels, nor disregard their responses' (*Germania*, VIII, *The Works of Tacitus*, Bohn's Classical Library, II [London, 1887], p. 296).

[45] F. L. Lucas, *The Decline and Fall of the Romantic Ideal* (Cambridge: CUP 1936), p. 18.

⁴⁶ Jean Pierre Papon, *Histoire générale de Provence* (4 vols, Paris, 1777–86), II, p. 466. Arthur Johnston has a chapter on Warton in *Enchanted Ground. The study of medieval romance in the eighteenth century* (London: Athlone, 1964).

⁴⁷ See Thomas R. Hart, 'Friedrich Bouterwek. A pioneer historian of Spanish literature', *CL*, V (1953), 351–61.

⁴⁸ This is a reversal of the conventional theory, according to which Provençal was the literary idiom imitated by the Catalans.

⁴⁹ See N. F. Haym, *Notizia de'libri rari nella lengua italiana . . . anessori tutto il Libro della Eloquenza Italiana di . . . G. Fontanini* (London, 1726).

⁵⁰ 'In matters of music . . . Andrés was well informed, for he was in touch with Casiri's school in Spain, and had used Banqueri's translation of a musical treatise by al-Fārābī' (Monroe, 1970, p. 41). Al-Fārābī was cited by numerous theorists from the thirteenth century onwards. Yet no medieval Moorish music survives. The problem is still a controversial one. See Chapter II, p. 72.

⁵¹ See González Palencia, *And*, XI (1946), 241–5; Augustin and Aloys de Backer, *Bibliothèque de la Compagnie de Jésus*, new edn. by Carlos Sommervogel, I (1890), *s.v.* 'Jean Andrés', pp. 242–350; 'Étienne Artiaga', pp. 590–1; Pedro Sainz y Rodríguez, *Las polémicas sobre la cultura española* (Madrid, 1919).

⁵² See Janine R. Dakyns, *The Middle Ages in French Literature, 1851–1900* (London: OUP, 1973).

⁵³ François-René de Chateaubriand, *Génie du Christianisme, ou Beautés de la religion chrétienne* (2 vols, Paris: Migneret, 1802), I, Bk. 3, ch. 9, p. 158. This section served as a prologue to the novel *René*.

⁵⁴ Sismondi's colleague, Friedrich von Schlegel (1772–1829), spoke of the inclination to locate the golden age prior to any recorded period of history in his lectures at Vienna in 1812. See Curtius, *European Literature*, p. 269.

⁵⁵ Ibn Abī Hadjala (1325–75), author of the *Dīwān al-Sabāba*, a history of celebrated lovers, with a selection of erotic poems.

⁵⁶ There is still considerable disagreement over Andreas' intentions: whether he was in jest or earnest; whether he was expounding the theory of *fin' amors* or deliberately undermining it; whether he was writing a moralistic work or a manual of seduction. The popularity of the work is nevertheless undeniable: it was twice translated into French (by Drouart la Vache in 1290 and Enanchet in the early thirteenth century); twice into Italian and German in the fifteenth century; once into Catalan, by Domenic Mascó, for John I of Aragon in the late fourteenth century. See A. D. Deyermond, 'The textbook mishandled. Andreas Capellanus and the opening scene of *La Celestina*', *N*, XLV (1961), 218–21.

⁵⁷ Barthélemy Herbelot, *Bibliothèque orientale, ou dictionaire universel contenant généralement tout ce qui regarde la connoissance des peuples de l'Orient* (Paris: Compagnie des libraires, 1697).

⁵⁸ For his life and works see Pompeo Giannantonio, *Bibliografia di Gabriele Rossetti (1806–1958)* (Florence: Sansoni Antiquariato, 1959). See also R. D. Waller, *The Rossetti Family* (Manchester: MUP, 1932), and E. R. Vincent, *Gabriele Rossetti in England* (Oxford: Clarendon, 1936).

⁵⁹ Similar ideas had been voiced by Protestant writers since the sixteenth century. Dante and Petrarch were among the anti-papalists listed by Mathias Flacius Illyricus in his *Catalogus testium veritatis, que ante nostram aetatem reclamarunt Papae* (Basle, 1556; Strasbourg, 1562), and by Bishop John Jewel in his *Apology for the Church of England* (London, 1560). Amongst those whom John Foxe cites, in *The Acts and Monuments* (London, 1563), are Joachim da Fiore, the Albigenses, Raymond of Toulouse, Marsilio of Padua, Arnald of Villanova, Robert Grosseteste, William of Ockham, Jean of Jandun, Buridan, Dante, Petrarch, Nicholas Oresme, Nicholas of Lyra, Cardinal Cusanus, Aeneas Sylvius, Wyclif, Gower, Chaucer, Huss, Savonarola, Lorenzo Valla and Pico della Mirandola. See Frances A. Yates, *Astraea. The imperial*

theme in the sixteenth century (London: RKP, 1975), pp. 39–45. The earliest history in which the Cathars were portrayed in a favourable light was by a Calvinist, Chassonion de Monistrol, *Histoire des Albigeois* (Geneva, 1595). See René Nelli *et al.*, *Spiritualité de l'hérésie* (Paris: PUF, 1953), pp. 209 ff.

60 Dante believed that only a world ruler was capable of establishing a reign of universal peace. In *De monarchia*, III, he maintained that this ruler, the monarch, derives his authority directly from God, without the necessity of having to rely on the Pope's mediation. See Frances Yates, *Astraea*, pp. 2–20. It would thus be easier to make out a case for Dante the heretic than for Dante the socialist. This was not the opinion of Ferjus Boissard, who answered Aroux with *Dante révolutionnaire et socialiste, mais non hérétique; Révélation sur les révélations de M. Aroux et défense d'Ozanam* (Paris: C. Douniol, 1854).

61 Rougemont identified the troubadours with the Cathars but stressed that the latter were Manichaean heretics. See below, pp. 37–9.

62 See Edward K. Rand, *Ovid and his Influence* (Boston, Mass.: Longmans, 1925), p. 112. Schrötter's ideas were summarised and favourably received by Antonio Viscardi in *Le origini* (1939). The following analogies between courtly and Ovidian love were mentioned. (1) Love is a bond or chain: *praeda, recens, vincula, captiva mens*, and *catena*. (2) One of the chief problems for both the Ovidian and the courtly lover is that of overcoming timidity: Bernart de Ventadorn, 'Quant ieu la vey . . . / aissi tremble de paor / cum fa la fuelha contra'l ven'. The dichotomy *temer/auzar, paor/ doptansa* was a common one in troubadour poetry. (3) Love diminishes a person's sensitive and spiritual faculties. The troubadours use the terms *esbahit* and *marit*; Dante speaks of his *spiriti smarriti*. (4) Love is a malady, the symptoms of which are insomnia, pallor and emaciation. This malady can be fatal: *amore mori, periturus amando, conveniet mors*. (5) Love is an art or technique with codifiable rules. (6) The lover must conceal his secret. (Viscardi, pp. 581–3.) Verbal borrowings from Ovid are traced in troubadour poetry by Jessie Crosland (1947), and by Gordon Michael Shedd (1965). See also Shapiro (1971). The troubadours took from Ovid what accorded with their tastes, but they seem to have missed his irony (Lewis, 1936, p. 7). The pathological symptoms of love are not specifically Ovidian; they belong to the Graeco-Arabic physiological tradition; see below, pp. 67–8. Since it is generally agreed that Ovid could not have been more than a formative influence, the Ovidian theory has not been classified as a separate theory of origin.

63 See above, p. 4 n.1.

64 Chrétien mentions his translation in his prologue to *Cligès*; it has not survived.

65 Jeanroy, *La Poésie lyrique* (1934), I, pp. 93–7; Lewis: 'We come much nearer to the secret [i.e. of origins] if we can accept the picture of a typical Provençal court drawn many years ago by an English writer, and since approved by the greatest living authority on the subject [Jeanroy]' (Lewis, 1936, p. 12).

66 Paget's theory was labelled 'la thèse marxiste' by Davenson in *Les Troubadours* (1961), p. 132. For a genuinely Marxist view of Courtly Love see Schlauch (1956), pp. 138–42.

67 Cf. Moller's sociological thesis, below, pp. 43–5.

68 See below, pp. 30–2.

69 If an axis were drawn between the two poles of scholarship the spiritual pole might be represented by Violet Paget, Myrrha Lot-Borodine or Denis de Rougemont, the sensual by Robert Briffault, Moshé Lazar and Keith Whinnom. Play theorists, such as Huizinga, Charles S. Singleton and John Stevens, would stand at the centre.

70 Ahsmann (1929) spoke of a mutual affinity between Marianism and Courtly Love. Anitchkof (1931) discussed possible affiliations between Courtly Love and Bernardine mysticism. Schoeck (1951) noted parallels between the twelve steps of love in Andreas Capellanus' *De amore* and St Bernard's twelve steps of humility. Foster (1963) and Russell (1965–66) insisted that Courtly Love can be understood

only as a deviation from Christian principles. Deroy (1971) has shown that St Bernard borrowed some of the words and themes associated with *fin'amors* in his commentary on the Song of Songs.

[71] Ribera gave an inaugural address on Ibn Quzmān to the Spanish Academy in 1912. This study was reprinted in *Disertaciones y opúsculos* (1928), I, pp. 3–92. 'La clave misteriosa que explica el mecanismo de las formas poéticas de los varios sistemas líricos del mundo civilizado en la Edad Media, está en la lírica andaluza, a que pertenece el *Cancionero de Abencuzmán*' (*ibid.*, I, p. 71).

[72] For a discussion of this question see below, p. 72.

[73] See also, by the same author, *Germanisch-romanisches Mittelalter* (Zürich and Leipzig, 1935). Similarities have been found between the plot of Tristan and that of the Persian romance *Vis u Rāmin*: Schröder (1961). See Rosenthal in *The Legacy of Islam*, ed. Schacht, pp. 341–5.

[74] *Civilization and its Discontents*, trans. J. Rivière, revised by James Strachey, International Psycho-analytical Library, 17 (London: Hogarth, 1973), pp. 14–22.

[75] See above pp. 7–8.

[76] The phrase 'a new manner of loving' was used by Paget (1884), p. 126. Louis Gillet, *Dante* (Paris: Fayard, 1965): 'C'était une véritable création morale, la plus originale invention du moyen âge . . . C'était une sorte d'amour entièrement détaché de la génération et de la reproduction de l'espèce, de tout intérêt utilitaire comme de l'attrait des sens et de l'amitié conjugale. C'était moins l'amour que de l'adoration. La femme devenait une religion' (p. 20). This passage was cited by Briffault, *The Troubadours*, p. 103. It betrays the influence of Denis de Rougemont.

[77] See above, pp. 55 n.24.

[78] See E. O. James, *The Cult of the Mother Goddess* (London: Thames & Hudson, 1959). It has been suggested that Courtly Love was the survival of the cult of Cybele (C. B. Lewis, 1934); see below, p. 88. Marianism was the consequence, rather than the cause, of Courtly Love; see pp. 84–6.

[79] Some twenty years later Lewis saw the great cultural divide in a different place. 'I have come to regard as the greatest of all divisions in the history of the West that which divides the present from, say, the age of Jane Austen and Scott . . . somewhere between us and *Persuasion* the chasm runs' ('De descriptione temporum' [Cambridge inaugural lecture, 1954], in *They asked for a paper* [London: Bles, 1962], pp. 9–25, at p. 17).

[80] Peter Lombard attributed this saying to Sextus Pithagoricus in his *Sentences*, IV, xxxi. It was quoted by Alanus de Insulis (*Epitome of the Art of Preaching*, ch. xlv), by Jerome (*Against Jovinian*, I, p. 49), and by Clement of Alexandria (*Pedagogue*, II, x). The nobleman in Andreas' Sixth Dialogue perversely uses this saying as a justification for extra-conjugal adultery (Andreas, trans. Parry, p. 103). The problem of adultery is discussed by Keith Whinnom in his introduction to Diego de San Pedro's *Cárcel de Amor* (Madrid, 1971), p. 10. Whinnom notes that, according to St Thomas Aquinas, such ardour is more reprehensible within marriage than without: 'magis quam ille qui est amator alterius mulieris'.

[81] This article, in *BH*, XL (1938), 337–423, was reprinted as a chapter in a book with the same title in 1941.

[82] *Poesía árabe*, pp. 18–47. It was commonly accepted, when this article was written, that the two genres differed only in the language employed: the former is composed in classical Arabic, the latter in vulgar Arabic or even Romance. Samuel M. Stern has since demonstrated that they are not identical in structure. The scheme of the *muwashshaḥ* is AA bbbAA cccAA or AB cccAB dddAB, whilst that of the *zajal* is AA bbbA cccA. See Stern (1974), pp. 52–6.

[83] Bezzola summarises, but rejects, Ecker's thesis in *Les Origines*, II, pp. 187–202.

[84] Nykl translated Ibn Ḥazm's *Tawq al-Hamāma* (*The Dove's Neck Ring*) in 1931 and Ibn Quzmān's *Diwān* in 1933. The *Tawq* was more elegantly translated into English by

Arberry and into Spanish by García Gómez. See Bibliography. This treatise on love is of central importance in the polemic over the origins of Courtly Love.

[85] *La Civilisation arabe en Espagne. Vue générale* (Cairo, 1938; Paris, 1948).

[86] *Civilization and its Discontents* (1973), pp. 59 ff.

[87] *Man's Western Quest. The principles of civilization* (London: Allen & Unwin, 1957), p. 63.

[88] 'La passion est cette forme de l'amour qui refuse l'immédiat, fuit le prochain, veut la distance et l'invente au besoin, pour mieux se ressentir et s'exalter' (*Les Mythes de l'amour*, 1961, p. 51).

[89] See Pitangue (1946); Closs (1947); Paul Imbs, 'A la recherche d'une littérature cathare', *RMAL*, V (1949), 289–302; Dora Baker, 'Poésie manichéenne', *CEC*, XIII (1953); Pierrefeu (1957); Russell (1965–66). The other chief exponent of the Crypto-Cathar thesis in the twentieth century was Otto Rahn, whose arguments were refuted by P. Breillet in *Recherches albigeoises* (Albi, 1948). De Rougemont speaks of Déodat Roché and René Nelli as members of a French neo-Catharist school; see Roché, *Études manichéennes et cathares* (Arques, 1952), and René Nelli *et al.*, *Le Catharisme. Spiritualité de l'hérésie* (Paris, 1953). Hannah Closs was the author of a trilogy inspired by Cathar legends and history: *High are the Mountains*, *And Sombre the Valleys*, and *The Silent Tarn* (London, 1949–55). Nelli thought it significant that this novel should simultaneously provoke comment at the Indian Institute of Bangalore and l'Institut d'Études Occitanes at Toulouse: 'Le climat spirituel de la France méditerranéenne ne serait-il pas, en définitive, le climat du regret-de-l'orient?' (*Le Catharisme*, p. 222). Nelli's major work on Courtly Love, *L'Érotique des troubadours* (1961), attached less importance to the Cathars; see below pp. 48–9. A number of articles were published in *La Table Ronde*, XCVII (1956), which stressed links between Tantric Buddhism and the Cathars or explored de Rougemont's theory of a 'confluence of heresies': de Rougemont, 'Tableau du phénomène courtois', 16–29; Mircea Eliade, 'Note sur l'érotique mystique indienne', 28–33; Henry Corbin, 'Soufisme et Sophiologie', 34–43; Robert Amadou, 'Les théories dualistes et la sexualité', 48–59; Michelle Meyer, trans., 'Contre les hérétiques albigeois' (fragment of *Contra hereticos* by Alanus de Insulis), 60–3.

[90] This suggestion is singularly unconvincing. The structure of the work was determined by Ovid's *Art of Love* and *Remedies for Love* and by the traditional technique of dialectical reasoning. The courtly ethic was not based on 'natural reason' but was opposed to 'naturalism'. See Scaglione (1963). The works of Averroes (d. 1198) did not, in any case, reach Paris until after 1210, when he came to be known as 'the Commentator' of Aristotle. See *The Legacy of Islam*, ed. Schacht (Oxford, 1974), pp. 383–5.

[91] 'Les vers finaux en espagnol dans les *muwaššaḥs* hispano-hébraïques. Une contribution à l'histoire du *muwaššaḥ* et à l'étude du vieux dialecte espagnol mozarabe', *And*, XIII (1948), 299–346.

[92] S. M. Stern, ed., *Les Chansons mozarabes. Les vers finaux ('kharjas') en espagnol dans les 'muwashshaḥs' arabes et hébreux* (Palermo, 1953; repr. Oxford: Bruno Cassirer, 1964); Emilio García Gómez, ed. *Las jarchas romances de la serie árabe en su marco* (Madrid: Sociedad de Estudios y Publicaciones, 1965); Brian Dutton, 'Some new evidence for the Romance origins of the *Muwashshaḥas*', *BHS*, XLII (1965), 73–81; Vincent Cantarino, 'Lyrical traditions in Andalusian *Muwashshaḥas*', *CL*, XXI (1969), 213–31; Stern (1974). It has been argued that the *kharjas* contain the rudiments of Courtly Love: Cluzel (1960); cf. Dronke, *Medieval Latin*, I, pp. 26–32. For a detailed bibliography see Heger (1960).

[93] 'Esistono dei rapporti letterari tra il mondo islamico e l'Europa occidentale nell'alto medio evo?', *Settimane di studio del Centro italiano di studi sull'alto medio evo XII. L'Occidente e l'Islam nell'alto medio evo, 2–8 aprile 1964* (Spoleto, 1965), II, pp. 639–66; 811–31; reprinted in English ('Literary connections between the Islamic world and Western Europe in the early Middle Ages: did they exist?'), Stern (1974), pp. 204–30.

[94] Américo Castro had asserted that the lyric was incompatible with the Castilian temperament in *España en su historia* (Buenos Aires: Losada, 1948), pp. 490 ff.

[95] Alonso attempted to reconcile Ribera's position with that of Hartmann, who derived the *muwashshaḥ* from the *musammaṭ*. See Monroe (1970), pp. 216–19. The article was also published in French in *Arab*, V (1958), 113–44.

[96] He did not accept the view of C. S. Lewis that modern romantic love was an emotional discovery of twelfth-century Europe, nor did he believe that Courtly Love had any significant impact on relations between the sexes or on the status of women.

[97] *Collected Papers*, trans. J. Rivière, IV (London: Hogarth, 1925), pp. 203–16.

[98] Quoted by Moller, pp. 42–3.

[99] See Shota Rustaveli in Bibliography. The 'Panther's Skin' is the correct reading.

[100] Review by Peter Dronke, *MAe*, XXXV (1967), 51–8. Dronke's chief criticism was that Bezzola ignored the part played by oral traditions in the genesis of literary works and the nature of literary influences.

[101] Ed. J. Buchanan-Brown (revised edn., London, 1973), I, pp. 407–72.

[102] 'Paien unt tort e chrestiens unt dreit.' Courtly Love is in fact inherently ambiguous. See below, pp. 66–7, 106–7, 113, and Appendix II.

[103] See Pierre Guiraud, *La Seméologie*, 'Que sais-je?' (Paris, 1973). Guiette (1960), Dragonetti (1960) and Vinaver (1970) have studied the stylistic and aesthetic aspects of troubadour poetry.

[104] Denomy (1949). *Cf.* Duby (1964) and Köhler (1966).

[105] For a collection of Köhler's articles see Köhler, *Trobadorlyrik* (1962).

[106] This theory was cited with approval by Jean Frappier (*R*, XCIII, 1972, 183–6).

[107] 'One may write about fascism, for instance, from a fascist's point of view without oneself being a fascist' (Askew, p. 20). Despite protests to the contrary, the obvious implication of this analogy is that a literary work can never be great because of, but only in spite of, Courtly Love. This being so, it follows that the best poets writing within this tradition were hypocrites.

[108] *Fin'amors* was incompatible with jealousy; see Köhler (1970).

[109] *Collected Papers*, IV (London, 1925), pp. 192–202.

1　HISPANO-ARABIC

Courtly Love was either imported into the south of France from Muslim Spain, or was strongly influenced by the culture, poetry and philosophy of the Arabs.

(a) *Scholarship and culture of the Islamic world.*　It was from the Arabs, from the tenth century onwards, that Christian Europe became better acquainted with Hellenic culture. Europe, which was still emerging from barbarism, assimilated the literary, scientific and technological achievements of a civilisation which had already reached its maturity. Lampillas (1778–81); Andrés (1782–1822); Bouterwek (1801–50); Sismondi (1813); Dawson (1935).

(b) *Chivalry of the Arabs.*　The institution and the ideal of chivalry was initially unconnected with the feudal system; it was introduced into Europe from Moorish Spain or from the Middle East, together with Arabian prose romances, through cultural, commercial and military contacts, and as a consequence of the Crusades. Huet (1671); Sismondi (1813); Hammer-Pürgstall (1849); Ghali (1919); Nelli (1963); Graves (1967); Burckhardt (1972).

(c) *Music.*　The music to which the European troubadours set their songs was Arabic in inspiration, and the instruments which they used derived from the Arabs. Ribera y Tarragó (1922); Farmer (1930); Briffault (1945).

(d) *Rhyme and poetic forms.*　The Arabs were the first to compose rhymed verse, and Provence learnt the art from Moorish Spain. Barbieri (d. 1575); Huet (1671); Sismondi (1813); Briffault (1945). Certain reputedly Arabic methods of versification, in particular the *zajal*, have been traced in early Provençal, Galician–Portuguese, and Castilian poetry. Ribera y Tarragó (1928); Nykl (1939); Menéndez Pidal (1941); Nelli (1963).

(e) *Etymology of 'trobar'.*　The verb *trobar*, 'to compose poetry', derives from *ṭarab*, 'music', 'song', or from the root *ḍaraba*, 'to strike'. The Arabic for minstrel or 'troubadour' was *ṭarabī*. Ribera y Tarragó (1928); Lemay (1966); Monroe (1970); Hussein (1971).

(f) *Poetic themes.*　Hispano-Arabic and medieval European love poetry share a number of themes and motifs, some of which may be enumerated: the use of the pseudonym or *senhal* to conceal the identity of the lady addressed; the masculine form of address, *midons*, instead of *madomna*; the same *dramatis personae*, such as the guardian, the slanderer and the confidant; the same pathological symptoms of love, namely insomnia, pallor, emaciation and melancholy; a belief in the fatal consequences of this malady, known as '*ishq* or *amor hereos*; and the use of the spring or nature prelude. Ecker (1934); Nykl (1939); Menéndez Pidal (1941); Pérès (1947); Lévi-Provençal (1948); Nelli (1963); Dutton (1968); Hussein (1971).

(g) *The concept of love in poetry.* Some, if not all, the essential features of Courtly Love can be discerned in Hispano-Arabic (and even Middle Eastern) poetry: the insatiability of desire; the description of love as exquisite anguish; the elevation of the lady into an object of worship; the poet's submission to her capricious tyranny; and the emphasis on the need for secrecy. Sismondi (1813); Schack (1865); Burdach (1918); Gibb (1931); Nykl (1939); Menéndez Pidal (1941); Pérès (1947); Daniel (1975).

(h) *Theoretical works on the nature of love.* There are a number of analogies between Courtly Love and the Arabic theory of profane love, which constitutes a distinct Arabic literary genre. The works most frequently cited are Ibn Dāwūd's *Kitāb al-Zahra*, Ibn Ḥazm's *Ṭawq al-Ḥamāma* and Avicenna's *Risāla fi'l-'Ishq*. These works formulated a Platonic ethic which might explain the origin of *fin'amors*. Nykl (1931); Gibb (1931); Denomy (1945); Lévi-Provençal (1948); García Gómez (1952); Hussein (1971).

There are, on the whole, strong grounds for supporting this theory, even if some of the arguments used are false. The cultural supremacy of the Islamic world in the period immediately preceding the rise of the troubadour lyric is indisputable, and the importance of Arabic scholarship as a medium for the transmission of Greek classical texts is widely acknowledged.[1] More important still, poetry was an art in which the Arabs, according to their own estimate, excelled.[2] In order to prove that Arabic poetry exercised a decisive influence on the development of the Romance lyric, parallels must be established between court poetry composed in Muslim Spain (or in the Middle East) and that which was composed in Provence or elsewhere in Europe. It must then be demonstrated that channels of communication existed between the Islamic world and Christian Europe, and that poets from southern

France could have had access, directly and/or indirectly, to Arabic poetry. This proof is necessary in order to refute the argument, advanced by Stern, Dronke and others, that the similarities are purely coincidental.

The parallels are of three kinds: first, there are formal and stylistic elements; secondly, there are common themes and motifs; thirdly, there are analogies between the concept of love in both lyrical traditions. Poetic forms are easily transferable and offer conclusive evidence for cultural interaction in the Iberian Peninsula. Classical Arabic poetry, which was based, like Latin and Greek poetry, on a quantitative system of prosody, and which had tended to become artificial and over-refined, was revitalised by contact with popular strophic genres indigenous to Spain and Portugal. The Spanish *villancico* is the Romance equivalent of the *zajal*, a poetic form which has been traced in Provence, Italy, northern France and England.[3] This form consists of a rhymed couplet, followed by stanzas which are monorhymed, except that the last line of each rhymes with the initial couplet. The bilingual *kharjas*, in which the principal constituent is Romance, provide evidence for the existence of a native Romance lyric which influenced the *zajal* and the *muwashshah*. The theory that the metrical forms of troubadour poetry were borrowed from the Arabs has thus been discredited. However, these facts do not justify S. M. Stern's scepticism with regard to literary connections between the Islamic world and Western Europe. Stern himself speaks of the symbiosis of Arabic and Romance dialects (Stern, 1974, p. 210), a term which implies reciprocity. In the homogeneous culture of Moorish Spain there must have been a constant exchange of themes, concepts and stylistic devices between courtly and popular poetry. It was, above all, popular poetry, composed by Mozarabs, Jews and the Christians of the north, which must have formed a link between Muslim Spain and Provence (Watt, 1972, p. 27). One should not expect to find the rudiments of Courtly Love in the *kharjas*, because these passionate confessional utterances are self-consciously popular.[4]

Arabic and troubadour poetry are linked by many thematic affinities. 'No belief could be more uninformed,' wrote Briffault, 'than the notion, not infrequently entertained, that the Arabs knew nothing of love beyond its sensual aspect' (*Troubadours*, p. 25). In fact he believed that if Arabic poetry was uncongenial to the troubadours it was because of its idealism, not because of its sensuality. The development in Al-Andalus of a concept of love akin, in many respects, to Courtly Love has been ascribed to the cultural tradition of the Zāhiris (Grunebaum, 1952, p. 237). Three of the most famous Arabic theoretical works on the nature of love were written by members of the Ẓāhirite sect: the *Kitāb al-Zahra* by Ibn Dāwūd (d. 909);[5] the *Tawq al-Hamāma* by Ibn Ḥazm (d. 1064);[6] and the *Tarjumān al-Ashwāq* by Ibn Arabī (d. 1240).[7] With the exception of Ibn Arabī, who was a Ṣūfī, the Ẓāhirites adhered to the orthodox view that the transcendent Deity is emotionally inaccessible to man on earth. Love was cultivated as a highly subjective ideology, a substitute for divine grace, which was, in existential terms, absurd. The decision to obey love's precepts was entirely arbitrary and gratuitous; moreover the lover contrived to conceal his feelings from the lady, the ostensible cause of his suffering: 'l'idéal d'Ibn Dāwūd est de souffrir dans la plus grande liberté morale possible, pour autant que la nature et le Créateur le permettent' (Vadet, 1968, p. 310). This extravagant anti-natural theory of love took as its premise the *ḥadīth* imputed to the Prophet: 'He who loves and remains chaste, never reveals his secret, and dies, dies the death of a martyr.' This love was said to have been practised by the tribe of the Banū Udra, a tribe of the Hijaz in western Arabia. In fact Ibn Dāwūd, Ibn Ḥazm and other theorists, most of whose works have never been translated out of Arabic,[8] codify and philosophise the themes and concepts expressed by the '*Udhrī* poets of seventh-century Arabia. *Ḥubb 'udhrī* has been described as 'a literary and philosophical theme related to the "platonic love" of the Greeks from which it derived, and to the *amour courtois* of the western Christian middle ages which it inspired'.[9] '*Udhrī* love and Courtly Love share the same basic tenets: fidelity, suffering, secrecy, servitude and submission (Hussein, p. 118). Both lyrical traditions conceived of love as an ennobling but potentially destructive force and a counterfeit religion; in neither case could the relationship between lover and beloved be described as interpersonal or mystical. Qays Ibn al-Mulawwaḥ, known as *Majnūn* or the 'Mad One', was the prototype of the hero of courtly romance and an *exemplum* for the Ṣūfī mystic.[10]

Another work which may have contributed to the formation of Courtly Love is Avicenna's *Risāla fī'-l-'Ishq*, with its chapter 'On the love of those who are noble-minded and young for external beauty' (Denomy, 1945). Avicenna (980–1037), a philosopher and physician deeply influenced by Neoplatonic doctrines, envisaged the possibility of an ethical code based on a compromise between concupiscence and the craving for the source of all beauty:

If a man loves a beautiful form with an animal desire, he deserves reproof, even condemnation and the charge of sin, as, for instance, those who commit unnatural adultery and in general people who go astray. But whenever he loves a pleasing form with an intellectual consideration, in the manner we have explained, then this is to be considered an approximation to nobility and an increase in goodness. [Trans. Fackenheim, *MedS*, VII, p. 221]

Avicenna insisted that it is man's moral obligation to integrate the lower with the higher faculties in the quest for perfection. The sexual act was condemned as a function of the animal soul, yet kissing and embracing were permitted as a means towards intellectual union.[11] This doctrine, which is remarkably analogous to the Platonism of the Florentine Academy, as defined, for example, in Castiglione's *Il Cortegiano*, was probably known to the early Provençal troubadours (Denomy, 1945). Andreas' definition of *amor purus* suggests that he was familiar with these ideas: 'This kind [of love] consists in the contemplation of the mind and the affection of the heart; it goes so far as the kiss and the embrace and the modest contact with the nude lover, omitting the final solace, for that is not permitted to those who wish to love purely' (*De amore*, trans. J. J. Parry, p. 122). Marie de Champagne's insistence, in a letter quoted by Andreas (*ibid.*, p. 107), that the morality of human love rests on the free exercise of the rational faculty and that, consequently, marriage is incompatible with love may also reflect the ideas of Avicenna.

To Avicenna, Ibn Arabī, Dante and Ficino the insatiability of desire signified the attraction of an infinite Good. Dante's Beatrice was an analogue of the Supreme Beloved. Desire cannot be appeased by sight or touch, because lovers fear and venerate the glow of divinity which they perceive in the beloved's countenance. Ibn Arabī dedicated some love poems to a lady whom he met at Mecca in 1201, but he found it advisable to write a commentary on them, explaining them in a mystical sense. The *Tarjumān al-Ashwāq* and the *Dhakhā'ir* have been compared to the *Vita nuova* and the *Convivio* of Dante.[12] The courtly lover did not, on the whole, follow the example of Ibn Arabī or Dante; he aspired to perfection without the necessity of forfeiting sensuality. The 'paradoxical asceticism' of Abū Ḥamza al-Baghdādī (d. 882), of Ibn Arabī, and other mystics of Islam nevertheless appears to have influenced the troubadour lyric, the *trobar clus* in particular. Almost all the dichotomies of late medieval European love poetry can be found in the mystical works of Ibn Arabī: delight and torment; life and death; absence and presence; sickness and medicine; hope and despair; secrecy and self-expression; freedom and slavery; memory and oblivion; human and divine; or everything and nothing.[13]

The theory of love as an experience of contradiction or a *concordia discors* is linked with the Graeco-Arabic theory of love-melancholy or *amor hereos*.[14] Avicenna analyses this malady in his *Canon of Medicine*, a standard textbook for European medical students during the Middle Ages.[15] The Arabic word for passionate love is *'ishq*, possibly derived from *'ashaqa*, meaning a creeper which twines round a tree and gradually causes its death.[16] The verb *'ashiqa* means 'to love' or 'to stick to'. Etymologically the word 'anguish', from the Latin *angere*, conveys the same notion of contraction or constriction, which was interpreted by doctors as an introversion of the vital spirits within the heart.[17] The term *'ishq*, as used by Avicenna, referred to a mental disorder, caused by excessive meditation on the image of a woman who is sexually unattainable. A modern psychiatrist might diagnose this malady as a form of manic depression, because the victim of *amor hereos* and, according to Aristotle, melancholic persons in general would oscillate between extremes of exhilaration and despair.[18] This theory is implicit in the Petrarchan metaphor of the 'icy fire', since black bile, the cause of melancholia, was regarded as a vehicle of extremes of heat and cold. Aristotle had suggested, in Problem XXX, that an excess of black bile produces intoxicating, contradictory and erotic effects, similar to those produced by wine, so that 'melancholy persons are out of the ordinary, not owing to illness, but from their natural constitution'.[19] Aristotle's *Problemata physica* were not known to the Middle Ages, but his ideas were preserved, modified and amplified by Arab physiologists, whose works were translated into Latin from the tenth century onwards. The Arabs frequently reversed Aristotle's relationship between physical cause and spiritual effect, and gave special emphasis to love-melancholy: a person was not necessarily predisposed to melancholy by his natural constitution; he might become melancholic through love or intellectual over-exertion. Men of keen wit and outstanding intellect were considered particularly susceptible to this psychic ailment because they are endowed with a superior sensibility and a lively imagination.[20] Mystics were also believed to be prone to melancholy on account of their great yearning to be united with God and the fear which God inspires in their hearts.[21] The opening words of Andreas Capellanus' *De amore* were borrowed from this medical tradition: 'Amor est passio quaedam innata, procedens ex visione et immoderata cogitatione formae alterius sexus' (ed. Trojel, p. 3).[22] The description, in Andreas' *De amore*, of love's paradoxical virtues is also incomprehensible without reference to the Graeco-Arabic theory of love-melancholy: 'Love causes a rough and uncouth man to be distinguished for his handsomeness; it can endow a man even of the humblest birth with nobility of character; it blesses the proud with humility; and the man in love becomes accustomed to performing many services gracefully for everyone' (Andreas, p. 31). Constantinus Africanus (1020–87), who was copying a late ninth-century treatise on melancholy by Isḥāq ben 'Amrān, 'never tired of picturing the boundless variety of the symptoms and, most important, their obvious contradictoriness in many cases. Men loquacious and quick-tempered become silent and pacific, the shy and quiet could become bold and eloquent . . . '.[23] The diversity of authors in whose works this theme occurs is itself an indication of the diffusion of Arabic thought: Ibn Ḥazm (d. 1027), Aimeric de Peguilhan (d. 1230), Francesco da Barberino (d. 1348), Juan Ruiz (*fl.* 1330), El Tostado (d. 1455), Rodrigo Cota de Maguaque (d. *c.* 1505), Equicola (d. *c.* 1525), and the anonymous author of the *Comedia Thebaida* (1521).[24] It could, furthermore, be argued that these medical theories explain the para-doxical tendency inherent in troubadour poetry, which prefigured the *conceptismo* of the seventeenth century. As Lynne Lawner says with reference to the *trobar clus*, 'this style and the tradition to which it gave rise have been little studied by scholars, partly because the very nature of the hermetic poetry is obscure, and often impenetrable, but also because hardly anyone has recognized the continuity of the *clus* tradi-tion, which extends past Dante and Petrarch to Scève, Donne, Góngora, and even Mallarmé' (Lawner, 1973, p. 485). This is clearly a subject which requires further investigation. That the Baroque style, both in literature and in the fine arts, originated in Spain is in itself significant.

The chief objection to the Hispano-Arabic theory of origins is that there is virtually no evidence that any Arabic poetry or treatises on love were translated into Latin or into any Romance language during the Middle Ages (Denomy, 1953). It is moreover doubtful whether the troubadours could have known enough Arabic to understand Arabic poetry (Stern, 1974, pp. 216–17). To this it may be replied that the ideas and themes could have travelled by word of mouth, and could have been acquired without a first-hand knowledge of Arabic. In the Iberian Peninsula there were many points of contact between Moors and Christians: war, trade, diplomacy, intermarriage, migration, cultural interchange and the activities of translators. 'It was probably through contacts with the courts of Aragon and Castile, through inter-marriage such as that of Guilhem of Poitou with Philippa of Aragon in 1094, and through political dealings, that knowledge of Hispano-Arabic love philosophies and love poetry of the tenth and eleventh centuries came to the courts and poets of the Midi' (Salter, 1973,

Plate I

Two lovers. Drawing from a fifteenth-century MS of 'Kalīlah wa-Dimna' and a collection of tales (completed in 1159) by the Sicilian Arab Muḥammad IbnʿAbd Allāh (Ibn Ẓafar), 'Sulwān al-Muṭā' (Waters of Comfort). Or. 4044, fol. 136r. (British Library)

Plate II

The Tree of Love. From a MS, *c.* 1400, of Matfré Ermengaud's 'Breviari d'amor', in Catalan (completed in 1288). Yates Thomson 31, fol. 8. (British Library)

Plate III

The Woman, symbol of the Church. From 'The Apocalypse'. Early fourteenth century. MS Royal 19 B XV, fol. 20v. (British Library)

Plate IV

Lancelot in conversation with a lady who holds a black and white dog on her knee. Early fourteenth century. MS Royal 14 E III, fol. 136. (British Library)

Plate V

Man and woman talking. From the 'Roman de la Rose'. Fourteenth century.
MS Egerton 881, fol. 114v. (British Library)

Plate VI

Two love scenes beneath a tree. Ivory mirror case. French; fourteenth century. (Victoria and Albert Museum)

Plate VII

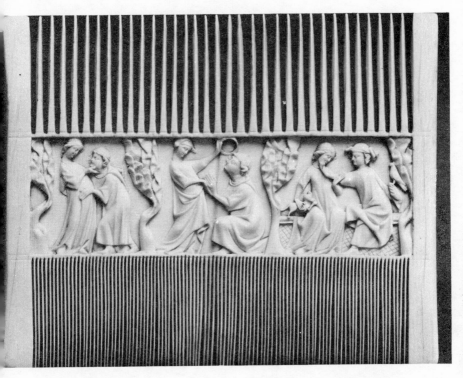

Lovers in a garden. Ivory comb. French; early fourteenth century. (Victoria and Albert Museum)

Plate VIII

Group of dancers. From 'Les hystoires des roumains'. Early fourteenth century. MS Add. 12042, fol. 7. (British Library)

Man encouraging a dog to dig up two mandrakes. From the Queen Mary psalter, 1310–20. MS Royal 2 B VII, fol. 119v. (British Library)

p. 424). One of Guilhem IX's sisters had married Pedro of Aragon; another had married Alfonso VI of Castile (Nelli, 1963, p. 44). These dynastic ties, forming a network across Europe, even extended in the tenth century to Muslim Spain.[25] No princely retinue was complete without Moorish musicians. A miniature in Alfonso el Sabio's *Cantigas de Santa Maria* of a Christian and a Moorish lute player rehearsing together over the same jug of wine suggests that musical collaboration was by no means uncommon (Marrou, 1947, p. 88). Moorish musicians and singers were invariably present at wedding festivities. It is even recounted by Ibn Baṣṣam, in his *Dhakhīra*, that Sancho of Castile arranged that his daughter be married to Raymond of Catalonia in the palace of an Arab prince, Mundhir Ibn Yaḥyā, in the presence of a mixed gathering of Muslims and Christians (Pérès, 1937, pp. 386–7).

The eleventh century was a period of remarkable tolerance, during which several towns and strongholds fell to the Christians. When Alfonso VI recaptured Toledo, the ancient capital of Gothic Spain, in 1085 he adopted on occasion the title 'Emperor of Spain and of the Two Faiths'. According to the lost *Cantar de la Mora Zaida* he fell in love, after the death of his fifth wife, with the daughter of the king of Seville, Muḥammad al-Muʿtamid ibn ʿAbbād. It is significant that, like Jaufré Rudel and the Countess of Tripoli, they fall in love by hearsay. A policy of religious coexistence was pursued by Alfonso X in the thirteenth century. It is stated in his law book *Las siete partidas* that 'by good works and appropriate teaching the Christians should seek to convert the Muslims and make them believe our faith . . . not by force or through bribery'.[26] The *mudéjares*, Muslims who found themselves under Christian rule, were permitted to retain their traditional way of life. In Aragon they formed one-fifth of the population. The County of Barcelona had suzerainty over Muslim communities, such as Tarragona, and was related by marriage to the ruling families of Languedoc and Provence (Dawson, 1935, p. 136). 'Arabs were often feudatories of Europeans, who might send their sons to spend some time in Arab households' (Daniel, 1975, p. 101). The movement of women, as slaves or captives of war, was also an important factor. Guillaume de Montreuil is said to have received a thousand girls captured at the siege of Barbastro in 1064, many of whom may have become singers and concubines in the courts of southern France: 'Il n'est pas impossible que quelques barons occitaniens . . . aient entendu chanter, dans leurs propres cours, des poèmes d'amour sur des airs andalous' (Nelli, 1963, pp. 45–6).

Furthermore most of the early troubadours, including Guilhem IX,

Marcabru, Cercamon, Peire d'Auvergne, Aimeric de Peguilhan, Arnaut Daniel and Peire Vidal, frequented the courts of Aragon and Castile (Briffault, *Troubadours*, pp. 71–2). Both politically and culturally southern France was more Spanish than French, especially after 1112, when Ramon Berenguer IV, a celebrated patron of troubadours, succeeded Gilbert, Count of Provence (Barbieri, p. 45; Dawson, p. 136; Briffault, *T.*, p. 5). This region was exceptionally prosperous and comparatively immune from ecclesiastical interference, and these conditions favoured the spirit of free inquiry and the growth of secular poetry in the vernacular. The coastal belt from Marseilles to Barcelona 'possessed wider international contacts and a more cosmopolitan type of culture than any other region of Western Europe, apart from the Norman kingdom of Sicily' (Dawson, p. 147).

The Norman–Saracen court at Palermo under Roger II (*c.* 1095–1154) and Frederick II (1194–1250) was no less important than the courts of Castile and Aragon as a bridge between East and West. Frederick II has been described as 'the first and only medieval Emperor who drank of the spirit of the East and came home to fuse it with the Holy Roman Empire, the Empire of the Salians and the Hohenstaufens'.[27] He was served by astrologers from Baghdad, Moorish musicians, Saracen ballerinas and Jewish translators. Many of his counsellors and court officials were Muslims: 'the Muslims were amazed when at the time of the midday prayer almost all the Emperor's servants and one of his teachers stood up and went through the orthodox Muhammadan ritual as true believers: they were the Sicilian Saracens of the Emperor's household' (Kantorowicz, p. 191). In the Holy Lands he had learned discussions with Muslim philosophers, much to the scandal of pious Christians, and he is known to have dispatched a series of metaphysical problems to Egypt, Syria, Iraq, Asia Minor and Yemen, which were finally answered by the Hispano-Arabic Ṣūfī Ibn Sab'īn. Frederick wrote poetry and encouraged his court officials to follow his example. This poetry was closely modelled on Provençal.[28] A Provençal grammar was composed for the emperor by Hugues de Saint-Circ; Provençal was studied by one of his favourites, Jacob of Morra (Kantorowicz, p. 330). The emperor's first wife was Constance of Provence, who arrived in Palermo in 1209 accompanied by 500 knights. Arabic poetry was also written at his court.[29] His predilection for Arabic culture, a useful weapon for the supporters of the Papacy against the claims of Empire, was inherited by his son Manfred, who, according to Mateo Spinello, would wander through the streets of Barletta by night singing *estrambotes* (Schack, II, pp. 249–53). It is possible that the poetic contests celebrated by Frederick resembled the Floral Games at Toulouse and Barcelona, and further research might point to a common ancestry in certain Arab poetic institutions.[30]

Schools of translators were established at Salerno, Toledo, Barcelona, Tarazona, Seville, Palermo and Montpellier. According to the author of the ninth-century *Hisperica famina*, young men flocked to Spain, dressed in Arabic apparel and carrying quivers for their pens, in order to study rhetoric.[31] Gerbert d'Aurillac, later Pope Sylvester II (999–1003), studied mathematics and astronomy in Catalonia (967–70), probably at the monastery of Ripoll (Watt, 1972, pp. 58–9). The main period of translation was, however, the twelfth century, when Arabic manuscripts were discovered in the wake of the Reconquest. Among the foreigners who were attracted to Spain as scholars or translators were Campanus of Novara, Robert of Ketton, Hugo of Santalla, Hermann of Carinthia, Robert of Retines, Plato of Tivoli, Gerard of Cremona, Adelard of Bath, Michael Scot, and Albert and Daniel of Morlay (Sismondi, I, p. 184; Schack, I, p. 204; Watt, pp. 60–3).[32] Whilst it is true that the interests of these men were primarily scientific and philosophical, a more accurate image of Islamic culture must have been diffused through this channel. These foreigners collaborated with Mozarabs, Jews and in some cases Muslims from whom they could have acquired some knowledge of Arabic poetry. Bishop Alvaro of Córdoba was probably exaggerating when he complained, in A.D. 854, that in the 'college of Christ', scarcely one man in a thousand could write a decent letter in Latin, whereas most could compete with the Arabs themselves in the composition of monorhymed poetry in Arabic, but his words prove that many Christians in Al-Andalus had completely assimilated the culture of their political masters (Bouterwek, p. 4; Sismondi, I, p. 96; Barbieri, ed. Tiraboschi, p. 14; Schack, II, p. 200).[33]

Under the patronage of Raymond I, Archbishop of Toledo (1126–51), Dominicus Gundisalvi (Domingo González), Selomo ibn David (christened Juan Hispalensis), and Avendeath or Ibn Dāwūd (likewise a converted Jew) translated the works of al-Ghazālī, Ibn Sīnā and Ibn Gabirol. Juan Hispalensis[34] also wrote a commentary on the Bible in Arabic for Mozarabs who were ill acquainted with Latin (Sismondi, I, pp. 96–7). The *Disciplina clericalis*, a collection of tales and fables, written in Toledo by an Aragonese Jew, Pedro Alfonso (b. 1062, baptised 1106),[35] consists principally of material which he translated from Arabic into Latin. A later Archbishop of Toledo, Rodrigo Jiménez de Rada (1170–1247) wrote a *Historia Arabum*,[36] and his disciple Mark was commissioned to translate the Koran.[37] Another school of translators was founded by Alfonso el Sabio at Seville, where once again Jews played the mediatory role. Constantinus Africanus, a Tunisian convert to Christianity, made Latin paraphrases from the Arabic of 'Alī ibn al-Abbās, Ibn al-Jazzar, Isḥāq al-Isrā'īlī and Ḥunayn ibn Isḥāq, and from Arabic versions of Hippocrates and Galen for the school of medicine at Salerno in the eleventh century (Daniel, 1975, p. 144). Montpellier was later to become a centre for the study of Graeco-Arabic medicine and astrology. A number of Greek works reached Sicily from Byzantium, including Plato's *Meno* and *Phaedo*, both of which were translated into Latin.

Arabian musical treatises were translated into Latin at Toledo and elsewhere. The works of al-Fārābī (*c.* 872–950) were quoted by many theorists in the West, including Vincent of Beauvais (d. 1264), Robert Kilwardby (d. 1279), Roger Bacon (d. 1280), Ramon Llull (d. 1315), and Gregor Reisch (d. 1525). Ribera y Tarragó sought to infer the nature of medieval Arabic music from the study of Alfonso el Sabio's *Cantigas de Santa Maria* on the basis of these treatises. It has been objected that this music 'can scarcely have been Moorish when every song in the entire collection celebrates the Virgin and her miracles'.[38] Since no written medieval Arabic music survives, it is impossible to ascertain to what extent the troubadours were indebted to Arabic musicology. However, Ribera's thesis is supported by the names of musical instruments which Europe inherited from the Arabs: 'lute' (*'ūd*), 'rebec' (*rabāb*), 'guitar' (*qīthāra*, from Greek *kithara*), and 'naker' (*naqqāra*). Spanish contains a large number of Arabic loan words related to music.[39] Sancho of Castile (ruled 1284–94), Peter III of Aragon (r. 1276–85), and Alfonso IV of Aragon (r. 1336–87) engaged Moorish musicians: players of the *añafil* (a straight trumpet), *ajabeba* (tranverse flute), *canón* (psaltery) and *rabel* (rebec). The general appearance of Arab minstrels, with their long hair, painted faces and particoloured dress, left its mark on the European *jongleurs*. There does not, therefore, seem to be any justification for dismissing the case for the influence of Arabic music as 'unconvincing in face of the obvious influence of Gregorian chant and popular song'.[40] These influences are not mutually exclusive. If it could be proved, as some suggest, that the word 'troubadour' itself derives from *ṭarab*, 'music', *ṭarabī*, 'minstrel', or from the root *ḍarab*, 'to strike', 'to play a musical instrument', then of course the Hispano-Arabic theory of origins would be considerably strengthened.[41]

Some scholars have claimed that chivalry was a Christian–Islamic institution, and that chivalric practices were introduced into Europe by crusaders returning from the Holy Land or adopted by Spaniards in the wars of the Reconquest. The pledge to defend women, to succour the oppressed and to avenge wrongs, an essential part of the ritual of the European orders of knighthood, is said to be Arabic in origin (Schack, I, p. 76; Graves, p. 184). In earlier times knights merely swore an oath of fealty to their king or overlord. It has been conjectured that the Christian military orders in Spain were formed as a counterpart to the monastery-fortresses which had been established by the Moors along the line of *ribāt*, the military borders of Islam, during the eleventh century. The term *futuwwa*, which was applied to the brotherhoods of devout young men who defended these fortresses, resembled the Western ideal of chivalry.[42] The purpose of the *jihād* or holy war was not evangelical; war was justified by the right to recover territory wrongfully held. It was in this sense that the protracted war of the Reconquest was, for Spaniards, a 'holy war'. *Courtoisie* was a formal code which 'may have provided the framework for relations between Arab and European lords' (Daniel, 1975, p. 168). The science of heraldry appears to have been unknown in the West before the First Crusade. There might therefore be some truth in Robert Graves's assertion that heraldry is of Saracen origin: 'The Saracens and the Moors, to whom we owe the origin of so many of our recognised heraldic charges and the derivation of some of our terms (e.g. "gules", from the Persian *gul*, and "azure", from the Persian *lazurd*) had evidently on their part something more than the rudiments of armory.'[43]

In the aristocratic ideals of European and Arabic society there was a considerable overlap in the period of the Crusades, which facilitated the passage of poetic techniques and concepts. 'The chivalrous aspect of European tradition blended particularly well into the situation of the East' (Daniel, 1975, p. 184). The ideals of *urbanitas*, *affabilitas* and *liberalitas* were virtues extolled by Christians and Muslims alike. Chivalry was not, however, imported into Europe by the Arabs; it emerged as an institution distinct from feudalism when, in the twelfth century, knighthood became dissociated from land tenure by the constant subdivision of fiefs, the promotion of new men into the ranks of the nobility, and the development of a more stable monetary economy.[44]

One of the traditional objections to the Hispano-Arabic theory of troubadour origins, raised by Schlegel, Jeanroy and others, is that mutual hostility between Muslims and Christians and the abject status of Muslim women would not have permitted cultural interchange between Arab and Christian poets (Schlegel, p. 67; Jeanroy, *La Poésie lyrique*, I, pp. 70–1). This argument carries little weight. Prior to the intervention of the fanatical Almohads in the middle of the twelfth century there was constant social intercourse between Muslims, Jews and Christians; within the sphere of religion there was confrontation rather than interchange, but cultural elements which did not threaten religious identity were easily transferable; even in the fifteenth century Henry IV of Castile was able to employ numerous Moors at court and to adopt a Moorish style of life, much to the astonishment of some Bohemian travellers who visited him in 1467.[45] Women in Muslim Spain were comparatively free: they could meet in public and often wore no veil; their social position was no worse than that of Provençal women, who were kept under the surveillance of a *gardador* (the counterpart to the Arabic *raqīb*) (Menéndez Pidal, *Poesía árabe*, pp. 48–9). Intermarriage and a trade in Christian slaves resulted in a greater degree of freedom for women in Muslim Spain than in other parts of the Islamic world: 'the customs of the Spanish Arabs may well have been as much influenced by Christian infiltration, often involuntary, as the other way round' (Daniel, 1975, p. 101).

It has been argued that parallel themes and poetic forms might arise spontaneously in different places, especially in view of the fact that Western Europe and the Islamic world share the same Hellenic heritage and a Semitic monotheistic religion (Bezzola, II, p. 198). It has even been maintained that Courtly Love is itself polygenetic, that is to say its essential features are timeless and transcend geographical boundaries (Dronke, *Medieval Latin*, I, p. ix). Whilst it is true that few of the motifs in the concordances of Ecker and Nykl are exclusive to Arabic and Provençal poetry, the accumulation of analogies is persuasive. Most scholars would, of course, agree that rhyme is polygenetic, and occurs, for instance, in ancient skaldic poetry and in early Christian hymns, but this does not invalidate the main lines of the argument in favour of the Hispano-Arabic theory.

One point should, however, be emphasised. Muslim society was not familiar with that aspect of feudalism which, in medieval Christendom, conditioned all human relations: the bond between a vassal and his feudal lord (Bezzola, II, p. 198). Feudal terminology acquired a specialised meaning in the troubadour lyric (Sutherland, 1956), but the feudal element in Courtly Love has perhaps been exaggerated (Dronke, *Medieval Latin*, I, p. 55). Love service tended to imply an exchange of favours for services rendered, although it was customary, from the thirteenth century onwards, for love poets to disclaim the right to any reward. The Arab theory of profane love was adapted to suit the needs of a petty nobility, and thus attained a social significance which it appears to have lacked in the more autocratic environment of Muslim Spain.

2 CHIVALRIC–MATRIARCHAL

Courtly Love was the product of the interaction of Christianity and a primitive Germanic/Celtic/Pictish matriarchy, which ensured the survival of pre-Christian sexual *mores* and a veneration for women amongst the European aristocracy.   'adore, worship.

(a) *The privileged status of women in pagan Europe.*   Women enjoyed a position of authority amongst the peoples of northern Europe, because they participated in public affairs and were credited with divine or prophetic powers. Warton (1775–81).

(b) *The Gothic spirit of chivalry.*   Women were served and revered amongst the Gothic tribes. A code of morals, based on the service of woman, was a source of moral refinement and heroic action. Millot (1774); Warton (1775–81); Vossler (1929).

(c) *A subterfuge to avoid ecclesiastical censorship.*   The European aristocracy resented having an ascetic morality imposed upon it by the early Church. Courtly and chivalric ideals were devised as a subterfuge to prevent ecclesiastical interference, since 'they gave to customary sex relations the sanction of cultivated taste'. Briffault (1927).

The Chivalric–Matriarchal theory clearly raises more questions than it can solve. Warton, Vossler and most nineteenth-century theorists took it for granted that chastity is a virtue which women universally impose upon their menfolk, whereas Briffault asserted that 'wherever individual women enjoy . . . a position of power, far from imposing or observing chastity, they avail themselves of their independence to exercise sexual liberty' (*Mothers*, ed. G. R. Taylor, p. 387). To the former, troubadour love was chaste and romantic; to the latter, it was sensual and essentially adulterous. Briffault's description of the barbaric behaviour of medieval knights, later romanticised in Arthurian legends, was more realistic than Warton's rosy picture of the Gothic barbarians. Similarly his conviction that troubadour love was basically lascivious would meet with the assent of many medievalists at the present moment. Warton, Vossler and Briffault were, however, agreed that women played an active part in the creation of a new art of gallantry.

In the affluent aristocratic society of Provence and Languedoc women must have been called upon to act as arbiters of fashion and literary taste. Twelfth-century France produced some outstanding women, such as Eleanor of Aquitaine, Marie de Champagne and Ermengarde de Narbonne. There were instances of women who waged war, owned land, ruled principalities and dubbed knights. Yet it must be emphasised that women as a whole never enjoyed anything other than a secondary status in medieval society (Valency, p. 2), and it is uncertain whether pagan Europe was genuinely matriarchal. Throughout the Middle Ages women were simultaneously adored and denigrated (Petrarch, for example, wrote, 'Foemina . . . est diabolus'), and it was paradoxically during the very period when Courtly Love flourished that this ambivalence was most evident. Courtly Love counterbalanced clerical misogyny, but it could scarcely have had a liberating influence. The most that can be said is that the courtly ethic presupposed a certain degree of freedom between the sexes, and that it had a civilising effect on manners (Power, 1926, p. 406). If, as Briffault argued, women were under a moral obligation to reward services performed on their behalf, then it would seem that women had less freedom in the early days of 'chivalry' than they did at a later date. The theory that matriarchy universally precedes patriarchy has, in any case, been refuted by most social anthropologists.[46] It has even been demonstrated that some primitive peoples have passed from patriarchy to matriarchy. Furthermore a period during which women are venerated and socially predominant is not necessarily matriarchal. Matriarchy must be defined in terms of actual 'mother rule', inheritance through the female line, 'matrilocy', and other specific factors.

Warton was perhaps justified in believing that chastity was itself an object of veneration in primitive times (Warton, diss., p. 67). Briffault had himself suggested that Marianism represented the resurgence of the cult of the Virgin Mother Goddess or Magna Mater which had once prevailed in pagan Europe. There is a primitive chivalrous asceticism, evident in the oaths whereby knights were prepared to do penance until they had performed a particular deed, which probably antedates Christianity. Tacitus, discussing the customs of one of the Germanic tribes, writes, 'The bravest among them wear also an iron ring (a mark of ignominy in that nation) as a kind of chain, till they have released themselves by the slaughter of a foe . . . They have no house, land or domestic cares: they are maintained by whomsoever they visit' (*Germania*, XXXI, Bohn's Classical Library, p. 322). This type of asceticism is illustrated by the activities of a lay institution called the Fraternity of the Penitents of Love, mentioned by Warton, and described by the Chevalier de la Tour Landry in a book of admonition to his daughters (Huizinga, *Waning*, p. 87). This institution was possibly a late survival of the pagan cult of Cybele.[47] The desire to incur danger as a proof of love was an essential ingredient of Courtly Love, which was very far from being a cover for promiscuity.

There is perhaps a case for distinguishing, as René Nelli has done, between chivalrous and courtly love. The former, which was devoid of the morbid sensibility and the lively sense of status which informs the latter, would approximate to the matriarchal *mores* about which Briffault speaks. Yet it is impossible to draw a hard-and-fast distinction between these two species of love, or to argue that there was a definite evolution from the former to the latter. The troubadour revival in the late Middle Ages was, after all, inseparable from the revival of chivalry which occurred during this same period. Chivalric gallantry was not, as Hearnshaw imagines, 'a gigantic system of bigamy, in which every lady was expected to have both a husband and a *paramour*'.[48] Rather it was, to use Huizinga's phrase, 'a dream of heroism and love'. This dream or ideal does not enable us to infer that medieval society was ruled by women. Women ruled the imaginations of men and motivated their conduct, but it is doubtful whether the position of women in society was greatly altered by Courtly Love.

3 CRYPTO-CATHAR

Courtly Love grew out of the Cathar or Albigensian heresy, either as an actual vehicle for Catharist doctrines or as an indirect expression of Cathar sentiments.

(a) *Coincidence in time and place.*   The Cathar heresy flourished in the south of France in the eleventh and twelfth centuries; troubadour poetry reached its apogee between 1150 and 1250 in this same region, at a time when the Cathars were increasingly the victims of religious persecution.

(b) *Coincidence of anti-papalist sentiments.*   The Cathars and the troubadours were 'protestant' or anti-papalist sectarians, who sought to return to the simplicity and the purity of the primitive Church. The troubadours were, in short, harbingers of the Reformation. Rossetti (1832); Aroux (1854); Méray (1860); Péladan (1906).

(c) *Coincidence of attitudes to love and marriage.*   The Cathars recommended sexual continence; marriage was condemned by the

Perfect as an attempt to vindicate the procreative function of sexuality, which, in their eyes, was responsible for perpetuating the work of the evil demiurge. Courtly Love, being chaste and adulterous, corresponded more closely to the morality of the Cathars than to that of orthodox Christianity. De Rougemont (1939); Nelli (1963).

(d) *Obscurity of poetic diction.*   The deliberately enigmatic style of *trobar clus* lends itself to interpretation on several levels. The emphasis on secrecy, service, suffering and death indicate that Courtly Love was a vehicle for Catharist doctrines. Rossetti (1832); Aroux (1854); de Rougemont (1939).

(e) *The ecstatic impulse of Eros.*   Courtly Love and the Cathar heresy were both inspired by Eros: the soul's nostalgic and insatiable desire to dissolve itself in the Unity whence it sprang. Death is the ultimate obstacle to which passion irrevocably leads. De Rougemont (1939).

The main argument in favour of the Crypto-Cathar thesis is that the environment in which the early troubadours were writing was predominantly Cathar. There is no *prima facie* evidence that they were not Cathar sympathisers. The enigmatic *trobar clus* (or closed style) and the occurrence of the love–death equation, extolling death as a form of liberation, obviously leave room for conjecture. The Cathar condemnation of marriage provided the troubadours with an excellent moral pretext for celebrating extra-conjugal love, and it is possible, as René Nelli suggests, that some of them simulated chastity, either as a respectful tribute to the morality of the Perfect or as a necessary expedient in poetry addressed to castle ladies who were very often Cathar believers 'whose bad consciences had to be pacified by song' (quoted in de Rougemont, *Passion*, p. 114). This hypothesis is not improbable, because, according to Steven Runciman, an authority on the Manichees, 'one of the most spectacular aspects of the Cathar movement in southern France was the enthusiasm with which it was supported by the great ladies of the country'.[49] Women no doubt imagined that Catharism protected their interests. There is, for example, the case, reported by Runciman, of a girl who was accused of being a Cathar because she resisted the advances of the canon, Gervase of Tilbury. 'Good young man,' she protested, 'God doesn't wish me to be your lover or that of any man, since if I should lose my virginity and my flesh should once be corrupted, without doubt I should fall irredeemably into eternal damnation.'[50] She was found guilty of heresy and burnt at the stake. By exalting the preservation of the human species as the noblest function of love Jean de Meun directed a double-edged assault against Courtly Love and the Cathar heresy: 'Pansez de mener bone vie, / aut chascuns anbracier s'amie, / et son ami chascune anbrace / et bese et festoie et solace.'[51] The courtly lover and the Albigensian heretic were both liable to be charged with Forced Abstinence.

The recurrent troubadour theme of 'la mort-par-l'amour' may be taken as supporting the Crypto-Cathar thesis. Nelli believed that this theme was Arabic and mystical in origin, but he noted that it was employed in two contradictory senses. The lover longs for death, either because he knows that his love could never be fulfilled by the pleasures of this world or because these same pleasures have been denied him:

Tantôt, c'est l'excès même de son désir—le *Joi*—qui est censé faire mourir l'amant, la mort étant souhaitée par lui comme réalisant l'amour. (Et il y a bien là une sorte de transposition de la théorie arabe selon laquelle l'amour pur, *insatisfait par essence*, ne peut s'exprimer en ce bas monde que sous forme d'aspiration à la mort.) Tantôt, ce qui amène, au contraire, la mort de l'amant, c'est tout simplement l'insatisfaction sur le plan terrestre: la dame le désespère par sa rigueur, et comme elle ne lui accorde rien de ce qu'il désire, il souffre au point d'en mourir. (*L'Érotique*, p. 73)

The identification of love and death may be found in Arabic love poetry, in the Cathar *consolamentum*, in the *mors osculi* of the Cabbala, and in the *hieros gamos* of the Hellenistic mysteries. It is also, of course, present in the Christian biblical tradition, and is expressed in the idea of the seed that must die to be reborn.[52]

The theory that the Cathar heresy was a formative influence on the troubadour ideal of *fin'amors* accords with the Hispano-Arabic thesis, since, according to Jean-Claude Vadet, there were definite links between Manichaeism and early Arabic love poetry (Vadet, 1968, pp. 171–8; 436–7). The eighth-century Iraqi poet Bashshār b. Burd (d. 783) was condemned to death as a *zindīq* or crypto-Manichee, because he identified the lady to whom he addressed his poetry with the Spirit or *rūḥ*, an intermediary between man and God. The *mu'tazalite* sect to which Bashshār belonged developed the theory of *'ishq*, which sought to reconcile the materialism of Persian and Ionian physics with the belief in a single Divinity. In the ninth century the cosmic principle of *'ishq* was modified by the influence of Plato's *Timaeus* and the *Symposium*. It is significant that the *zindīq* practised *ẓarf* or courtliness, which means that he was generally from the upper strata of society. The expression 'more elegant than a Manichee' is proverbial in the Middle East. 'Par la prédominance qu'il donne à la vie intérieure l'esprit courtois paraît très enclin au dualisme si ce dernier est . . . un refus délibéré du monde extérieur' (Vadet, p. 437). The chaste and suicidal love codified by Ibn Dāwūd and Ibn Ḥazm was probably influenced by Manichaean habits of mind. It is thus possible that the Provençal troubadours were well disposed to the Cathars partly as a result of the Arabic theory of *'ishq* (or vice versa).

During the twelfth century the Church had little power to intervene in the daily lives of those who lived in the principalities of southern France. The clergy had acquired a reputation for greed and debauchery; many of the troubadours were in consequence violently anti-clerical, and some became ardent supporters of the Ghibelline cause. Anti-clericalism should not, however, be confused with Catharism, nor should the Cathars be confused with Ghibellines, Lollards and Fran-ciscan 'Spirituals', as though they were all members of one vast con-spiracy. Furthermore the coexistence of Catharism and Courtly Love does not in itself prove that they were genetically linked.

Little is actually known about the Cathars, because few documents have survived. According to the Abbé Foncaude, the Cathars 'differed from the Church of Rome merely in denying the sovereignty of the Pope, the powers of the priesthood, the efficacy of prayers for the dead, and the existence of purgatory' (Sismondi, I, p. 216). If this is true an analogy could be drawn between the Cathars and the Protestants of the Reformation. Whether or not the Cathars were genuine Mani-chees, the Church never accused the troubadours, as a group, of Catharism (Russell, 1965–66, p. 36), nor can it be proved that Cathars were more tolerant to *fin'amors* than orthodox Christians. Moreover the Cathars were not persecuted before 1210, so there was no need for elaborate concealment (Jackson, *The Literature*, p. 241). The worst charge against Crypto-Cathar theorists is that they systematically ignore the literal meaning of a text: 'Le sophisme fondamental est celui de tous les maniaques de l'ésotérisme; on prend un texte, on en refuse le sens obvie, on y infuse un sens secret et on se redresse triomphant: "Prouvez-moi qu'il est impossible" ' (Davenson, *Les Troubadours*, pp. 142–4). The attractiveness of the theory is also considerably diminished if, as many critics now agree, Courtly Love was not essentially extra-conjugal nor necessarily chaste.

Denis de Rougemont's thesis lays itself open to criticism. The observation that passion thrives on obstacles scarcely justifies postula-ting the existence of a self-destructive impulse; still less can such an impulse be defined by the term Eros, Freud's life principle. In proposing that this impulse was historically determined, de Rougemont mixed bad history with bad psychology. He failed to differentiate carefully between *fin'amors*, which was based on a pledge of faith, and the fatal passion of Tristan and Iseult, which was initiated by a love potion, an extraneous device precluding freedom of choice. Nor was it ever adequately explained how the myth of Tristan could have been affiliated with Catharist doctrines. The *matière de Bretagne* was certainly known to the troubadours, but it was only of marginal importance, and was not Manichaean. The tension between mind and matter or soul and body is probably at the root of all love poetry, and the germ of dualism is latent within all religions that stress the transcendence of the Deity.[53] The most that can be said in favour of the Crypto-Cathar thesis is that the early troubadours may have attempted to make their songs conform, at least superficially, to the morality of the Cathars. The cult of 'la mort-par-l'amour' and the image of the *belle dame sans merci* may owe something to the Cathar environment, but both can be accounted for in other ways.

4   NEOPLATONIC

Courtly Love was fostered by Neoplatonism, which conceived of the soul as a substance, divine in origin, yearning to be liberated from the prison of created matter in order to ascend to the First Principle, the source of beauty and goodness.

(a)   *Contact with Neoplatonism.*   The currents of thought which reached the south of France between the late tenth and the early twelfth centuries were primarily Neoplatonic, which means that the troubadours must have been exposed to such influences. Denomy (1944).

(b)   *The thought pattern of Courtly Love.*   The basic thought pattern underlying the poetry of the troubadours, namely the supremacy of the love object, the upward surge of the lover and the insatiability of desire, is Neoplatonic. Denomy (1944).

(c)   *The amorality of the courtly ethic.*   Although Courtly Love developed in a Christian milieu (twelfth-century Languedoc), it was amoral in the sense that its moral standards were not those of Christianity. Dawson (1935); Denomy (1944); Lazar (1964).

(d)   *The ascent of Eros.*   Plotinus reinterpreted the Platonic Eros as a compound of need and abundance, which participates in matter

and yet desires the Good from the moment of its birth; Courtly
Love was similarly intended to pass through frustration to sublimation. De Rougemont (1939); Denomy (1944); D'Arcy (1945).

(e) *The ennobling effects of love and beauty.* According to Neoplatonism, created beauty acts as an incentive to the Godhead; similarly
the courtly lover improves his conduct and his character by con-
templating his lady's moral and physical excellence. Denomy
(1944).

The Platonism of the Middle Ages was largely Neoplatonic and
Augustinian. Neoplatonism reached the Latin Middle Ages from a
variety of sources. Arab philosophy, including the works of Avicenna,
was imbued with Neoplatonic thought, largely owing to the mis-
apprehension that Aristotle was the author of two works, the *Liber de
causis* and the *Theologia aristotelica*, which in fact comprised extracts
from the *Institutio theologica* of Proclus and the *Enneads* of Plotinus
respectively. Neoplatonism was present in Boethius, in Macrobius, in
the Christian adaptations of Dionysius the Areopagite and Scotus
Eriugena, and was fused in the theology of St Augustine and St Thomas
Aquinas. The Cathars, whose doctrines were Gnostic in origin, shared
Plotinus' view that human existence represents a descent of the soul
into matter: 'By its presence, matter is the cause of the soul's exerting
its generative powers, and being led thus to suffering.'[54] It should,
however, be emphasised that, for Plotinus, matter is created by the
Soul and has no independent existence. The naturalistic current in
Neoplatonism, which was prominent in Arab philosophy, conceived of
the cosmos as a series of emanations from the First Principle, which
could be studied through mathematics and the natural sciences. The
mystical current, exemplified in pseudo-Dionysius, in St Augustine and
in the works of the Ṣūfīs, stressed the inwardness of religious experience
and hence the independence of the individual from external authority.
Augustinian and Avicennist schools of thought were replaced by
Aristotelianism in the thirteenth century, but the Neoplatonic tradition
was never eradicated. However, until Marsilio Ficino began to translate
the works of Plato in 1463, and to write his *Theologica Platonica*, there
was no such thing as a single coherent Neoplatonic system.

Neoplatonism, which was, after all, a 'religion of Eros', might
explain how a love which for Christians was sinful could have been
exalted as pure and ennobling. In modern theological terms, Courtly
Love could be defined as a love of Eros rather than a love of Agape,
because the lover was prompted by an ecstatic impulse to submit him-

self to the sovereignty of a lady, who, as a consequence of her beauty, virtue, rank and, very often, married status, was unapproachable or sexually unattainable. The lover's growth in worth was considered, in theory, to be a sufficient compensation for the pains of love service. Thus in many ways the ideology of the troubadours reflects a Neo-platonic mentality: 'L'idéal d'amour que les troubadours introduisent dans une société christianisée depuis des siècles, a été formé et développé par toute une tradition néo-platonicienne' (Lazar, 1964, p. 13). Neoplatonism is especially evident in Matfré Ermengaud's *Lo breviari d'amor*[55] and, of course, in Dante's *Divina Commedia*. The condemnation of jealousy by the early troubadours is, for example, consistent with Platonism: 'Que gelosia es fols ressos / don totz lo mons brai e crida'.[56]

Although the general intellectual background of the troubadour lyric could be described as Neoplatonic, Courtly Love was not mystical: there was no movement from individual to universal beauty, nor was there, as in Dante's works, any ascent from the human to the divine. There are also chronological reasons for doubting whether the early troubadours could have had access to Arab Neoplatonism before about 1130, unless they were able to read or speak Arabic, which is not unlikely (Denomy, 1953). Theodore Silverstein noted that certain aspects of *fin'amors* are absent from Avicenna's doctrine of 'pure' love: there is no mention of what Andreas calls *zelotypia* (a fear lest love should not be reciprocated and an anxiety for the beloved's well-being), nor is there any reference to the state of exultation called *joy* in Provençal. The Provençal idea of *joy* was, however, accurately defined by the Neoplatonist Ṣūfī Ibn Arabī:

If union with the beloved is not personal union, and the beloved is a superior being who imposes obligations on the lover, then the fulfilment of these obligations sometimes takes the place of personal union, producing in him a joy which obliterates the awareness of sorrow from his soul.[57]

The spiritual aspirations of Ṣūfī and Christian mysticism were probably more important than the highly intellectual philosophical works which would not have been available at first hand.

5　BERNARDINE–MARIANIST

The mysticism of St Bernard and the cult of the Virgin Mary influenced the ideas and sentiments of troubadour poetry, and contributed to the birth of Courtly Love.

(a) *Nostalgia*. The courtly lover and the Christian mystic share the same yearning for a distant ideal: an *amor de lonh*. Spitzer (1944).

(b) *Spiritual aspiration*. Courtly Love was an effort, in response to Cistercian mysticism, to bring the physical appetites into harmony with the spirit. Wechssler (1909); Lot-Borodine (1928); Foster (1963).

(c) *Disinterestedness*. Profane love service was modelled on service to God; the troubadour, like the mystic, proved his love through suffering, and disclaimed any right to favours. Wechssler (1909); Lot-Borodine (1928).

(d) *Ecstasy*. The courtly lover, like the Christian mystic, seeks to merge himself in the object of his love; he falls into a trance at the sight of his beloved, or loses himself in the contemplation of her image. Wechssler (1909).

(e) *Martyrdom*. The romantic glorification of agony, a trope rooted in Christianity, was a central feature of the medieval love lyric. Wilhelm (1965).

(f) *Redemption*. The courtly lover begs his lady to offer him a sign of recognition, a *salute*, because his fate rests in her hands. If she accords him this blessing he is transformed by *joy* into a 'new man'. Russell (1965–66).

(g) *Marianism*. Courtly Love was a profane aristocratic counterpart to the cult of the Virgin Mary. Symonds (1883); Adams (1913); Power (1926); Ahsmann (1933); Wilhelm (1965).

(h) *Appropriation of religious terms*. The use of religious terms, concepts and metaphors implies a transfer of religious emotion. Lot-Borodine (1928); Russell (1965–66).

It should be stated at the outset that, although Marianism and Bernardine mysticism are related phenomena, St Bernard himself did not approve of the new cult of Mary. When a Feast of the Immaculate Conception of Our Lady was celebrated at Lyons in 1140 he protested against 'this new feast of which the custom of the Church knows nothing, which reason does not approve, and that tradition does not authorize' (de Rougemont, *Passion*, p. 111). Since, however, the Order of St Bernard placed its churches under the special protection of the Virgin Mary, there is a case for conflating the two theories. The knights of St Bernard were, after all, 'knights of Mary'.[58] Furthermore Bernardine mysticism was closer to the popular devotion of the people than other contemporary intellectual developments.

It could be argued that the Cistercian movement, which began in

1098, coincided, and was therefore linked, with the birth of Courtly Love. St Bernard, having joined the Order in 1112, founded the Abbey of Clairvaux in 1115. The activity of St Bernard and Hugh of St Victor began towards 1120–30; the first great poets whose poetry displays mystical elements appeared towards the middle of the century: Jaufré Rudel, Bernart de Ventadorn and Pierre Rogier. Between 1170 and 1270 the French built eighty cathedrals and nearly 500 churches of the cathedral class, most of which were dedicated to the Virgin Mary (Adams, p. 92). It would indeed be surprising if certain general analogies could not be found between religious and literary movements during this period. There is a sense in which, both for the mystic and for the courtly lover, desire interposes a distance, in time or place, between the lover and the object of his love: 'l'éloignement est paradoxalement consubstantiel avec le désir de l'union' (Spitzer, *L'Amour lointain*, p. 21). In the words of Abbot Gilbert de Hoy, in his continuation of St Bernard's *Sermones super Cantica*: 'Ubi viget amor, ibi viget languor, si absit quod amatur' (Lot-Borodine, 1928, p. 232; Spitzer, p. 15). This stress on absence lent troubadour poetry a metaphysical slant: 'C'est le lointain qui donne à la tenue morale un rayonnement métaphysique et un sens à l'amour' (Spitzer, p. 16). Absence or non-attainment allowed the poet to concentrate on an inner vision of beauty; it was the means whereby the poet, in love with love and unwilling to risk disillusion, guaranteed the integrity of his ideal, in accordance with St Augustine's injunction 'Noli foras ire: in interiore animae habitat veritas' (Spitzer, p. 38). The lover regarded himself as a martyr subject to the whims of the person whom he 'adored'. She was the sole arbiter of his destiny, endowed with the power to kill or to save. This religion of profane love demanded patience, humility, abnegation, obedience and fidelity, and was a source of elegance and social refinement, but it was also self-consciously fictitious (Singleton, in Newman, p. 47).

Étienne Gilson has convincingly demonstrated that Bernardine mysticism could not have contributed to the birth of Courtly Love, because the activity of St Bernard coincided with the most flourishing period of troubadour poetry, in the middle of the twelfth century, not with its beginnings (Gilson, *The Theology*, p. 170). Scarcely any poetry was dedicated to the Virgin Mary before 1150 (Ahsmann, 1929, p. 110), and it was only after 1230 that Marianism reached its height (Jeanroy, *La Poésie lyrique*, II, p. 130).[59] The troubadours were under increasing pressure, when the Albigensian Crusade ended in 1229, to make their poetry conform to ecclesiastical requirements. It is therefore more probable that Courtly Love contributed to the rise of Marianism than the reverse: 'The worship of the Virgin responded to a vital necessity for the Church while under threat and pressure' (de Rougemont, *Passion*, p. 111). As with countless cults and customs, 'the Church adopted what she could not suppress' (Briffault, *The Troubadours*, p. 154).

Gilson has also proved, by means of selected passages, as Briffault and Lazar have done, that Courtly Love was far from being disinterested or Platonic in the vulgar sense. Even if it could be shown that it was a sensual interpretation of the mystical love of St Bernard the thesis would, he insisted, remain a sophism, because the two loves are mutually exclusive (Gilson, p. 179). The parallel between the *amor purus* of Andreas and the pure love of the mystic is entirely specious, because the 'purity of courtly love keeps the lovers apart, while that of mystical love unites them' (p. 193). *Amor mixtus* is, in some respects, more acceptable to a Christian theologian than *amor purus*, which permits everything short of the sexual act. As C. S. Lewis says, 'medieval theory', by which he means Church theory, 'finds room for innocent sexuality: what it does not find room for is passion' (Lewis, 1936, pp. 16–17). Andreas wrote, 'reddit hominem castitatis *quasi* virtute decoratum'. Special emphasis should be given to the word *quasi* (Gilson, p. 196). An even more important distinction between love directed to God and love directed towards a human being is that the former can never be unrequited, while the latter is never sure of requital. The courtly lover is thus a prey to fears and anxieties which are completely foreign to the mystic. 'Caritas mittit foras timorem' was a maxim, taken from the Gospel of St John, on which St Bernard frequently meditated (Gilson, p. 182). If Gilson is correct, one must conclude that those analogies which exist between Courtly Love and Bernardine mysticism are either of such a general nature that they prove nothing, or formulas which have acquired a totally different meaning in their new context.

6   SPRING FOLK RITUAL

Courtly Love evolved out of the folk traditions and ritual dance songs of Europe, particularly those associated with the rites of spring, or it was an actual survival of the pagan cult of Cybele or Maia, the Great Mother of the Gods.

(a) *Spring nature prelude.*   Many troubadour lyrics contain a description, usually in the opening stanza, of trees in blossom, singing birds, and a fountain of cool water. This picture of the rebirth of nature is appropriate to a lyrical tradition which originated in hymns to the goddess of Nature. Paris (1891–92); Anglade (1908); Chaytor (1912); C. B. Lewis (1934); Wilhelm (1965).

(b) *Easter: season of joy and regeneration.* Just as the May festival marks the rebirth of nature after the winter, so Easter, which occurs in late March or in April, commemorates Christ's resurrection. The terms *jovens* and *joy* are used repeatedly by the troubadours. It was in Holy Week that Dante, Petrarch, Boccaccio, Ausias March and many others met the lady with whom they fell in love.

(c) *Adultery or free love.* It was the convention in May Day songs and in *chansons de mal-mariée* to scoff at the odious bonds of matrimony, and to treat the husband as an easily outwitted enemy. The goddess, whose festival was at the vernal equinox, on 25 March, did not recognise marriage, but required free love from all her votaries. Courtly Love was extra-conjugal, and generally adulterous. Paris (1891–92); C. B. Lewis (1934).

(d) *Lack of individuality.* There is little difference between the lady of one poet and that of another. Cybele or Maia was the prototype of the Virgin Mary and of the lady addressed by the troubadours. C. B. Lewis (1934).

(e) *Humble adoration.* The courtly lover was the 'servant' of a *domna*, a lady of high rank, who represented an ideal of womankind. The worshipper of Cybele likewise declared himself a 'servant' of a goddess, who alone deserved the title of *Domina*. C. B. Lewis (1934).

(f) *Secrecy.* The practice of using a *senhal* or pseudonym originated in the worship of Cybele, whose name could only be pronounced in her innermost sanctuary. C. B. Lewis (1934).

(g) *Growth in virtue.* 'I have fled the bad, I have found the better' was a ritual formula used in the ceremonies of the Phrygian cult of Cybele, and one which occurs in the poetry of the troubadours. C. B. Lewis (1930).

In the eleventh and twelfth centuries courtly and popular genres were not as clearly differentiated as they were later to become. There must therefore have been a constant process of cross-fertilisation, as regards both form and content (Bec, *Mélanges Lejeune*, II, pp. 1310–15). The region of Poitou, from which the first known troubadour, Guilhem IX, originated, is particularly rich in popular verse, and his poetry and that of his contemporaries contains frequent allusions to the season of May. Love, spring, Christ's passion, and spiritual regeneration create a web of associations which were exploited by many medieval poets, including Dante in the *Vita nuova*. Holy Week was traditionally connected with the genesis of love, and an analogy was sometimes drawn between the suffering of love and the passion of Christ. It was also on May Day, soon after Holy Week, that the poetic academies of Toulouse and Barcelona celebrated their annual Floral Games. The coveted prize on these occasions was the golden replica of a violet, a flower which is said to have sprung from the blood of Attis,[60] when he was killed by a wild boar and transformed into a pine tree. The name of Attis was linked with that of Cybele, the great Asiatic goddess of fertility. The worship of Cybele had been adopted by the Romans in 204 B.C. and spread throughout the Roman Empire—along the northern coast of Africa and throughout southern Gaul. In Europe it survived in the May Day festival, when a tree, usually a pine tree, was cut down to serve as a maypole, which was wrapped in purple bands and decorated with violets. The mysterious apostrophe to the 'flowers of the pine tree' in the famous song by King Dinis of Portugal, 'Ai flores, ai flores do verde pino',[61] is therefore possibly associated with the sacred drama of Cybele and Attis. In the twelfth century there existed in Languedoc an institution called the Fraternity of the Penitents of Love, whose members were known as Galois or Galoises. The term *Galli* was applied to the castrated priests of Attis who scourged themselves to the accompaniment of drums, pipes and deafening cries.[62] It is therefore not impossible that vestigial traces of the cult of Cybele can be discovered in troubadour poetry. It is significant that Cybele was served by singers, crowned in laurel, and that at Rome they were trained at a *Schola cantorum* (C. B. Lewis, 1934, p. 26). It is doubtful, however, whether this theory could account for any of the essential features of Courtly Love.

May Day theorists tend to belong to that class of critics, which includes Denis de Rougemont and Jessie Weston, whom Silverstein has described as 'literary *peelers*' (Newman, 1968, p. 85): it is argued that by stripping a poem of its individual traits and courtly accretions one may infer the existence of a single primal sub-genre, from which, it is deduced, all European vernacular poetry is descended. This regressive and inductive method of reasoning was criticised by Joseph Bédier in a review article on Gaston Paris' theories (Bédier, 1896). In fact popular genres, such as *pastourelles* and *reverdies*, were artificially adapted to a courtly environment, and are, for that reason, quite distinct in tone from court love songs. C. B. Lewis must be charged with sophistry of a different kind; he can be classed, once again with de Rougemont, among 'les maniaques de l'ésoterisme' (Davenson, *Les Troubadours*, p. 144) because he expects every poem to fit an obscure hypothesis. This does not mean that the theory is totally invalid, but merely that no theory can claim a monopoly of the truth.

A more serious objection to the Folk Ritual thesis is that it cannot explain one of the most important features of Courtly Love, namely the belief in love's ennobling power (Bédier, 1896, p. 172). C. B. Lewis countered this objection by quoting the Roman historian Diodorus Siculus, who wrote, with reference to the cult of Cybele, that 'those who took part in the mysteries of the goddess were looked upon as having become more devout, more just and better in all respects'.[63] These sentiments are scarcely applicable to the May festivities in medieval Europe. The anti-matrimonial character of May Day has little bearing on Courtly Love, because if a poet addressed his verses to a married woman (which was by no means always the case), he never proclaimed the right to rebel against the institution of marriage; he merely pretended to be unaware of the existence of social constraints. Courtly Love did not liberate women from their parents and husbands, nor did it promote sexual licence. The Folk Ritual theory may explain certain extraneous aspects of Courtly Love, but as a theory of origin it is unconvincing.

7   FEUDAL–SOCIOLOGICAL

Courtly Love may be explained by certain sociological factors operating within the feudal environment of twelfth-century Europe, chief of which was the rapid promotion of new men into the ranks of the nobility.

(a) *The practice of arranged marriages.* In a society where marriages were arranged by the parents of the bride and bridegroom, in accordance with political and mercenary interests, it was inevitable that love and marriage should have been considered mutually exclusive. Courtly Love was, as a consequence, an extra-conjugal affair. Paget (1884); Lewis (1936).

(b) *The feudal contract.* Love service or *domnei* was constituted on the analogy of the feudal relationship between a vassal and his over-lord: the lover swore an oath of allegiance to his lady, and made a pledge to obey her and to abide by certain rules, such as secrecy, patience and moderation. Fauriel (1846); Wechssler (1909); Chaytor (1912); Lewis (1936); Jackson (1960).

(c) *The absence of men on crusades.* A woman of noble birth whose husband or brother was absent on a crusade or a military expedition might be called upon to act, in his stead, as a feudal suzerain, thus facilitating the transference of feudal concepts to love. Chaytor (1912); Jackson (1960).

(d) *Social mobility and the decline of feudalism.* The troubadours generally belonged to the lower nobility, a class comprising *ministeriales* and court officials who had recently been promoted. Lacking the prestige of inherited wealth and noble birth, they argued that nobility was a potential virtue which had to be earned by courtesy, valour and personal merit. The courtly ethic was thus sponsored by the very classes whose basis it undermined. Valency (1958); Köhler (1964).

(e) *A high sex ratio.* A shortage of females in the upper strata of society, which was a consequence of upward social mobility, made it difficult for knights to marry. In those regions where this phenomenon occurred women were idealised and love poetry prospered. Moller (1958–59). Males were predominant within the confines of the medieval castle because it was a place of training for novice knights, and few men could afford the luxury of a wife. Paget (1884).

(f) *The dream of hypergamy.* It was essential that a knight should not demean himself by marrying beneath his station. In the south of France, where the daughters of noblemen had the right to inherit property and where the nobility, in the twelfth century, remained an open class, hypergamy was particularly tantalising, whilst women, in such circumstances, could afford to be haughty and capricious. Moller (1958–59).

(g) *Social anxieties.* The fluidity of class barriers created a sense of insecurity, both for the social upstart and for the nobleman of ancient lineage. The troubadour of humble origin regarded his lady as a figure of authority, capable of allaying his social anxieties and his fear of detractors, whilst the aristocrat was obliged to prove that he was worthy of his status. Moller (1958–59).

(h) *The aristocratic 'juvenes'.* The courtly and chivalric literature of twelfth-century France (and of Europe as a whole in succeeding centuries) was conditioned by the tastes and ideals of a large group of young men, recently dubbed or aspiring to knighthood, who were without children or material commitments, and who were, in many cases, deprived by the principle of primogeniture from the prospect of inheritance. Heer (1962); Duby (1964).

Even if Courtly Love were a mere literary fantasy, divorced from the realities of everyday life, it would still be important to ascertain what social factors caused poets to turn their backs on life. Courtly and chivalric ideals were not in fact confined to literature, but informed the manners and conduct of the aristocracy. The courtly lyric was moreover the symptom of a social activity practised at court (Jackson, 1958; Stevens, 1961), which was fashioned, to some extent, by feudal concepts. No theory that purports to explain the origin of Courtly Love can afford to ignore sociology. The analysis of quantifiable changes in the structure of medieval society in relation to social institutions and cultural ideals is a subject which is still in its infancy. Earlier theorists such as Fauriel, Wechssler and C. S. Lewis concentrated on feudalism as a static institution, and exaggerated the feudal overtones of Courtly Love.[64] Most social theorists would now agree that the new ideology was formulated by a recently ennobled class, and that social mobility was therefore important as a background to the courtly mentality. The theory that a preponderance of males in the upper classes or, more specifically, in the court environment contributed to the birth of Courtly Love is one which deserves more serious consideration. Moller's research into the sex composition of different European populations in the twelfth century was inevitably based on unreliable data, but his findings were at least partially anticipated by Violet Paget in 1884. It might be worth studying whether a similar correlation could be established between social mobility and the revival of troubadour poetry in late medieval Spain and elsewhere.

It is important to remember that changes in the sex or class composition of different social groups are mostly the consequence of socioeconomic factors. An increment in the wealth of the ruling classes in the south of France during the twelfth century permitted an influx of persons into the service of princes and barons. At the same time this wealth, derived from the development of manufacturing industries, increasing trade links with the Orient and the introduction of new agricultural methods,[65] created a powerful bourgeoisie which threatened to undermine the feudal basis of the aristocracy. The establishment of a more stable currency made it gradually possible to replace or supplement payments and services in kind by an exchange of money, thereby loosening personal ties of dependence and permitting the individual more freedom of movement. Furthermore the inhabitant of a burgh township enjoyed rights, as a member of a community, which were denied to the feudal vassal, who was bound to render onerous services in return for protection. A 'feudalisation of love' thus occurred when feudalism was beginning to decline. The principle of primogeniture, which was adopted by the aristocracy of the twelfth century as a means of avoiding the constant subdivision of fiefs, was another socio-economic factor which indirectly influenced the cultural ideals of the period, since it increased the number of unattached landless knights, who were debarred by prescriptive custom from stooping to productive labour. In an age when the feudal contract ceased to exercise the same sense of moral compulsion over lords and vassals, and when rapid changes in the structure of society resulted in friction and insecurity, Courtly Love, itself a patron–client relationship, may have acted to some extent as a cohesive force between the ruling élite and those who were affiliated to them. The courtly lover was, to adapt Veblen's phrase, 'conspicuously subservient', while women of noble birth, having been endowed with that 'prerogative of leisure which is the mark of gentility', required entertainment.[66] It was in the interests of the princes and magnates to promote the new ideology because it guaranteed fidelity from their noble subjects and prevented them from stirring up trouble on their rural estates. Moreover it may, as Köhler suggested, have served to neutralise the conflict at court between the old hereditary nobility and the petty nobility of recent origin. These are all factors which might be studied more carefully. Huizinga noted that ideals, however delusory, are no less important to the cultural historian than the real but hidden socio-economic forces which are known in retrospect to have shaped the course of history. However, like most theorists of Courtly Love, he underestimated the influence of the latter upon the former.

The materialistic and utilitarian character of medieval marriage is one of the few socio-economic factors which has been considered relevant. 'Any idealization of sexual love, in a society where marriage is purely utilitarian, must,' according to C. S. Lewis, 'begin by being an idealization of adultery' (Lewis, 1936, p. 13). This argument is obviously fallacious. If love was not normally connected with marriage, we must conclude that love was extra-conjugal, which is not to say that it was necessarily adulterous. There is, in any case, a more fundamental reason for this situation: in the words of Andreas, 'the easy attainment of love makes it little prized' (Andreas, trans. Parry, p. 184). It may also be observed that conjugal love was not immune from amatory ideals. There were no doubt some husbands in the Middle Ages who sought to follow the example of the Franklin in *The Frankeleyns Tale*, and shared his opinion that 'Love wol nat been constreyned by maistry'.[67] Since, however, the *fin amant* did not, at least ostensibly, woo his lady with a view to marriage, it is doubtful whether any significance can be attached to the practice of hypergamy.

The chief objection to a purely sociological approach is that society is not the only context within which poetry should be judged; it is also the product of an intellectual environment, shaped by philosophical and religious ideas and by literary traditions and influences. The sociologist tends to be concerned with poetry only in as much as it reflects certain aspects of society. This theory would nevertheless appear to be one of the most important theories of origin.

NOTES

[1] For a summary of the present state of scholarship consult Watt, *The Influence of Islam*. See also *The Legacy of Islam*, 2nd edn., ed. Schacht and Bosworth (Oxford, 1974); Aldobrandino Malvezzi, *L'islamismo e la cultura europea* (Florence, 1956); Jean Paul Roux, *L'Islam en Occident* (Paris: Payot, 1959); Youakim Moubarac, *Pentalogie Islamo-Chrétienne* (5 vols, Beirut: Editions du Cénacle Libanais, 1972–73).

[2] Vicente Cantarino, *Arabic Poetics in the Golden Age. Selection of texts, accompanied by a preliminary study* (Leiden: E. J. Brill, 1975).

[3] The oldest extant *zajals* date from the late eleventh and twelfth centuries. Whether they were disseminated from Andalusia or whether they occurred spontaneously in the popular lyric of different countries is uncertain. M. Hartmann argued that the *muwashshaḥ* and *zajal* originated in certain metrical forms of Eastern Arabic poetry such as the *musammaṭ* which occur in pre-Islamic and Abbasid poetry (*Das Arabische Strophengedichte*, I, *Das Muwaššaḥ* [Weimar, 1897]). Stern has demonstrated that these poetic forms were almost certainly inspired by poetry which was indigenous to Spain. Guido Errante discovered an eighth-century inscription in Latin with the rhyme scheme aaab:

> Te semper sobrium
> Te cernebamus modestum
> Tu tribulantium
> Sis consolatio vera

(Errante, 1948, p. 73.). This poem requires a prelude or refrain to form the rhyme scheme of the *zajal*; see Stern (1974), pp. 208–14.

[4] 'The *kharja* is the last of the *qufls* (lines ending in a common rhyme) of the *muwashshaḥ*; it is a separate unit . . . The lines of the *kharja* are placed in the mouth of a character other than the poet. In most cases it reproduced the words of women (probably of singing girls), of young men, of drunkards, or even of doves cooing in the branches' (Ibn Sanā'al-Mulk, in Stern, 1974, p. 126).

[5] Ibn Dāwūd al-Iṣfahānī al-Ẓahirī (868–909), *Kitāb al-Zahra*, MS Cairo, IV, 260, analysed in Louis Massignon, *La Passion d'al-Hosayn-ibn-Mansour al-Hallāj, martyr mystique de l'Islam* (Paris: P. Geuthner, 1922), I, pp. 170–9; Nykl, *Hispano-Arabic Poetry*, p. 123; Vadet (1968), pp. 264–316. Massignon translates the title as *Book of Venus*, which Gibb accepts, whereas Nykl, who edited the work in 1932, translates it as *Book of the Flower*. Ibn Dāwūd describes his intentions in his preface: 'J'y ai placé

cent chapitres,—et, dans chaque chapitre, cent vers; dans les cinquante premiers chapitres je rappelle les aspects de l'amour, ses lois, ses variations, et ses cas;—dans les cinquante autres, je fais mémoire des autres genres de poésie . . . L'amour est le fait d'une élite, le privilège des caractères délicats, c'est une affinité intellectuelle' (quoted from Massignon, La Passion d'Al-Ḥallāj, pp. 175–6).

[6] Abū Muḥammad Alī ibn Aḥmad ibn Said, called Ibn Ḥazm (994–1064). See Bibliography.

[7] Abū Bakr Muḥammad ibn Alī Muhyi ad-Din al-Andalusī, called Ibn Arabī (1165–1240). This work was translated by Reynold A. Nicholson with a commentary (London, 1911).

[8] Lois Anita Giffen has made a preliminary study of some of these works in Theory of Profane Love among the Arabs. The development of the genre (New York University Studies in Near Eastern Civilization, No. 3) (London and New York, 1971). See also Hellmut Ritter, Der Islam, XXI (1933), 84–109. The following 'arts of love' may be mentioned. (1) (a) Abū 'Uthmān 'Amr b. Baḥr al Jāḥiẓ (c. 776–868), Risāla fi-'l-Ishq wa'n-Nisā' ('Treatise on passionate love and woman'), abridged translation in Charles Pellat, ed., The Life and Works of Jāḥiẓ, trans. from the French of Pellat by D. M. Hawke (London: RKP, 1969); (b) Jāḥiz, Risālāt al-Qiyān ('The treatise on singing girls'); see C. Pellat, 'Les esclaves-chanteuses de Ğaḥiẓ'', Arab, X (1963), 121–47 (a French translation with notes). (2) Abū 't-Tayyib Muḥammad b. Aḥmad b. Isḥāq al-Washshā 'al-A'rābī (860–936), Kitāb al-Muwashshā, ed. Rudolph E. Brünnow (Leiden, 1886). (3) Abū Bakr Muḥammad b. Ja'far al-Kharā'iti as-Sāmarrī (d. 938), I'tilāl al-Qulūb ('The malady of hearts'). (4) Abū Isḥāq Ibrāhīm b. 'Ali b. Tamīm al-Ḥusrī (d. post-1022), Kitāb al-Maṣūn fi Sirr al-Hawā al-Maknūn (What has not been revealed about the secret of hidden love'). (5) Abū Muḥammad Ja'far b. Aḥmad b. al-Ḥusain as-Sarrāj al-Qarī (1026–1106), Maṣāri' al-'Ushshāq ('The calamities of lovers').

[9] 'Udhiri', in Encyclopédie d'Islam, ed. E. Lévi-Provençal. Hassan Soleiman Hussein insists that 'Udhri love should not be confused with Platonic love; see Hussein, pp. 109–11. His reasons are as follows. 'Udhri love did not imply any philosophical system or sophisticated culture; 'Udhrī love is against nature, 'a sick love by people in an abnormal situation' (p. 110); the love object was a specific woman, not an abstract ideal; 'Udhrī poets had no guide; they were aimless wanderers, dominated not by reason but by emotions. 'Udhrī poetry contains many of the themes of Courtly Love, such as the anguish of separation and the fear of the slanderer. It was a religion coexisting with religion: 'O my God, make her love and cherish me . . . /When I pray I turn my face towards her place though the right direction is the opposite one./ I do not do that from polytheism, but because my lovesickness resisted the cure of the doctor' (A. Kinany, The Development of Gazal in Arabic Literature [Damascus, 1950], pp. 297–8). This type of sacro-profane hyperbole was extremely common in European court poetry, especially in Spain. See María Rosa Lida, 'La hipérbole sagrada en la poesía castellana del siglo XV', RFH, VIII (1946), 121–30. The Ṣūfīs made the tale of Majnūn and Laylā a parable of man's quest for God.

[10] It is recounted by Ibn Arabī that Majnūn was so deep in meditation on the image of Laylā that when she called to him he sent her away, saying that he had no time for her. The mystic lost in contemplation is, like Majnūn, a narcissist, because he strives to participate in the paradox of God's self-love. See Miguel Asín Palacios, El Islam cristianizado. Estudio del 'sufismo' a través de las obras de Abenarabi de Murcia (Madrid, 1931), pp. 466–7.

[11] This idea was expressed by Aḥmad b. at-Tayyib as-Sarakhsi (833/7–899), whose words are quoted in an anonymous untitled essay on love. 'Kissing offers the nearest contact with the soul of the beloved, because it is the mouth and nostrils which carry the breath which has had recent contact with his nature and the powers of his soul' (Giffen, Theory of Profane Love, p. 7). The theory is based on Graeco-Arabic physiology:

the vital spirit, generated in the heart, 'receives the powers of the soul and transfers them to the body' and 'receives through the instruments of the senses the images of external bodies'; it could also pass from the blood stream of one person to that of another, causing his heart to become sick with love. See Marsilio Ficino, *Commentary on Plato's Symposium*, trans. S. R. Jayne, UMS, 19 (1944), p. 189. *Cf.* Dronke, *Medieval Latin*, II, pp. 449–50. See Gaselee (1923–24). The idea of 'fascination' through the *spiriti* is important for an understanding of the *Vita nuova*.

12 M. Asín Palacios, *La escatología musulmana en la 'Divina Comedia'* (Madrid: E. Maestre, 1919), pp. 339–49.

13 See *Al- Futūhāt*, in M. Asín Palacios, *El Islam cristianizado*. These abstract dilemmas were to become the stock-in-trade of the fifteenth-century Spanish love poet, and passed into the poetry of Boscán, Garcilaso, Camões, Maurice Scève, Marguerite de Navarre and John Donne.

14 See Appendices I and II.

15 'As it continued in use until after 1650, it has been claimed the most studied medical work in all history' (Watt, *The Influence of Islam*, p. 67). See O. Cameron Gruner, *A Treatise on 'The Canon of Medicine' of Avicenna* (London: Luzac, 1930); Charles Homer Haskins, *Studies in the History of Medieval Science* (Cambridge, Mass., 1924; repr. New York, 1960); D. Campbell, *Arabian Medicine and its Influences on the Middle Ages* (London: Kegan Paul, 1921).

16 This etymology is given in a seventeenth-century Persian medical work, *Tibb-i-Akbarī*, by Muḥammad Akbar, largely copied from a treatise, no longer extant, by the ninth-century physician Najab ad-Din Unhammad. *Haram*, caused by impure love, is distinguished from *pak*, caused by pure love carried to excess. See Gregory Zilboorg, *A History of Medical Psychology* (New York: W. W. Norton, 1941), p. 124. In a glossary of Arabic terms appended to the 1582 edition of Avicenna's *Liber Canonis* is written: '*alhasch* sicut scribit Ebenesis est species volubilis quae involuitur super arbores, et exicca est, et ad eius similitudinem alhasch dicitur de quodam aegritudine quae exiccat patientem ipsam [*sic*], et removet ab eo colorem splendidum vitae'. The same explanation is given in a fourteenth-century work, Ad-Damiris, *Ḥayāt al-Ḥayawān* (a zoölogical lexicon), under the word *al-Fākhitah* (a species of collared dove), where it is also said that the '*ashaqa* was a plant which is first green, then shrivels and turns yellow. See Lowes, 'The Loveres Maladye', 22 n. Mario Equicola uses the term *hilisci*: 'ne le infermità melancolice Avicenna questa pazia numera nominandola hilisci' (Equicola, fol. 114*v*); the term was incomprehensible to the French translator, Gabriel Chappuys Tourangeau, who wrote (Paris, 1584, fol. 213*v*): '& descrit la guarison d'icelle'.

17 Extremes of joy and grief were both considered a threat to life: the former, associated with the sanguine temperament, caused an exodus of the vital spirits, whilst the latter, in conjunction with the melancholy humour, caused their withdrawal into the heart: 'Pues en el cuerpo proprio muy claro es que puede la triste ymaginación matar y la alegre también con la violencia de la una y la otra. La alegre echando fuera todos los espíritus: y dexando el hombre sin vida. Y la otra de los apretar y ahogar violentíssimamente' (Pedro Mexía, *Silva de varia lección* [Antwerp: Martin Nucio, 1544], fol. 124*r*).

18 Aretaeus of Cappodacia (A.D. *c.* 30–*c.* 90) was possibly the first to regard *mania* and *melancholia* as expressions of a single pathological disorder. Thenceforward manic-depressive psychosis was generally recognised by physicians (Zilboorg, *A Hist. of Med. Psych.*, pp. 73–4).

19 Raymond Klibansky, Erwin Panofsky and Fritz Saxl, *Saturn and Melancholy. Studies in the history of natural philosophy, religion and art* (London: Nelson, 1964), p. 29.

20 In the second century A.D. Rufus of Ephesus, whose ideas were embraced by Galen and by ninth-century Arabic writers, wrote, 'illi qui sunt subtilis ingenii et multae perspicationis, de facili incidunt in melancolias, eo quod sunt velocis motus et multae

praemeditationis et imaginationis' (Klibansky *et al.*, *Saturn*, p. 49). The grief-stricken mother of Leriano, in Diego de San Pedro's *Cárcel de Amor*, believes that those who possess 'el entendimiento agudo' are fated with 'el sentimiento delgado' (*Obras completas*, ed. K. Whinnom, II, p. 15).

21 'There are very many holy and pious men who become melancholy owing to their great piety and from the fear of God's anger, or owing to their great longing for God until this longing masters and overpowers the soul. They fall into melancholy as do lovers and voluptuaries, whereby the abilities of both soul and body are harmed, since the one depends on the other' (Constantinus Africanus, copying Isḥāq ben 'Amran, in Klibansky *et al.*, *Saturn*, p. 84). According to Juan Huarte de San Juan, 'el rezar, contemplar y meditar enfría y deseca el cuerpo y lo hace melancólico' (*Examen de ingenios para las ciencias* [1575], ed. Rodrigo Sanz [2 vols, Madrid, 1930], I, p. 89). Religious melancholy is discussed by Robert Burton in his *Anatomy of Melancholy* (1621), ed. Floyd Dell and Paul Jordan-Smith (New York: Farrar & Rinehart, 1927), Third Partition.

22 Avicenna, 'Haec aegritudine est solicitudo melancholica similis melancholiae, in quo homo sibi iam induxit incitationem seu applicationem cogitationis suae continuam super pulchritudine ipsius quarundam formarum, et gestuum seu morum, quae insunt ei' (*Liber Canonis*, Liber III, Fen. I, Tractatus iv, cap. 23).

23 Klibansky *et al.*, *Saturn*, p. 83.

24 See Appendix II.

25 Aurora, the wife of al-Ḥakam II (961–976), was Navarrese. In 980 Sancho Garcés, king of Navarre, offered his daughter in marriage to al-Manṣūr, and she subsequently became a fervent convert to Islam. In 993 Bermudo II of Leon sent his daughter, Teresa, to al-Manṣūr, who received her as a slave. He later released her in order to marry her, but she remained a Christian, and retired to a monastery in León after her husband's death in 1002. See Menéndez Pidal, *Historia y epopeya* (Madrid: Centro de Estudios Históricos, 1934), pp. 18–21.

26 Quoted by Richard Hitchcock, 'Muslim Spain (711–1492)' in *Spain. A companion to Spanish studies*, p. 58.

27 Ernst Kantorowicz, *Frederick the Second, 1194–1250* (London: Constable, 1957), p. 197.

28 See Torraca (1902); V. de Bartholomaeis, 'La "metgia" di Aimeric de Peguilhan . . . osservazioni sulle poesie provenzali relative a Federigo II', in *Memorie della R. Accademia delle Scienze dell'Instituto provenzali storiche relative all'Italia*, series 1, VI (1911–12), pp. 69–123; id., *Poesie provenzali storiche relative all'Italia*, Istituto Storico Italiano, Rome (vols 71–2 of the *Fonti per la storia d'Italia*), 1931 (*cf.* intro.); Jeanroy, *La Poésie lyrique*, I, pp. 254–8 and pp. 260–5; Ruggero Ruggieri, 'La poesia provenzale alla corte di Federico III di Sicilia' in *BCSS*, I (1953), pp. 228 ff.; and Palermo (1969).

29 M. Amari, *Storia dei Musulmani di Sicilia* (1868–72), III, pp. 738 and 889; G. Cesareo, *Le origini della poesia lirica e la poesia siciliana sotto gli Suevi* (1924), pp. 101 and 107.

30 A poetry festival was held annually at 'Okaz in Arabia from 500 B.C. until it was suppressed by the prophet Muhammad as a relic of idolatry. This institution was later assimilated by Islam: poets competed at Fez on the birthday of the Prophet, and the winner, the Prince of Poets, was showered with gifts (Huet, p. 51; Sismondi, II, p. 53).

31 Otto Wiener, *Contributions towards a History of Arabico-Gothic Culture* (London, 1917), pp. 90–1. 'The reference to the rhetoricians and the crowd of dandies who follow them is identical with that made by Alvarus in the middle of the ninth century' (*ibid.*, p. 90).

32 According to Watt, about a hundred translations are ascribed to Gerard of Cremona, who probably had a team of translators under him. He worked for many years in Toledo and died there in 1187. Adelard of Bath studied in France, Sicily, Syria and perhaps also Spain in the late eleventh and early twelfth centuries. Michael Scot was

in Toledo in 1217, then in Bologna, in Rome and finally in Sicily, where he was court astrologer to Frederick II. He died c. 1236. Daniel of Morlay was a pupil of Gerard of Cremona. See Richard Lemay, 'Dans l'Espagne du XIIe siècle. Les traductions de l'arabe au latin', *AESC*, XVIII (1963), 639–65.

33 'Arabico eloquio sublimati, volumina Chaldaeorum avidissime tractant, intentissime legunt, ardentissime disserunt . . . Heu, proh dolor! linguam suam nesciunt Christiani, et linguam propriam non advertunt Latini, ita ut omni Christi collegio vix inveniatur unus in milleno hominum numero, qui salutatorias fratri possit rationabiliter dirigere litteras. Et reperitur absque numero multiplex turba, qui erudite Chaldaicas verborum explicet pompas. Ita ut metrice eruditiori ab ipsis gentibus carmine, et sublimiori pulchritudine, finales clausulas unius litterae coarctatione decorent, et juxta quod linguae ipsius requirit idioma, quae omnes vocales apices commata claudit et cola, rythmice, imo uti ipsis competit, metrici universi alphabeti litterae per varias dictiones plurimas variantes uno fine constringuntur, vel simili apice' (Paul Alvar, *Indiculus Luminosus*, ed. J. P. Migne, in *Patrologiae Cursus Completus*. *Series Latina* [1852], CXXI, cols. 555–6). This passage cannot be taken as evidence of the peaceful coexistence of Christians and Muslims. Bishop Alvar identified Muhammad with the Antichrist, and he was a protagonist in the martyr movement of Cordova. See Edward P. Colbert, *The Martyrs of Córdoba, 850–859. A study of the sources* (Studies in Mediaeval History, 17, Washington, D.C.: Catholic University of America Press, 1962).

34 John of Seville is sometimes identified with John of Spain. See Watt, *The Influence of Islam*, p. 60.

35 He later became a physician to Henry I of England.

36 See Daniel, *The Arabs and Medieval Europe*, pp. 90–3.

37 His translation (done between 1209 and 1213) was better than that of Robert of Ketton but was 'negligible in its influence' (*ibid.*, p. 238 and p. 270). See Marie-Thérèse Alverny, 'Deux traductions latines du Coran au Moyen Âge', *Archives d'Histoire Doctrinale et Littéraire du Moyen Âge*, XVI (1947–48), 69–131.

38 Robert Stevenson, in *Spain. A companion to Spanish studies*, p. 549.

39 *Ibid.*

40 J. A. Westrup, 'Medieval song', in *New Oxford History of Music*, ed. Dom Anselm Hughes (London: OUP, 1954), II, pp. 220–69, at p. 225. *Cf.* Farmer (1930), Ribera y Tarragó (1922), Schneider (1946) and O. Wright in *The Legacy of Islam* (1974), pp. 489–505. The controversy created by Ribera's interpretation of the *Cantigas de Santa Maria* has still not been settled. See Higinio Anglés, *La música de las Cantigas* (Barcelona: Diputación provincial, 1943).

41 For the etymology of *trobar* see Appendix I.

42 See Fr. Taeschner, 'Futuwwa', *Encyclopaedia of Islam*, n.s., II (Leiden and London, 1965), pp. 961–9, and Américo Castro, *The Spaniards. An introduction to their history*, trans. W. F. King and S. Margaretten (Berkeley, Los Angeles and London: University of California Press, 1971), pp. 471–83.

43 A. C. Fox-Davies, *A Complete Guide to Heraldry*, revised by J. P. Brook Little (London: Nelson, 1969), p. 10.

44 See Marc Bloch, *Feudal Society*, trans. L. A. Manyon (2 vols, London: RKP, 1962, repr. 1971), and F. J. C. Hearnshaw, 'Chivalry and its place in history', in *Chivalry*, ed. E. Prestage (London, 1928).

45 *Viaje del noble bohemio León de Rosmital de Blatna por España y Portugal hecho del año 1465 a 1467*, trans. J. García Mercadel, in *Viajes de extranjeros por España y Portugal* (Madrid, 1952), p. 298. The poet Fernández de Jerena obtained permission from John I of Castile to marry a Moorish *juglaresa*, who had recently been baptised, believing that she was immensely rich. He settled in Granada, became a Muslim and took his wife's sister for a second wife. Thirteen years later he returned to Castile and reverted to Christianity (Schack, II, pp. 219–22). The *Cancionero de Baena*, ed. José M. Azáceta

(3 vols, Madrid, 1966), contains his poems and those of a Moor, Mahomat el Xartosse de Guardafaxara.

46 See V. Gordon Childe, *Social Evolution* (London, 1951), p. 28. It would have been wiser if, as Gordon Rattray Taylor says, Briffault 'had confined himself to asserting that in every patriarchy the existence of a previous matriarchal state can be shown or inferred' (intro. to abridged edition, *The Mothers*, p. 14).

47 See C. B. Lewis in Bibliography; and below, p. 88. Warton's source (I, pp. 461–2 in main text, *History of English Poetry*) was Claude de Vic and Jean Joseph Vaissette, *Histoire générale de Languedoc* (5 vols, Paris, 1730–45), IV [by Vaissette], pp. 184 ff.

48 *Chivalry* (1928), p. 18.

49 *The Medieval Manichee. A study of the Christian dualist heresy* (Cambridge: CUP, 1947), p. 131. 'Dualism necessarily disapproves of the propagation of the species. It therefore disapproves of marriage far more than of casual sexual intercourse, for the latter represents merely one isolated sin, while the former is a state of sin' (*ibid.*, p. 176).

50 Quoted from Benton, in Newman (1968), p. 34. The source is Ralf of Coggeshall, *Chronicon anglicanum*, Rolls series, 66 (London, 1875), pp. 121–4. Benton concludes that the Cathars 'made it more difficult to advocate chastity', implying that this was what the troubadours did. Briffault argues that, on the contrary, the troubadours spoke of chastity because they wished to *avoid* ecclesiastical censorship. The above anecdote is in Runciman, *The Med. Manichee* (1947), p. 121.

51 *Le Roman de la Rose*, ed. Félix Lecoy, CFMA (3 vols, Paris: H. Champion, 1965–70), III, p. 97, ll. 19855–8.

52 See 'Amor as a god of death' in Wind, *Pagan Mysteries in the Renaissance*, pp. 152–70. Wind mentions the love–death equation in Lorenzo de Medici's poetry, but no reference is made to the Cathars or the troubadours.

53 Simone Pétrement, *Le Dualisme dans l'histoire de la philosophie et des religions* (Paris: Gallimard, 1946), p. 127. Certain courtly works may allegorise Cathar doctrines. The enigmatic *Razón de amor con los denuestos del agua y el vino* (thirteenth century) is a case in point. See Enrique de Rivas, 'La razón secreta de la *Razón de amor*', *AnFi*, VI–VII (1967–68), 109–27, reprinted in *Figuras y estrellas de las cosas* (Maracaibo, 1969), pp. 93–110.

54 Quoted from Denomy (1944), 201 n. (*Enneads*, ed. Bréhier [6 vols, Paris, 1924–38], I, p. 129).

55 Ed. Gabriel Azaïs (2 vols, Béziers: Société archéologique, scientifique et littéraire de Béziers, 1802 [composed *c.* 1288]). Through the contemplation of the circle of nature and natural law man reaches the circle of God and the angelic hierarchy. The theory is expressed in a diagram at the start of the work.

56 Gaucelm Faidit, quoted by Erich Köhler, 'Les troubadours et la jalousie', *Mélanges . . . Frappier*, I, pp. 543–59, at p. 543. According to Köhler this attitude can be explained as a protest against private property.

57 Asín Palacios, *El Islam cristianizado*, p. 501. I translate the quotation.

58 During the Albigensian Crusade Simon de Montfort, learning that King Peter of Aragon had dedicated his life and death to a lady of the Languedoc, is said to have exclaimed, 'S'il a sa Vénus pour le protéger, nous, nous avons la Sainte Vierge!' (R. P. Benoist, *Histoire des Albigeois et des Vaudois* [Paris, 1691], I, p. 235, quoted by René Nelli, *L'Amour et les mythes du coeur*, p. 86). This anecdote may be taken as an illustration of what Oswald Spengler calls 'pseudomorphosis'. The Virgin Mary supplied a psychological need to counteract Courtly Love, just as St James of Compostela countered Muhammad in the Spanish wars of the Reconquest and King Arthur was disinterred to challenge Charlemagne.

59 The Virgin Mary occupied a secondary position in early Christianity: 'It was only in the Gnostic Ophite sects that the Virgin Mary was actually worshipped as a goddess' (E. O. James, *The Cult of the Great Mother Goddess* [London: Thames & Hudson, 1959], p. 201). As the instrument of the Incarnation Mary became the key figure in the

Christological debate which culminated in the defeat of Arianism at the Council of Nicaea in 325. At the council held at Ephesus, a city notorious for its devotion to Artemis or Diana, the title Theotokos, Mother of God, was bestowed on the Virgin Mary (*ibid.*, pp. 205–7).

60 James George Frazer, *The Golden Bough*, abridged edn. (London: Macmillan, 1971 [first edn., 1922]), p. 459.

61 *Cantigas d'amigo dos trovadores galego-portugueses*, ed. José Joaquim Nunes, II (Coimbra University Press, 1926), pp. 19–20.

62 James, *The Cult*, p. 107, and Frazer, *The Golden Bough*, p. 458. An altar to Cybele in white Carrara marble was erected in Arles in the first or second century A.D. with the following inscription:

Bonae Deae

Caiena Priscae Lib. Attice

Ministra

'To the Good Goddess, Caïena Attice, liberated by Prisca, priestess'. (Caïena was a Greek slave girl, whose name was Attice until she was released by Prisca. She then took the name of her protectress and became a priestess of Cybele.) On the altar was a bust of the goddess, symbolised by her large ears and earrings, dating from the sixth century A.D. See Charles Lenthéric, *La Grèce et l'Orient en Provence* (Paris: E. Plon, 1878), pp. 274–8.

63 Quoted by H. Graillot, *Le Culte de Cybèle, Mère des dieux* (Bibliothèque des Écoles Françaises d'Athènes et de Rome, 107, Paris, 1912), p. 187, and by C. B. Lewis (1934), p. 28.

64 Dronke states bluntly that 'the ideas of *amour courtois* are not the product of chivalric social conditions', and quotes from an article by Scheludko (*NMi*, XXXV [1934], pp. 1 ff.): 'Nowhere in the romances do we find a poet in love with his married patroness. The romances reflect every aspect of the life of their time, yet nowhere do they show us a troubadour of the kind Fauriel and Wechssler depicted . . . The troubadours' cult of their lady in the accepted chivalric sense is a legend' (*Medieval Latin*, I, p. 55 n.).

65 These economic changes are discussed in Baret (1857), pp. 45–50. The expulsion of the Jews from France in 1306 was a serious setback.

66 Thorstein B. Veblen, *The Theory of the Leisure Class* (Boston, Mass.: Houghton Mifflin, 1973 [first edn. 1899]), p. 53. This book is essential for the understanding of the crisis of the aristocracy and the troubadour revival in the late Middle Ages.

67 *The Complete Works of Geoffrey Chaucer*, ed. F. N. Robinson (London: OUP, 1933), l. 764, p. 163. These words are very close to those of a poem by Bernart de Ventadorn: 'Mas en amor non a om senhoratge, / e qui l'i quer vilanamen domneya, / que re no vol amors qu'esser no deya' (*The Songs of Bernart de Ventadorn*, ed. Stephen G. Nichols, Jr, and John A. Galm, UNCSRLL, 39 [Chapel Hill, N.C., 1962], No. 42, ll. 15–17). Chaucer's Franklin secretly swore 'as a knyght / That nevere in al his lyf he, day ne nyght, / Ne sholde upon hym take no maistrie / Agayn hir wyl, ne kithe hire jalousie, / But hire obeye, and folwe hir wyl in al, / As any lovere to his lady shal' (*The Complete Works*, ll. 745–50, p. 163).

III   Theories on the meaning of Courtly Love

1   COLLECTIVE FANTASY

Courtly Love was a collective fantasy or an institutionalisation of neurotic values, generated by a mother fixation of infantile origin, which was sufficiently widespread to alter the nature of social reality.

(a) *Reversal of sex roles.*   The lover assumed a childlike or feminine attitude, whereas the beloved, who was generally a married woman, was the dominant partner in the relationship, and was considered both morally and socially superior to her suitor. Moller (1960).

(b) *Dichotomy of tender and sensual feelings.*   Protracted yearning from a distance was necessitated by the forbidden nature of the love object. Desire could never be appeased, because an unconscious prohibition prevented the possibility of sexual fulfilment. Moller (1960); Cleugh (1963); Koenigsberg (1967).

(e) *Paradoxical quest for sorrow.* The lover cherished his suffering in order to alleviate unconscious guilt feelings arising from incestuous desires. Hostility, provoked by the traumatic discovery of the mother's participation in sexuality, was transformed into self-contempt. Moller (1960); Koenigsberg (1967).

(d) *Ambivalent attitudes to women.* The courtly lover repressed his secret contempt for the mother by idealising a married lady and by masochistically making his will subservient to hers. By thus recreating the Oedipal triangle he sought to come to terms, in adult life, with the basic trauma of his childhood. Courtesy was a 'reaction-formation' against an underlying sadism. This ambivalence is inherent in the structure of Andreas Capellanus' *De amore*. Askew (1965); Koenigsberg (1967).

(e) *Rivalry of siblings for a mother's favour.* The husband of the adored lady was rarely mentioned; the real enemies were the flatterers, watchers and slanderers; the lady herself was simultaneously an antagonist and a source of protection. The absence of a threatening father figure precludes an Oedipal interpretation of the mother fixation. The syndrome could be explained as a reversion to the rivalry of siblings. Moller (1960).

(f) *Rejection anxieties.* The courtly lover, fearing lest he should be rejected and abandoned, strove to earn the approval of the lady whom he loved. She acted, to some extent, as his conscience or *alter ego*. Moller (1960).

(g) *Voyeurism.* Some of the best known troubadours expressed the desire to contemplate the naked body of their *domna*, or longed to know whether she went to bed naked or dressed. Moller (1960).

(h) *Infantile identification of love and food.* The lady's kind words were, for several poets, a form of nourishment, capable of saving them from emaciation and death. Moller (1960).

Courtly Love was certainly a fantasy or fiction, shared by the aristocracy of medieval Europe from the twelfth century onwards, and its constantly reiterated themes must have fulfilled an important psychological function for poets and for contemporary audiences. This fantasy cannot, however, be easily reconciled with Freud's theory of art as wish fulfilment, nor is there sufficient biographical evidence to postulate the theory that the majority of court poets in the Middle Ages suffered from a mother fixation of infantile origin.

'The artist,' writes Freud, 'is originally a man who turns away from reality because he cannot come to terms with the demand for the renunciation of instinctual satisfaction as it is first made, and who then in phantasy-life allows full play to his erotic and ambitious wishes.'[1] The artist is, in short, a neurotic who uses his art as a therapy. Three dubious assumptions underlie this definition: first, that 'the mental apparatus endeavours to keep the quantity of excitation in it as low as possible';[2] secondly, that the work of art is primarily a substitute for reality, both for its creator and for its audience; thirdly, that the psychoanalyst is in a position to diagnose the unconscious motives which produced it. The courtly lover's choice of suffering in preference to gratification is incompatible with the Freudian 'pleasure principle'. As Arthur Koestler says, 'the sex drive in the Freudian system is essentially something to be got rid of—through the proper channels or by sublimation; pleasure is derived not from its pursuit, but from getting rid of it'.[3] An artificial distinction cannot be drawn between pleasure and desire, or between enjoying and wanting. There are, as the philosopher Gilbert Ryle has shown, many activities, most of which can be classed as play, which involve agitation of a pleasurable kind.[4] The theory which studies Courtly Love as a form of play is discussed below. Whether or not Courtly Love was a collective fantasy or a game, therapy was not its only or primary function. Persuasion, communication, imitation and indoctrination are no less important, and it is within the context of these conscious intentions that artistic performance can be assessed. Without detailed biographical information, or, better still, the artist or poet in person, a psychoanalyst is not in a position to diagnose his patient's unconscious motives. The paucity of data on the circumstances of composition does not make medieval poetry susceptible to this kind of treatment. Furthermore, even if such information were available, psychological methods might explain the process, but never the end product, of artistic creation, because they do not provide the critic with the instruments with which to form aesthetic or moral judgements.

Granted that Courtly Love was a collective fantasy, a more fruitful line of approach would be to study the social conditions which might have promoted it. A child of good family would generally enter the service of a local magnate as a page, and his education was entrusted to the women of the household until he reached the age of seven.[5] He would thus tend to form an attachment to a woman, who was both a teacher and a mother substitute, and this attachment might develop into a lifelong friendship. The males clustered around the lady of the castle could be compared to boys competing for their mother's attention. Moller's 'The social causation of Courtly Love' (1958–59) could have been more satisfactorily integrated with 'The meaning of Courtly Love' (1960) had he emphasised that the sex ratio created a mother–son analogue. However, there is no need to postulate the theory that unconscious feelings of incest prevented the possibility of sexual fulfilment. If the *domna* seemed totally inaccessible, it was because social taboos of age, rank and married status separated her from her admirer, and because there was a shortage of women in the upper strata of society. There is, in any case, a fundamental discrepancy between the sociological and Freudian approaches: either the medieval love poet loved a married (or unmarriageable) woman out of necessity, owing to the scarcity of unmarried women, and overvalued her for that same reason; or else he deliberately chose a woman whom he had no right to possess because he was sexually inhibited by a mother fixation.[6]

The courtly ethic must have had a socio-psychological basis. Courtly society was a 'shame culture': the lover or courtier was amiable, deferential and discreet in his relations with others, because he was motivated by the desire to please and by the fear of ridicule.[7] One has only to recall the mocking laughter in Dante's *Vita nuova*.[8] The psychologist must study the style of life at court, the manner in which children were educated, and the games people played.

2 PLAY PHENOMENON

Courtly Love was a manifestation of the play element in culture, comprising contest, chance, divination and make-believe, which constituted an aesthetic and socially acceptable ritual for the expression of nostalgia, passion and anxiety.

(a) *Duplicity.*   The player is aware at each stage in the game that he is only playing; he is simultaneously both agent and spectator. Henriot (1969).

(b) *Illusion.*   The player pretends that he is not playing; he makes himself and others believe that he is other than he really is (*in-lusio* is a word which, etymologically, means 'entering into the game'). Huizinga (1949); Caillois (1958); Henriot (1969).

(c) *Commitment.*   The player undertakes to abide by certain rules or conventions which are accepted as absolute and binding for the duration of the game. Huizinga (1949); Caillois (1958).

(d) *Virtuosity.*   The player displays his ingenuity by working within self-imposed restrictions, and derives pleasure from 'la difficulté vaincue'. Huizinga (1949).

(e) *Secrecy.*   The player employs a specialised and often recondite terminology which is comprehensible only to those who have been initiated into the rules of the game. The playground or circle of play is generally secluded or set apart from everyday life. Huizinga (1949); Caillois (1958).

(f) *Unpredictability.*   Suspense is created through the fear of losing and the hope of winning; the essence of play is lost when the outcome is certain. The element of uncertainty allows scope for improvisation and adventure. Henriot (1969).

(g) *Conservatism.*   Games ensure the survival of rituals and beliefs which belong to a past phase of civilisation. Tylor;[9] Gombrich (1974).

Given the conventional stylised character of the form and content of the medieval courtly lyric and the festive circumstances in which this type of verse was sung or recited, there is a strong case for analysing Courtly Love in terms of a theory of play. Love, play and poetry are clearly interrelated phenomena, which can be defined by the features listed above. It was taken for granted that the troubadour should write about love,[10] and that he should adopt the *persona* or mask of the stereotype lover. In his prologue to a collection of poems, compiled for John II of Castile before 1454, Juan Alfonso de Baena maintained that a poet who was not in love should at least be prepared to play the part.[11] Courtly Love was a conventional, but anti-Establishment, sentiment; it was a style of expression which was capable of generating its own emotion. The medieval audience was invited to enter into 'gamelike revolt against traditional morality' (Howard, 1966, p. 102), or to pretend that the ordinary world no longer existed. Those who played the game were expected to abide by the rules. The lover, in his conduct, and the poet, in his choice of poetic themes and forms, were both expected to follow conventions. The former freely pledged to abide by love's precepts, including the injunction to be faithful, discreet and moderate. The latter selected a difficult rhyme scheme, a limited vocabulary and a set motif. In love and in poetry there was a spirit of noble emulation. Formal debates were held in which a contestant was required to answer his interlocutor in the same rhyme scheme, sometimes with the help of a rhyming dictionary.[12] The poet would often express himself in a deliberately enigmatic style, either because he wished to convey a private message without impropriety or fear of scandal (Ibn Ḥazm, trans. Arberry, pp. 65–6), or because he wished to provide the connoisseur with the pleasure of exegesis.[13] Words in common usage thus acquired a specialised meaning within the context of the troubadour tradition (Sutherland, 1956). The court was an enclosed environment from which sickness, ugliness, old age and death were excluded. However, the ideal world of play was the *hortus conclusus*, the walled garden where the lover meets the lady of his dreams.[14] The garden is surrounded by hostile forces, and the element of risk and uncertainty is never absent.[15] Love is a perpetual dilemma, an experience of contradiction. The lover is never sure whether his services will meet with his mistress's approval.

Huizinga noted that in troubadour poetry play forms, based on warfare, competition and litigation, were predominant: the *castiamen* (rebuke), the *tenzone* (dispute), the *partimen* (antiphonal song), and the *joc partit* (game of question and answer) (*Homo Ludens*, p. 147). This play element is even more marked in the riddles, mottoes, *glosas* and debate poems which were composed in Burgundy, Spain and other European countries in the fifteenth century. In the late Middle Ages chivalry became, increasingly, 'a game which nobility played and the others watched' (Gombrich, 1974, p. 1085) and every event at court tended to assume the character of a spectacle: the effects of joy and grief were theatrically exaggerated; the colour and quality of the cloth which a person wore indicated his status and even his state of mind (Huizinga, *Waning*, p. 240). The nobility was essentially a 'leisure class', since it was debarred by the duty of non-derogation from engaging in productive and profitable activities, adhering to the ancient Greek principle that leisure is necessary for a person with political responsibilities.[16] Courtly Love was from the outset an aristocratic phenomenon, and the accentuation of the play element in late medieval culture can be attributed to those changes in the art of war and in the structure of society which undermined the nobility's *raison d'être*.[17]

Huizinga's ideas on 'the play element in culture' have been developed and modified by a number of critics, but no theory of play has been systematically applied to Courtly Love. Roger Caillois was inspired by *Homo Ludens* to devise a 'sociology of play', based on four play categories: *Agon* (Greek for contest); *Alea* (Latin for dice); *Mimicry* (a term used in the natural sciences for the tendency, in plants and animals, to imitate their surroundings); and *Ilinx* (Greek for waterfall, whence the word *ilingos*, 'dizziness', derives). The last of these categories, covering such activities as skiing, motor racing or going on a roundabout, can obviously be dismissed as irrelevant to the study of higher forms of culture. The other three categories, associated with contest, chance and make-believe respectively, can be usefully applied to Courtly Love. Caillois doubted whether secrecy could be classified as essential to play, since play is generally spectacular and ostentatious. He also maintained that, if gambling is to be included as play, then play is not disinterested. He therefore preferred the adjective 'improductive' (Caillois, 1958, pp. 15–17). Furthermore a game need not have fixed rules; in many games of mimicry, such as that of a child playing an adult role, 'as if' performs the function of a set of rules. Apart from these minor reservations, Caillois' definition was closely modelled on the first chapter of *Homo Ludens*.

The features of play enumerated by Huizinga and Caillois were subjected to a careful analysis by Jacques Henriot, and redefined from an existentialist standpoint.[18] Volition was rejected as a defining principle on the grounds that work, as well as play, demand the agent's consent. However, what Huizinga actually meant (*Homo Ludens*, p. 26) was that play implies a temporary freedom from physical necessity and from the sense of moral obligation. Henriot also observed that work, like play, has its rules and has a special time and place reserved for it. In a society based on a work ideology, play can be more accurately defined as a non-remunerative and non-productive activity. Duplicity, uncertainty and illusion are, he concluded, the essential features of play (Henriot, 1969, pp. 57–65). He stated categorically that there can be no play without lucidity: 'Un jeu dont on n'est pas conscient n'est pas un jeu' (p. 9). To be more precise, play is 'l'acte de jouer à jouer' (p. 10). The point had already been made by Huizinga: 'Genuine play possesses, besides its formal characteristics and its joyful mood, at least one further very essential feature, namely the consciousness, however latent, of "only pretending"' (*Homo Ludens*, p. 41). The course of a game is unpredictable and irreversible: it is 'une suite d'opérations possibles' (Henriot, p. 27). It is implicitly understood that a play attitude must be adopted, which means that the player must be prepared to enter into the spirit of the game, without losing his self-awareness: 'Le risque que court Don Juan est de se laisser lui-meme séduire' (pp. 90–1).

Huizinga's research into the etymology of play in different languages reveals some more primitive traits of play which are not discussed by Caillois and Henriot, but which link play very closely to Courtly Love. In several Semitic, Germanic and Slavonic languages the verb 'to play' may denote a swift movement of the fingers such as a musician would use. The word *la'iba* in Arabic is used for the playing of a musical instrument (*Homo Ludens*, p. 55). French is the only Romance language which has 'jouer' in this sense (p. 62). The German *Spielman*, like the troubadour, not only played an instrument, but also composed the tune. Neither Greek nor Latin applies the idea of play to music. Many words for play, such as the Old Saxon *plegan*, the German *pflegen* or the Dutch *plegen*, evoke the idea of danger, risk or pledge. The oldest meaning of these words is 'to vouch or stand guarantee for, to take a risk, to expose oneself to danger for someone or something' (p. 59). These concepts are important for an understanding of courtly and chivalric ideals. David L. Miller, in an article 'Playing the game to lose' (in Moltmann, 1972), noted that the verb 'to win' derives from the Indo-European root *wen* or *ven*, 'to desire', whilst the verb 'to lose' derives from the root *los*, 'to loosen' or 'set free'. Similarly in Spanish the verb *ganar*, 'to win', derives from the Gothic verb *ganan*, 'to covet', whilst *perder* comes from the Latin *perdare*, which, according to Corominas, initially meant 'to give completely'.[19] The courtly lover clearly played to lose, often creating obstacles to fulfilment. Huizinga, in his discussion of play in relation to the erotic, writes, 'It is not the act as such that the spirit of language tends to conceive as play; rather the road thereto, the preparation for and introduction to "love"' (p. 63). The term 'play' generally refers to aspects of flirting and courtship: 'the deliberate creation of obstacles, adornment, surprise, pretence, tension, etc.' (p. 63). 'The term "play",' added Huizinga, 'is specially or even exclusively reserved for erotic relationships falling outside the social norm' (pp. 63–4). He finally rejected the erotic use of the term as a 'conscious metaphor', because, as Gombrich says, 'it fell outside his definition' (Gombrich, 1974, p. 1088). He thus failed to connect the lover's ascetic endurance of tension in the ritual of courtship with the primitive connotations of *pflegen*. 'But as for pleasure,' wrote León Hebreo, 'its delights consist not in possession nor enjoyment nor complete acquisition, but in a certain tension bound up with privation.'[20]

'Life must be lived as play,' wrote Plato, 'playing certain games, making sacrifices, singing and dancing, and then a man will be able to propitiate the gods, and defend himself against his enemies, and win in the contest' (*Homo Ludens*, p. 239). This ethic of play still prevailed during the Middle Ages, before it was replaced by the capitalist or bourgeois morality. In this sense, therefore, Courtly Love was a survival rather than a new departure. Mankind has lost this sense of play. Yet, for Huizinga, 'real civilization cannot exist in the absence of a certain play element' (p. 238).

The problem of interpreting Courtly Love *sub specie ludi* is that play is exceedingly difficult to define. There is also the danger of assuming that, if it is a manifestation of the play element in culture, then it is, as Peter Dronke believes, a universal phenomenon. The critic should not ignore contemporary beliefs on the psychology and physiology of love, nor should he overlook the specific religious and sociological factors that influenced the courtly mentality of twelfth-century Europe.

3   COURTLY EXPERIENCE

The sensibility which gave rise to *amour courtois* is universally possible, and is not confined to a learned or an aristocratic milieu.

(a) *Universality*.   *Amour courtois* was not, as critics have traditionally maintained, an emotional discovery of twelfth-century Europe. The whole problem of origins as previously understood is therefore irrelevant and misleading. Frings (1949); Valency (1958); Dronke (1965).

(b) *Unity of the popular and courtly love lyric*.   The 'courtly experience' is not exclusively aristocratic; it is implicit in many love songs written from the man's point of view. Frings (1949); Dronke (1965).

(c) *Unity of human and divine love*.   The religious language of profane love implies that finite love can be transcended through the mediation of the beloved, and that, ultimately, human and divine love are one. Dronke (1965).

(d) *Learned development of love themes.*   Research into European courtly poetry should be concerned with its intellectual content and development. The critic might study the way in which the language of love was enriched by mystical, noetic and Sapiential terms derived from Jewish, Christian, Hellenistic and Islamic sources. Dronke (1969).

'The study of comparative literature would seem to prove that romantic love is possible in any age or place or milieu.'[21] Some of the themes and sentiments of *amour courtois* can indeed be traced in the love songs of Egypt, Byzantium, Georgia, Mozarabic Spain and Iceland. In ancient Egyptian love poetry the woman is several times addressed as a semi-divine creature who alone is endowed with the capacity to cure love's malady. In one poem, quoted by Dronke (*Medieval Latin*, p. 10), the hieroglyph for 'health' is written with a Sacred Eye, which gives it the same physical–spiritual ambivalence as the Latin *salus* and its Romance equivalents. In Icelandic skaldic poetry of the tenth century A.D. the beloved was portrayed as the cause of insomnia and love-sick longing, and as a source of poetic inspiration and of courage against death. Icelandic poets also cultivated an esoteric style, resembling the *trobar clus*, and treated the theme of *amor de lonh* (pp. 39–42). In the case of Egyptian poetry of the second millennium B.C. and of Icelandic poetry of the tenth century these resemblances must be coincidental, whereas in the case of Byzantium and Georgia this would be more difficult to demonstrate—Byzantium, Georgia and Mozarabic Spain all inherited the lyrical tradition of the Arabs which developed in the seventh century.[22] Chinese and Japanese poetry might have provided Dronke with further evidence for the universality of what he calls the 'courtly experience'.

Although Dronke has convincingly demonstrated that analogies can be found between the male conception of love in the love lyric of many different countries, these analogies do not detract from the novelty of the troubadour movement in twelfth-century Europe.[23] As P. Boyde says, 'Dronke is concerned exclusively with the experience of those . . . who in his view are writing out of intense personal experience. Earlier scholars have on the whole been occupied with what was common to the many—the public things, the gradually crystallizing stock of ideas, attitudes, situations, epithets and metrical forms that could be and were imitated. *Amour courtois* for them is the "content" of a well-defined literary genre.'[24] The idea that a love which contravened the religious and legal establishment should form the basis of social refinement and well-being was entirely new to twelfth-century Europe, although it was already familiar to the Arabic ruling elite in Baghdad and Al-Andalus. 'In short, *amour courtois* and the "courtly experience" of love are distinct notions and must be recognized as such.'[25] Furthermore, if the latter is not confined to courtly or chivalric society, then there does not seem to be any justification for the retention of the adjective 'courtly'.

The majority of medieval courtly lyrics do not imply that human and divine love are one. In fact the appropriation of religious concepts, such as salvation, eternity, paradise, perdition and consolation, tends to draw attention to the discrepancy between the finite and the infinite. The language of religion was an accepted part of the *stilo de loda*, which was usually intended to shock and to flatter. It was not customary for European court poets to elevate their mistresses into symbols of Philosophy or analogues of the Supreme Beloved, as Dante had done. The practice of writing palinodes would appear to indicate that poets regarded this cult of woman as a form of idolatry and a truancy from true religion. Courtly Love was, in short, a make-believe religion. This is not to deny that it was the source of some genuine virtues: humility, constancy, patience and fortitude. The lady was extolled as the sole repository of morality: she was responsible for whatever merit the lover acquired, and she alone was capable of assessing his worth.

Dronke assumes that the essential features of *amour courtois* are universal and therefore non-transferable, and that a researcher should consequently restrict his study to formal and thematic elements and intellectual ideas. Yet it is improbable that a clear-cut distinction can be made between those responses which are innate or universal and those which are culturally conditioned (Whinnom, *Obras de San Pedro*, II, pp. 8–9). The religious and philosophical background to the development of the courtly lyric can illuminate only one aspect of Courtly Love. It is by studying military, sporting, feudal and medical terms that a critic will be able to understand the social reality and the psycho-physiological theories underlying the poetry.

4 STYLISTIC CONVENTION

Courtly Love was a European literary and rhetorical tradition from which the medieval writer could draw certain themes and stylistic devices.

(a) *Formal rearrangement of inherited elements.* The poet's scope for inventiveness was limited to the rearrangement of established topics, themes, motifs and key words. Dragonetti (1960); Guiette (1960); Zumthor (1963); Bec (1969).

(b) *Integrity of individual works.* Courtly Love was neither a social institution nor a uniform doctrine but a literary constituent in certain works. The tone and the organic structure of the individual work should be respected. Lazar (1964); Dronke (1965); Whinnom (1968–69); Silverstein (1968).

(c) *Freedom from prejudice.* Texts should not be cited in order to demonstrate a general hypothesis about Courtly Love. In order to appreciate the medieval courtly lyric, critical and theoretical preconceptions must be discarded. Whinnom (1968-69); Silverstein (1968).

(d) *Statistical analysis.* The aesthetic criteria by which a medieval audience judged a poem's worth can be established by means of quantitative analysis: the frequency of words and poetic forms is indicative of contemporary taste. Whinnom (1968–69).

(e) *Ambiguity and sexual euphemism.* Intentional ambiguity, which enabled a poem to be read at a number of different levels without running the risk of impropriety, was a device whereby the medieval love poet could overcome the semantic limitations of a restricted and predominantly abstract vocabulary. Many apparently innocuous words convey sexual innuendoes to the initiated.[26] Lazar (1964); Whinnom (1968–69).

Critics within this category share the conviction that the autonomy and integrity of literary objects should not be sacrificed for the sake of an extra-literary system. Special emphasis is given to problems of linguistics and morphology and to the need for reassessment on the basis of close textual analysis. The virtue of this approach is that it avoids generalising hypotheses and *a priori* reasoning. The reader must be prepared to re-educate his sensibility if he wishes to understand the literature and the aesthetic ideals of a period which may, at first, seem remote. It has been noted, for example, that the poems selected by the modern anthologist for their immediate appeal are not necessarily those which were most highly regarded during the Middle Ages (Whinnom, 1968–69).

The danger of a purely formalistic literary approach is that it ignores the relationship between literature and life. Literature is not a semi-autonomous universe. The courtly lyric cannot, therefore, be isolated from its social context. Computer data, correctly programmed and analysed, may yield useful results, but these results will tend to confirm an impression which might occur to any attentive reader. Polysemia cannot be studied mathematically; the critic must decide which connotations of a word are appropriate in a given context. For example, the word *muerte* in Spanish poetry may, as Whinnom points out, refer to the 'living death' of absence, the death of moral perdition, the selflessness of 'dying to others', the sexual act, or death itself.[27] The meaning of *muerte* in a particular poem must be assessed within the resonance of the text. A poem may be understood at several levels simultaneously. This discovery will alter a number of prejudices about this type of poetry, namely that it is insipid, monotonous and platonic. The possibility of discerning sexual undertones does not mean that a spiritual meaning is not also intended; it is important to remember that the lyric of Courtly Love is founded on a tension between spiritual aspiration and sexual desire. The term 'Courtly Love' should not refer merely to a literary constituent of medieval works, nor should it be limited to the stock of common themes and stylistic devices from which a poet could draw.

5   CRITICAL FALLACY

Courtly Love is an illusion of modern criticism and a serious impediment to the understanding of medieval texts.

(a) *An imprecise and controversial term.*   Courtly Love has been stretched to cover such a wide range of moods and genres that it has lost whatever utility it once had as a critical concept. The validity of the term has been undermined by the absence of any consensus of opinion on its meaning (i.e. whether it is a critical term or a medieval institution; whether it is adulterous or chaste), on its origins (i.e. which factors contributed to its formation), and on the subsequent effects which it had on European literature and social customs. Robertson (1962).

(b) *Absence of historical evidence.*   Historical sources, which should provide reliable data on medieval attitudes to love, sex and marriage, do not bear witness to the existence of Courtly Love. They reveal that adultery was not tolerated, that the social status of women during the Middle Ages was one of complete inferiority, and that, according to physiologists, the sexual needs of women are as great as, if not greater than, those of men. Benton (1968).

(c) *Victorian connotations.*   Courtly Love distorts criticism because it evokes 'a sentimental passion only faintly and enticingly tinged with sex' which properly belongs to the realm of Victorian fiction. Applied to Chaucer, the term destroys all humour and conceals the author's moralistic intentions. Donaldson (1965); Robertson (1968).

(d) *Idolatry.*   There is no shortage of literary evidence that women were the objects of an exaggerated devotion, verging on idolatry, a 'chronic human weakness' by no means peculiar to the Middle Ages. Chaucer's *Troilus and Criseyde*, Chrétien de Troyes' *Lancelot* and Andreas Capellanus' *De amore* all satirise, with varying degrees of humour and irony, the folly of idolatrous passion. Robertson (1968).

(e) *Charity and concupiscence.*   During the Middle Ages a rigid distinction was drawn between two species of love: charity and concupiscence. The former is a chaste friendship, compatible with social and religious laws; the latter is a carnal desire, which is a source of sin and error. A medieval audience would never make the mistake of confusing the two; if they enjoyed ambiguity it was not because they believed that the nature of love was inherently ambiguous. Robertson (1962); Benton (1968).

Jean Frappier has clearly demonstrated in his review article on *The Meaning of Courtly Love* (1972) that Courtly Love is not an imaginary construct which critics have superimposed on medieval literature. Those who have upheld this view have failed to define what they understand by the term they wish to abolish, and they have ignored the poetry of the early Provençal troubadours. Robertson's findings were based on Andreas Capellanus' *De amore*, which, if it does not deliberately set out to undermine *fin'amors*, is at any rate 'une doctrine pour exportation',[28] and on *The Book of the Duchess* and *Troilus and Criseyde*, works by Chaucer which display a moralistic concern for the destructive effects of passionate love: subjection to love and fortune leads to a loss of courage, moral integrity and chivalric virtue. If these works can be shown to parody Courtly Love, this scarcely proves that the latter never existed. 'Comment, d'ailleurs, parodier ce qui n'aurait jamais existé?' asks Frappier (Frappier, 1972, p. 149). Robertson starts from the premise 'that any serious work written in the Middle Ages that does not overtly promote St Augustine's doctrine of charity will be found, on close examination, to be doing so allegorically or ironically' (Donaldson, 1970, p. 159). Like the Christian theologian, he does not believe that sexual passion, however refined, can ever become a 'noble emotion' (Lewis, 1936, p. 8), nor could he conceive of any compromise between charity and concupiscence, despite the fact that the word *amor* served (and still serves) to designate both types of love. However, the medieval love poet was rarely a theologian, and his poetry shows that sentiment and sentimentality were not unknown to the Middle Ages. *Fin'amors* was, as Frappier says, 'un composé indissoluble, un tout global, où fusionnent la chair, le coeur, et l'esprit' (Frappier, 1972, p. 166). Karl D. Uitti remarked, in a review article on *The Meaning of Courtly Love*, that he could 'easily conceive of an individual, even an entire social class, capable of telling "the difference between love which [is] concupiscent and that which [is] not" and nevertheless experiencing, and dreaming ambiguously about, love' (Uitti, 1972–73, p. 84). Almost every courtly lyric is based on a dilemma: 'Dos terribles pensamientos / tiene turbada mi fe / ¿quál dellos yo tomaré? / . . . El uno tiene esperança / donde el otro se condena, / el uno quiere holgança / donde el otro quiere pena.'[29] Benton might at least have chosen a courtly work, not the *Chanson de Roland*, to illustrate the medieval tendency to think in rigid categories (Frappier, 1972, p. 152). It is doubtful whether he could have found a quotation to suit his argument. The principle of *discordia concors* was familiar to the poet, the mystic, the astrologer, the alchemist and the physician.[30]

Poetry does not belong to the world of scientific facts, dogmas or events that can be recorded. There is therefore no justification for inferring, as Benton does, that Courtly Love is a fallacy because it is not discussed in theological works, chronicles and non-fictional sources. To dismiss the testimony of poetry as less reliable than the above sources is to dismiss the most important evidence that we possess: Benton 'n'a pas compris que dans son essence l'amour courtois relevait d'une poésie de rêve et d'évasion' (Frappier, 1972, p. 153). He might, in any case, have discovered some useful evidence in sources other than the lyric and the prose romance had he looked in the right places. For example, the Spanish philosopher El Tostado discusses the 'vulgar' theory of love's ennobling and paradoxical effects, and even mentions the spiritual bright-eyed Cupid of Francesco da Barberino's *Documenti d'amore* (written before 1318), a work inspired by the troubadours of Provence.[31] The *Crónica de don Pero Niño* by Gutierre Díez de Games (c. 1378–c. 1450) describes how lovers are praised in royal households and how the ladies whom they love are honoured.[32] The former perform deeds of prowess in battle or in play and compose songs of love; the latter know that they are loved and that those who love them are ennobled by love: 'saben que por su amor son ellos mejores, & se traen más guarnidos, e hazen por su amor grandes proezas e cavallerías, ansí en armas como en juegos' (p. 90). The need for secrecy is mentioned: 'E otros ençelan e loan por figura, non osando declarar más, muestran que en alto lugar aman y son amados' (p. 91). The chronicler then adds that every woman wants the best lover and the best husband, and that if women were permitted to choose for themselves they would select a different husband from the one they have. He emphasises that Pero Niño's marriage was a love match. His distinction between three grades of love, *amor*, *dileción* and *querencia* or *caritas*, illustrates the ambiguity of Courtly Love. *Caritas* is not, in this context, Christian charity, because it is exemplified by the love which drove Dido to suicide for the sake of Aeneas. These two sources, a philosophical work and a chronicle, should suffice to prove that Courtly Love was not invented by Gaston Paris. The most convincing theories of meaning would thus appear to be those which interpret this phenomenon as a play activity and a literary tradition.

NOTES

[1] 'The relation of the poet to day-dreaming', *Collected Papers* (London, 1925), IV pp. 173–83.

[2] Freud, *Beyond the Pleasure Principle*, trans. J. Strachey (London, 1950), pp. 3–4.

[3] *The Act of Creation* (London: Pan Books, 1964), p. 500.

[4] 'People voluntarily subject themselves to suspense, fatigue, uncertainty, perplexity, fear and surprise in such practices as angling, rowing, travelling, crossword puzzles, rock-climbing and joking' (*The Concept of Mind* [Harmondsworth: Penguin, 1970], p. 95); 'an agitation requires that there exist two inclinations or an inclination and a factual impediment. Grief, of one sort, is affection blocked by death; suspense, of one sort, is hope interfered with by fear' (*ibid.*, p. 91).

[5] Sainte Palaye, *Memoirs of Ancient Chivalry*, 1784, pp. 3–6; Antoine de la Sale, *Jehan de Saintré*, ed. Jean Misrahi and Charles A. Knudson (Textes Littéraires Français, 117, Geneva, 1965); Gutierre Díez de Games, *El Victorial. Crónica de don Pero Niño*, ed. Juan de Mata Carriazo (Colección de Crónicas Españolas, 1, Madrid, 1940).

[6] The latter alternative is impossible to verify, even in those rare cases where a poet likens his lady to a mother. The Spanish poet Fernando de la Torre complained in 1449 that he had wasted ten years of his youth serving a pious lady, a *dama de religión*, whom he addresses as a cruel mother:

> O cruel madre sin par,
> sin jamás haver errado
> faze ser desanparado
> a su fijo singular
> sin gloria nunca dar

(*Cancionero y obras en prosa*, ed. A. Paz y Melia, Gesellschaft für Romanische Literatur, 16 [Dresden, 1907], p. 148). Dante sometimes conceived of Beatrice as a mother figure. In the *Vita nuova*, when Beatrice greets him for the first time, he retires to his room and weeps alone like a child after a beating: 'e quivi, chiamando misericordia a la donna de la cortesia, e dicendo "Amore, aiuta lo tuo fidele", m'addormentai come un pargoletto battuto lagrimando' (XII, 2–3). When he encounters her in Purgatory he looks upon her with the awe which a little boy would conceive for his mother: 'Così la madre al figlio par superba, / com' ella parve a me; perché d'amaro / sente il sapor de la pietade acerba' (*Purgatorio*, XXX, ll. 79–81, ed. C. H. Grandgent [Cambridge, Mass., 1972]).

7   See J. G. Peristiany, ed., *Honour and Shame. The values of Mediterranean society* (London: Weidenfeld & Nicolson, 1965).

8   'Io dico che molte di queste donne, accorgendosi de la mia trasfigurazione, si cominciaro a maravigliare, e ragionando si gabbavano di me con questa gentilissima' (XIV, 7).

9   Edward B. Tylor, *Primitive Culture* (2 vols, London: John Murray, 1871), I, pp. 72 ff.

10   See above, p. 53 n.4.

11   'e otrosý que sea amador, e que siempre se preçie e se finja de ser enamorado; porque es opynión de muchos sabyos, que todo omme que sea enamorado, conviene a saber, que ame a quien deve e como deve e donde deve, afirman e disen qu'el tal de todas buenas dotrinas es doctado' (*Cancionero de Juan Alfonso de Baena*, ed. José María Azáceta, CH [3 vols, Madrid, 1966], I, p. 15).

12   Alfred Jeanroy, 'La tenson provençale', *AMid*, II (1890), 281–304; 441–62. Cummins, 1963 and 1965. A rhyming dictionary, entitled *Gaya de Segovia*, was composed c. 1474–79 and dedicated to Alonso Carrillo, Archbishop of Toledo.

13   *Letter of the Marquis of Santillana to Don Peter, Constable of Portugal*, ed. A. R. Pastor and E. Prestage (Oxford, 1927), p. 70.

14   'The garden of love is used throughout Provençal love poetry as the secluded, ordered, beautiful setting for the seizure by, or the loss of, love. In its simplicity of motif and consecration to a kind of adoration, it reminds one of the earthly paradise— though one is always baffled by the question of specific literary sources for this poetry' (A. Bartlett Giamatti, *The Earthly Paradise and the Renaissance Epic* [Princeton: University Press, 1966], p. 60). See also H. R. Patch, *The Otherworld according to Descriptions in Medieval Literature* (SCSML, 1, Cambridge, Mass., 1950). Huizinga does not mention the *hortus conclusus*, but he does speak of the circle of play as an enclosed place where justice is pronounced (*Homo Ludens*, p. 98). The Spanish *Razón de amor* contains a good example of the courtly *locus amoenus*.

15   See Barron, 1965.

16   According to Aristotle, 'an ideal constitution . . . cannot have its citizens living the life of mechanics or shopkeepers, which is ignoble and inimical to goodness. Nor can it have them engaged in farming: leisure is a necessity, both for growth in goodness and for the pursuit of political activities' (*The Politics of Aristotle*, trans. Ernest Barker [Oxford: Clarendon, 1948], VII, ix, p. 301).

17   These changes created new forms of 'conspicuous leisure', partly as proof of abstention from labour, including games, sports, manners, proprieties of dress and furniture, the recitation of poetry, and various branches of higher or non-applied learning. See T. B. Veblen, *The Theory of the Leisure Class* (Boston, Mass., 1973), p. 43 *et passim*; and José Antonio Maravall, *El mundo social de 'La Celestina'* (Madrid: Gredos, 1972), pp. 32–58.

18   Jean-Paul Sartre defines existence as playing at being: 'Dès qu'un homme se saisit comme libre et veut user de sa liberté, quelle que puisse être d'ailleurs son angoisse, son activité est de jeu' (*L'Etre et le néant* [Paris: Gallimard, 1943], p. 669); he who questions this assertion lays himself open to the charge of 'mauvaise foi'. 'Le fait de jouer résulte de l'inquiétude profonde d'un être incapable, par nature, de coïncider avec lui-même et de se satisfaire de ce qu'il est' (Henriot, p. 98). The existentialist view of play is very close to Pascal's discussion of the need for *divertissement*. For Pascal the play instinct is a flight from the knowledge of the inner void, which

contradicts another instinct, deriving from the memory of man's prelapsarian happiness: 'Ainsi l'homme est si malheureux, qu'il s'ennuierait même sans aucune cause d'ennui, par l'état propre de sa complexion; et il est si vain, qu'étant plein de mille causes essentielles d'ennui, la moindre chose, comme un billard et une balle qu'il pousse, suffit pour le divertir' (*Pensées sur la religion et sur quelques autres sujets*, ed. Louis Lafuma [2 vols, Paris: Delmas, 1947], I, pp. 166–7). The deprecation of play as escapism is in total contrast to the attitude to play in ancient Greece or in medieval Europe.

19 James F. Burke, 'El juego de amor en el *Libro de buen amor*', paper read at the fifth Congreso de la Asociación Internacional de Hispanistas (Bordeaux, September 1974).

20 Judah Abravanel, called León Hebreo, *The Philosophy of Love*, trans. Friedeberg-Seeley and Barnes (London: Soncino Press, 1937), p. 19. This treatise (written *c.* 1502) displays an unusual compound of courtly and Neoplatonic elements. Even Ficino is familiar with the troubadour's experience of contradiction: 'Poor wretch, you seek yourself outside yourself, you cling to your captor so that you may recover your captured self. You do not wish to love madly because you do not wish to die; but you are unwilling not to love, because you think that you must pay lip service to this image of heaven' (*Commentary on Plato's Symposium*, ed. S. R. Jayne, UMS, 19 [1944], p. 202).

21 Gervase Mathew, Review of Dronke's vol. I, *MAe*, XXXVI (1967), 49–52, at p. 50.

22 Oswald Spengler speaks of 'a genuine troubadour and *Minne* poetry' at the courts of the Ghassanids and Lakhamids in northern Arabia in pre-Islamic times (*The Decline of the West*, trans. C. F. Atkinson [London: Allen & Unwin, 1922], II, p. 198).

23 It still remains to be proved that all the traits of the European troubadour lyric can be found elsewhere.

24 Review of Dronke's vol. II, *MAe*, XXXVI (1967), 171–6, at p. 174.

25 *Ibid.*

26 A. J. Foreman, 'The *cancionero* poet, Quirós' (unpublished MA dissertation, Westfield College, University of London, 1969), and Pierre Guiraud, *Le Jargon de Villon; ou le gai savoir de la coquille* (Paris, 1968).

27 Whinnom (1968–69), 373–4.

28 Marrou (1947), 87. 'Avant de se démasquer à la fin de son traité en écrivant un *De reprobatione amoris*, le Chapelain a longuement poursuivi un travail de sape, en usant à la fois d'une dialectique industrieuse et de la ruse du mimétisme (on le prendrait en maint endroit pour le doctrinaire et le penseur de la *fine amor*)' (Frappier, 1972, 177). See also Demats, 1970.

29 Juan del Encina, in Hugo Albert Rennert, 'Der spanische Cancionero des Brit. Museums (Ms. add. 10431)', *RF*, X (1895–99), 1–176, at pp. 138–9, rubric 'Villancico del actor deste libro'.

30 See Appendix II, pp. 134–9.

31 Alfonso de Madrigal (El Tostado), *Comentario sobre Eusebio* (Salamanca, 1506–7), III, ch. 3, fol. 35v. Erwin Panofsky discusses Barberino in his study of 'Blind Cupid' in *Studies in Iconology. Humanistic themes in the Renaissance* (New York: Harper & Row, 1967), pp. 95–128.

32 *El Victorial* (Madrid, 1940); see n. 5, above.

Conclusion

This work has attempted to describe and to assess the major trends in Courtly Love scholarship from the sixteenth century to the present day. In Chapter I these trends were surveyed chronologically. In Chapters II and III a distinction was made between theories of origin and theories of meaning, and the features of each theory were listed and analysed.

Chapter I showed that Italian scholars of the Renaissance were unexpectedly the first to take an academic interest in the troubadour movement. This interest was to a large extent a by-product of a debate, initiated by Dante nearly two centuries earlier, over the kinship of the Romance languages. Yet it appeared that Italian vernacular humanism owed a debt to Castile and Aragon for having preserved the theory and practice of the Provençal 'leys d'amors' as a living tradition. Cardinal Bembo formulated the theory, later disproved by Friedrich von Schlegel, Friedrich Diez and other nineteenth-century philologists, that Provençal was the archetypal Romance. The study of Provençal poetry was justified not only on linguistic grounds but also as a means of ascertaining the literary ancestry of those Italian writers (principally the triumvirate of Dante, Petrarch and Boccaccio) whom vernacular humanists had raised to the status of *auctores*. Medieval poetry was rarely discussed in Renaissance treatises on love. Mario Equicola's *Libro de natura de amore* was unusual in that it compared attitudes to love and modes of expression in the lyric of different countries. The contrast was here noted between the refined character of troubadour love and the disrespectful tone adopted by Latin poets. It is only during the last few decades that the novelty, the morality and even the existence of Courtly Love have been seriously called into question.

Of the theories of Courtly Love first expounded in sixteenth-century Italy, the most important for the future of scholarship was the Hispano-Arabic thesis. Giammaria Barbieri argued, on the basis of rhyme, that the Provençal poetic tradition originated in Muslim Spain, and that the cultural transmission could be dated from about 1130, when Ramon Berenguer IV, the ruler of Catalonia, inherited the County of Provence. Although Barbieri's treatise on the origin of rhymed verse was not published until 1790, his ideas were disseminated orally and had gained some currency prior to that date.

The seventeenth and eighteenth centuries were increasingly pre-occupied by the institution of chivalry and by the social implications of the troubadour lyric, but scholarship continued to be warped by Jean de Nostredame's highly romanticised biography of the troubadours, published in 1575. Pierre de Caseneuve believed that the Floral Games, which were still celebrated annually at Toulouse, were an offshoot of the courts of love about which Nostredame had spoken. Millot, the compiler and editor of the papers of La Curne de Sainte Palaye, was one of the first to cast serious doubts on Nostredame's reputation as a historian. Stendhal and many of his contemporaries persisted in regarding the courts of love as genuine legislative bodies. In the late nineteenth century it was generally acknowledged that these courts were merely an allegorical device and a parlour game. Nostredame's unreliability was fully exposed, and possibly even exaggerated, by Joseph Anglade in 1913.

Arabic studies were virtually non-existent during the seventeenth century. However, Pierre-Daniel Huet anticipated the eighteenth-century vogue for the Orient with an immensely popular essay, first published in 1671, which sought to prove that 'romance' was a literary genre introduced into Europe from Persia, Egypt, Syria and other Eastern countries. Reaction against Neoclassicism, the polemic over the relative merits of Spanish and Italian culture, and the rise of literary historiography were all factors which, in the late eighteenth century, contributed to the re-emergence of the Hispano-Arabic theory of troubadour origins. Miguel Casiri and his disciples at the Escorial library provided scholars with the documentary evidence which they required. Since it was widely believed, before the nineteenth century, that the concept of love expressed in European romances and in troubadour poetry was dictated by the 'spirit of chivalry' and by Germanic or Celtic veneration for women, claims for Arabic influence were confined to the question of literary genres, rhyme, music and other formal and stylistic elements, supported by the European debt in other spheres, such as medicine, astrology, philosophy and mathematics. Xavier Lampillas and Juan Andrés, both Spanish Jesuit expatriates living in Italy, agreed that Provençal poetry was modelled on that of Muslim Spain, and that Italy was consequently Spain's beneficiary as well as her cultural benefactor.

In the early years of the nineteenth century the troubadours were proclaimed the forerunners of Romanticism, because, according to Mme de Staël, they had been inspired by Christian and chivalrous ideals which were indigenous to Europe. Mme de Staël did not subscribe to the Hispano-Arabic thesis, nor did the philologist Friedrich von Schlegel. Orientalism was nonetheless an essential constituent of the Romantic movement. The ideas of Andrés and Lampillas were enthusiastically received by Simonde de Sismondi, a member of Mme de Staël's circle of friends and admirers, in his *Histoire de la littérature du Midi de l'Europe* (1813). Chivalry, both as an institution and as an ideal, was, in his opinion, a legacy from the Arabs, a theory which still finds a champion in Robert Graves.

By the middle of the nineteenth century it had become a conventional maxim of criticism that the Gay Science and the Provençal ideal of *fin'amors* derived from Muslim Spain. However, during the latter half of the century, when scholars endeavoured to rectify the excessively anti-classical attitudes of their predecessors, the theory suffered an eclipse. The negative judgements pronounced by Ernest Renan and by Reinhart Dozy must have also discouraged further investigation into the problem. Gabriele Rossetti had meanwhile proposed the theory that the troubadours were members of a 'protestant' and Cathar conspiracy against the Papacy and the *status quo*, and that their poetry was a vehicle for the propagation of heresy. These ideas were repeated and amplified by Eugène Aroux, Antony Méray and Josephin Péladan, and they formed the groundwork of Denis de Rougemont's celebrated work *L'Amour et l'Occident* (1939).

Research into the Latin Middle Ages prospered in the late nineteenth century, and some scholars, following Paul Meyer, were anxious to reconcile the rise of a cultured vernacular lyric in the twelfth century with the continuity of the classical tradition and the Carolingian renaissance. The importance of Ovid's *Ars amatoria* was widely acclaimed, but few scholars were convinced that Ovid was more than a formative influence. Medievalists therefore began to turn their attention to the feudal environment, folk-lore and Christian mysticism. Violet Paget argued that 'mediaeval love', a term comprising a wide range of literary genres from the popular *alba* or dawn song to the chivalric prose romance, is explicable in terms of the social conditions prevailing within the confines of the medieval castle, where there was a considerable preponderance of unmarried landless males. Gaston Paris, the inventor or populariser of the phrase *amour courtois*, suspected that the medieval courtly lyric had developed from the same primeval lyrical substratum as the dance songs of the May Day festival. Eduard Wechssler and Henry Adams were amongst those who, at the turn of the century, viewed Courtly Love as a secular counterpart to Marianism and as an ideology reflecting the influence of Bernardine mysticism. These scholars all tended to adhere to a vision of the Middle Ages which they had inherited from Romanticism. Courtly Love was thus regarded as a compound of chivalry, chastity and adultery.

C. S. Lewis long remained the established authority on Courtly Love. He more than anyone emphasised the revolutionary character of the troubadour movement and the permanent effects which it had on the literary taste, social customs and ethical standards of Western society. He agreed with Wechssler, Anglade and Chaytor that the troubadour's love service was based on feudal vassalage, and he suggested that 'Ovid misunderstood' is a useful formula for understanding medieval poetry. However, his discussion of Courtly Love in *The Allegory of Love* (1936) does not reflect the position of research at the time when he was writing, since it omits any reference to three important figures: Ribera y Tarragó, Johan Huizinga and Robert Briffault. Had he been familiar with the theories of these scholars he would have been less content with the validity of the term *amour courtois* as defined by Gaston Paris and Alfred Jeanroy.

In 1912 Ribera read a paper to the Spanish Academy on Ibn Quzmān's *Dīwān* in which he argued that Arabic-Andalusian poetry, itself influenced by the rhyme schemes and stress measures of contemporary Romance poetry, served as a model for that of Provence. This paper provoked a heated polemic over the origins of the Provençal lyric. Formal and thematic resemblances between the court poetry of Al-Andalus and that of Provence were noted by Nykl, Ecker, Pérès and Lévi-Provençal. Neoplatonism was studied as a background to the courtly mentality and the ideal of *fin'amors* by Father Denomy in a series of articles, the first of which was published in 1944. He concluded that the secular aesthetic doctrine propounded by Avicenna in his *Treatise on Love* was a 'possible source' for the troubadours. Stern's discovery of Mozarabic *kharjas* in 1948 confirmed Ribera's intuition of a Romance lyric prior to the *zajal*, and made it necessary to reject the conventional theory according to which the European lyric originated in Provence.

Huizinga's *The Waning of the Middle Ages* (1924) inaugurated a novel approach to cultural history which stressed the civilising influence of ideals. Observing the elements of risk, secrecy, emulation and make-believe in the aristocratic culture of the late Middle Ages, he arrived at the conclusion, in *Homo Ludens*, that courtly and chivalric themes were an expression of the play instinct in man. He nevertheless accepted the traditional view that Courtly Love was an emotional discovery of twelfth-century Europe, and that it gave rise to an ethical system which enabled the aristocracy to feel less dependent on religious admonition. Critics have only recently begun to apply Huizinga's ideas on play to the study of medieval poetry. These include John Stevens, Charles S. Singleton, Donald R. Howard, and James F. Burke.

In Robert Briffault's *The Mothers* (1927) the novelty and the morality of Courtly Love were dismissed as a fallacy. Courtly ideals were, according to Briffault, a means of eluding Christian precepts, ensuring the survival of the sexual *mores* of a pagan matriarchal society. They were, in short, a cover for sexual promiscuity. Étienne Gilson, Moshé Lazar, Keith Whinnom and others have followed Briffault (whether consciously or unconsciously) in discerning sexual innuendoes in medieval court lyrics, but the latter's matriarchal theory did not meet with the approval of many critics.

Within the last few decades the methods of sociology and psychology have been applied to Courtly Love. Literature has, of course, been studied in relation to social institutions since the end of the eighteenth century, but it is only comparatively recently that critics have begun to explore possible correlations between literary movements and changes in the sex and class composition of populations. This approach is illustrated by Herbert Moller's article 'The social causation of Courtly Love' (1958–59), which concluded that the troubadour lyric was disseminated in those parts of Europe where males far outnumbered females in the upper strata of society, and where women had, as a consequence, been idealised. Other sociological theorists, such as Valency and Köhler, shared Moller's opinion that the troubadour movement was a response to a sudden influx of commoners and *ministeriales* into the ranks of the nobility. Most poets, it was argued, were impecunious knights or young men aspiring to knighthood, excluded from the territorial hierarchy by their youth or by the principle of primogeniture. Some of these ideas had already been stated less systematically by Paget.

Moller distinguished between the social origin of the Courtly Love complex and its psychological function or meaning. His theory that Courtly Love should be interpreted as a collective fantasy caused by an infantile mother fixation has been accepted, in one form or another, by all those who have analysed medieval love poetry or Andrew the Chaplain's *De amore* in terms of Freudian psychology. Undeterred by the absence of a threatening father figure, Richard Koenigsberg referred to this 'fixation' as an expression of the Oedipal complex. Moller himself spoke of a reversion to the rivalry of siblings for a mother's favour. Donald Howard sought to integrate the sociological and psychological approaches by means of Huizinga's 'game theory': the troubadour played at what he could not do.

In recent years Courtly Love scholarship has suffered from the current intellectual malaise: fragmentation due to specialisation. Literary critics have, on the whole, preferred to ignore sociological and psychological speculations, but conventional assumptions about Courtly Love have come under attack from several quarters. There is, first of all, the formalistic literary approach, which concentrates on the structure of language. Extremists of this school of thought, betraying the mental habits of linguistic philosophy, assume that extra-literary matters are irrelevant to the genesis and the interpretation of literary texts. This point of view is represented by Paul Zumthor, author of *Langue et techniques poétiques à l'époque romane* (1963). Secondly there is the negative approach of D. W. Robertson and his disciples. Robertson has repeatedly maintained that in the Middle Ages love was either charitable or concupiscent, in accordance with Christian theology; consequently if a poet appears to extol sexual passion his intentions will prove, on closer inspection, to be ironical and moralistic. In his *Preface to Chaucer* (1962) he accused his fellow medievalists of projecting tension, ambivalence, drama and sentimentality into an age when such concepts would have been utterly incomprehensible, and in 1967 he delivered a paper in which he advocated that Courtly Love be discarded as a fiction of nineteenth-century scholarship. This paper set the general tone of the conference. Indeed, John Benton argued, in the second paper, that historical sources confirmed Robertson's thesis. Thirdly there is the comparative 'universalist' approach of Peter Dronke, as stated in the first volume of *Medieval Latin and the Rise of European Love Lyric* (1965–66). According to this view, *amour courtois* is not confined to a courtly environment but might occur at any time or place. The strength of this negative onslaught is that it comes from critics who insist that one should refrain from imposing grandiose hypotheses or inappropriate value judgements on medieval literature. But they have also provoked a mood of scepticism concerning the use of the term Courtly Love which it has been the intention of this book to dispel.

Chapter I was to a large extent a record of the permutations of literary taste. Theories on Courtly Love have inevitably been influenced by nationalist sentiments, religious convictions, contemporary literary movements and the availability of literary evidence. This chapter indicated the need for an exposition and analysis of all the theoretical positions, which would leave the reader with some scope for forming his own judgements.

Chapters II and III, assessing the wide spectrum of opinion on Courtly Love, arrived at the following general conclusions: no single hypothesis of origin or meaning can claim to be exhaustive, because each relies on the methods and assumptions of one intellectual discipline to the exclusion of other points of view; certain theories are controvertible, and, of the remainder, some are demonstrably more convincing than others; theories of origin are based on preconceptions about the meaning of Courtly Love, yet the meaning of the term has never been satisfactorily defined.

Two theories of origin were judged to be of primary importance: the Hispano-Arabic and the Feudal–Sociological. According to the former, Courtly Love was imported into southern France from Muslim Spain, or was strongly influenced by the culture, poetry and philosophy of the Arabs. According to the latter, Courtly Love can be explained by certain sociological factors operating within the feudal environment. Once it is conceded that the diffusion of cultural traits is a selective process, it will be seen that these two theories explore different aspects of the same problem. 'It is not the products that influence, but creators that absorb.'[1] Poets, artists and men of letters are predisposed by social, religious and intellectual circumstances to adopt certain foreign elements in their work and to reject others. Those elements which a poet assimilates from an alien literary tradition will be modified in accordance with his needs and the expectations of his audience; these in turn will be shaped by sociological factors, such as the feudal contract, the practice of arranged marriages, or the nature of court patronage. As Norman Daniel says, with reference to Courtly Love, 'the existing traditions of Europe were favourable to the new ideas; in particular, a dominating Lady is "feudally" intelligible, and the discursive, scholastic treatment of the theme, as by Andreas Capellanus, although it has Arab parallels in the love debates, is paralleled equally by contemporary philosophical methodology' (Daniel, 1975, p. 105). The poets of southern France would not have imitated and emulated their Arab and Mozarab contemporaries if they had not been encouraged to do so by conditions which favoured social intercourse and an attitude of receptivity. It is understandable that in the eleventh and twelfth centuries southern France should have been more receptive to the refinements of Arabic culture than Castile, which had to remain in a constant state of military alert, and which was more backward commercially and technologically. It is significant in this respect that in the eyes of a Castilian epic hero the troops of Ramon Berenguer were over-effete in their dress and their riding equipment.[2]

Many literary parallels have been established between the court poetry written in Muslim Spain (or even in the Middle East) and that which was written in Provence and elsewhere in Europe. These include the appearance of the same *dramatis personae*, such as the guardian or watchman (*gardador = raqīb*), the messenger (*mesager = rasūl*), the slanderer or spy (*lauzenger = wāshī*), and the jealous person (*enojos = hāsid*); the use of the *senhal* or pseudonym (*kunya*) to conceal the identity of the person addressed; the masculine form of address, *midons* (*sayyidī*), instead of *madomna*. Many characteristics of love, as expressed by the troubadours, are found in the lyrical tradition which originated among the *Udhrī* poets of seventh-century Arabia: the elevation of a lady into an object of veneration, humble submission to her capricious tyranny, the emphasis on the need for secrecy, the idea of love as a source of moral and social refinement, and belief in love's potentially destructive power. These aspects of love are classified and illustrated in two treatises, both by members of the orthodox Zāhirite sect: the *Book of the Flower* by Ibn Dāwūd (d. 910) and *The Ring of the Dove* by Ibn Ḥazm (d. 1064). The *Treatise on Love* by Avicenna (d. 1037) expresses an aesthetic amatory doctrine analogous to that of the troubadours and prefiguring the Neoplatonism of Castiglione's *Il cortegiano*. Works on courtly or profane love constituted a distinct Arabic literary genre.

The psychological and aesthetic principles, in particular the tendency to paradoxical expression, inherent in troubadour poetry are incomprehensible without reference to the Graeco-Arabic medical tradition. Avicenna's *The Canon of Medicine*, a standard textbook in European medical schools, contains a section on love-melancholy or *'ishq*. According to medical theory and popular opinion, 'dying of love' was more than a mere metaphor: if a man was in love with a woman who refused to bestow her *bel accueil* or some sign of recognition, then his condition was liable to deteriorate into *amor hereos* or *'ishq*, a species of melancholia and a disease of the imagination, leading ultimately to death. European and Arabic court poets were justified in their use of figures of contradiction, such as oxymora, hyperboles and dilemmas, by preconceptions about the nature of love itself. These same medical theories underlie the 'paradoxical asceticism' of Ṣūfī poetry, and were known to Ibn Arabī, who likened the stages of meditation to the phases of love-melancholy. The aesthetic principle of *concordia discors*, derived from the cosmology of Empedocles and Heraclitus, also played some part in the development of a paradoxical courtly style, justified by a theory of universal strife.

Evidence that Arabic modes of thought and expression were accessible to European poets either directly, through personal or bilateral contact, or indirectly, through the mediation of Jews and Mozarabs, makes it impossible to attribute these parallels to mere coincidence. In the late eleventh and early twelfth centuries political and economic changes opened up many new channels of communication between Christian Europe and the Islamic empire. The most important of these changes were the capture of Toledo in 1085, the First Crusade in 1096–99, the unification of Provence, Languedoc, Catalonia and Aragon under the Berenguers, the intermingling of Europeans and Arabs in the Norman kingdom of Sicily, the growth of trade links with Muslim Spain and the Orient, and the participation of French soldiers in the Spanish wars of the Reconquest. Furthermore many of the early Provençal troubadours are known to have visited the courts of Castile and Aragon, where they would have encountered Moorish and Jewish musicians and poets. Groups of Moorish musicians were employed to provide entertainment at weddings and other festivities, and they were free to travel from court to court. The European debt to Arabian music is still a controversial matter, but the origin of the words *lute*, *rebec*, *guitar* and *naker*, from the Arabic *'ūd*, *rabāb*, *qīthāra* and *naqqāra*, is well established, and indicates that this influence must have been considerable.

The differences between the Arabic and the European court lyric are no less important than the resemblances. Love service, in the latter, was constituted upon the analogy of the feudal contract. This notion of reciprocity was not one that was current in Arabic love poetry, which tended to be more extravagant in its cult of chastity. Yet feudal concepts must, as Daniel suggests, have facilitated the transference of that attitude of humble submission which characterised the Arab lover. Many of the conventional dichotomies of troubadour poetry, in particular the love–death equation, would appear to have been borrowed from Ṣūfī literature, but they were usually drained of their initial mystical significance. Western ideals of love and courtesy were formed by a petty nobility at a time of rapid social change, and presupposed a degree of freedom between the sexes which would have been unusual in Muslim Spain, even allowing for the fact that, in Spain, Muslim women were rarely confined to the harem or to the veil. In Christian Europe the lady to whom a poet addressed his verses was almost invariably of noble birth, whereas the Arab poet frequently loved a slave girl. Social mobility, which resulted in a shortage of women amongst the aristocracy, created a need for conventions of love outside marriage and forced the nobility of ancient lineage to redefine the moral basis of its authority. Troubadour poetry expressed the ideals and sentiments of a 'leisure class', debarred from participating in trade or commerce by the duty of non-derogation, detached from material responsibilities by the principle of primogeniture, and increasingly deprived of its military *raison d'être* by the decline of feudalism and by the mechanisation of warfare. The Arab theory of profane love thus acquired a social significance which it could never have possessed in Muslim society.

Those theories on Courtly Love which have been categorised as Neoplatonic, Crypto-Cathar, Bernardine–Marianist and Spring Folk Ritual cannot be considered genuine theories of origin, although they do introduce factors which are relevant to the subsequent development of Courtly Love. The basic thought pattern of Neoplatonism, which conceived of the soul as a substance, divine in origin, yearning to be liberated from matter, in order to return to the Unity whence it sprang, bears a vague resemblance to Courtly Love, with its emphasis on the insatiability of desire and the upward movement of the lover towards the beloved. Platonic and Neoplatonic doctrines had been assimilated by Arabic commentators on Aristotle. These philosophical ideas were, however, only marginally important to the troubadours.

The Cathars constituted a large religious minority in southern France during the twelfth century. Although the troubadours and Cathar heretics both depended for their survival on the patronage of an aristocracy opposed to ecclesiastical interference, their coexistence was coincidental. They were two sides of the same coin. Since the dualist heresy seems to have had a particular following among the ladies of the aristocracy, it is nevertheless possible that poets made their poetry conform, at least superficially, with the morality of the Perfect. In the eyes of the Cathars concubinage was less reprehensible than Christian marriage. Ladies who were Cathar sympathisers or believers may therefore have been well disposed towards the troubadours.

St Bernard (1090–1153), a contemporary of Guilhem IX (1086–1127), founded his religious order in 1115 in order to counteract the influence of the Cathar Goodmen or Perfect. It is impossible to establish a cause–effect relationship between Bernardine mysticism and Courtly Love, because the troubadour movement began before 1120–30, when St Bernard was active. Certain themes and formulas were borrowed from Christian mysticism in the middle of the twelfth century, but this does not alter the fact that, prior to Dante, no poet achieved a synthesis of Christian charity and Courtly Love. Marianism became associated with the Bernardine movement, although St Bernard himself was opposed to the doctrine of the immaculate conception of

Our Lady. The cult of the Virgin Mary, which prevailed throughout France during the thirteenth century, could not be subdued by the ecclesiastical authorities, and, in the opinion of the Church, it was clearly judged preferable to outright heresy or to the idolatry inherent in Courtly Love. Marianism was thus to some extent both a cause and a consequence of the decadence of troubadour poetry.

The May Queen, elected to preside over the joyful festivities of 1 May, and the Virgin Mary, as she was depicted in the popular imagination, derive many of their attributes from the Great Mother of the Gods, whose syncretistic cultus was once widespread in western Asia, the eastern Mediterranean and the Aegean. It was customary, among the aristocracy, to celebrate May Day with jousting and the recitation of poetry. The Floral Games at Toulouse, which were intended to promote a revival of troubadour poetry in the fourteenth century, were almost certainly linked indirectly with the pagan feast of Cybele and Attis. However, the sexual licence which marked the regeneration of nature is incompatible with Courtly Love. The courtly lover did not rebel against the institution of marriage; social constraints were merely ignored. Furthermore the courtly ethic, with its stress on fidelity and purity, was far from being a 'natural morality'. In short, the essential features of Courtly Love cannot be explained by studying the folk traditions and the ritual dance songs of Europe.

The Chivalric–Matriarchal thesis is the least convincing theory of origin, because it is based on assumptions which have little substance. It cannot be assumed that chastity is a virtue peculiar to patriarchy, and there is no evidence that pagan Europe was, in the true sense of the word, matriarchal. The Germanic tribes consulted prophetesses and venerated women, but it cannot be inferred from Tacitus that their womenfolk were socially predominant. According to this theory, Courtly Love was the product of the conflict between Christianity and pre-Christian sexual *mores*. While it could be argued that this conflict had existed ever since the emperor Theodosius condemned pagan rites in the fourth century, it was not until the twelfth century that the Church seriously attempted to consecrate marriage and chivalry to its own ends, and 'the exclusion of the pleasures of sex as in all circumstances profane, just when other motives were being idealized, made it inevitable that a special sanctity should be invented for them, outside marriage and outside the Church' (Broadbent, 1964, p. 18). However, Courtly Love was neither a pagan survival nor a cover for sexual promiscuity; it was a social and literary fiction which had a moral and civilising influence on the conduct of the medieval aristocracy. This fiction had a negligible effect on the status of women, which was never anything other than secondary. The woman raised on a pedestal by an admiring poet was scarcely more emancipated than the wife who was her husband's chattel, and she often fulfilled both roles simultaneously.

Two theories of meaning are of primary importance: the Play Phenomenon and the Stylistic Convention. The former claims that Courtly Love was a manifestation of the play element in culture, because it was a socially acceptable ritual for the expression of passion and anxiety. The latter claims that Courtly Love was a literary tradition from which the medieval writer could draw certain themes and stylistic devices. These two theories explore different aspects of the same phenomenon.

Play may be defined as a self-stimulating and self-rewarding activity, circumscribed within fixed limits of place and time, which must proceed according to certain rules or conventions which are accepted as absolute for the duration of the game, and which ceases to afford pleasure if and when the outcome is predictable. The pleasure of the game is in the tension between the hope of winning and the fear of losing. This definition of play expresses an essential truth about Courtly Love which would otherwise remain inexplicable: the choice of suffering or difficulty in preference to gratification. All the features of play, as defined by Huizinga and others, are present in the troubadour lyric: illusion, commitment, virtuosity, secrecy, unpredictability, risk, emulation, and the conservation of past rituals and beliefs. Poetry is itself associated with play: the poet plays with words, and within every poem there is a play of words on words. Courtly Love was a social fiction which governed life at court, in which poets competed and collaborated. Three categories of play can usefully be applied to literature: contest, chance and make-believe. These ideas deserve to be worked out systematically in relation to the medieval love lyric. The social and economic factors which created a 'leisure class' should also be studied. This theory of meaning is thus inseparable from the Feudal–Sociological theory of origin.

In addition to being a game, Courtly Love was a literary movement and an ideology with ethical implications. Just as many of Huizinga's disciples have ignored literature, so many literary critics have investigated medieval court poetry as though it belonged to a semi-autonomous universe, unrelated either to the social environment or to the culture of Muslim Spain. The troubadour movement, disseminated from Provence throughout most of Europe, was greatly indebted to the Arabic lyrical tradition. This theory, which views Courtly Love as a stylistic convention, is therefore inseparable from the Hispano-Arabic theory of origin.

Courtly Love must have fulfilled an important psychological function, but the reversal of the normal sex roles, the paradoxical quest for sorrow and the ambivalence displayed by poets in their attitudes to women can be explained more satisfactorily by the play and sociological theories outlined above than by the theory that Courtly Love was a collective fantasy generated by a mother fixation of infantile origin. Besides, it would be highly improbable if this literary phenomenon were attributable to a single form of mental aberration. This type of reductionism is dangerously simple. The methods of Freudian psychology are ill suited to the study of past literature, and they are impotent when it comes to forming aesthetic judgements. It is, however, significant that the symptoms of melancholia, as defined by Freud, bear a striking resemblance to the descriptions of this malady in medieval medical treatises and to the behaviour of the stereotype courtly lover.[3]

Two theories of meaning remain: Courtly Experience and Critical Fallacy. If the term Courtly Love is worth retaining, then it cannot refer to an experience which is, as Dronke maintains, universally possible. Ancient Egyptian and Icelandic poetry do not display all the essential features of Courtly Love; poems composed in Byzantium, Georgia and Mozarabic Spain are less convincing as evidence for the universality of *amour courtois*, because these countries inherited the lyrical traditions of the Arabs. Furthermore the religious concepts and formulas used by troubadours and *trouvères* do not necessarily imply that finite human love can be transcended through the mediation of the beloved. Dronke's Courtly Experience (which was not, incidentally, confined to courtly society) cannot be considered a useful theory of meaning. This critical study has, I hope, fully vindicated the use of the term Courtly Love in order to denote the complex of ideas and sentiments implicit in the troubadour movement. D. W. Robertson and John Benton are misguided in their assumption that the medieval audience was insensitive to the principle of ambiguity. Courtly Love is inherently ambiguous. Its aesthetic principles were inspired not by theology but by Graeco-Arabic physiology. Benton also misunderstood the nature of the phenomenon when he inferred, from historical sources, that it never existed. Poetry is fictitious; it belongs to a world of make-believe, not of scientific facts, dogmas or events that can be recorded. It is part of the fiction upon which civilisation is based.

Courtly Love was, we may conclude, a comprehensive cultural phenomenon: a literary movement, an ideology, an ethical system, a style of life, and an expression of the play element in culture, which arose in an aristocratic Christian environment exposed to Hispano-Arabic influences. This phenomenon occurred in the south of France and was first studied in Renaissance Italy, but Spain provides the key to its origins and to the origins of troubadour scholarship.

NOTES

[1] Oswald Spengler, *The Decline of the West*, II (London, 1922), p. 55.
[2] 'Ellos vienen cuesta yuso, e todos trahen calças; / e las siellas coceras e las cinchas amojadas; / nós cavalgaremos siellas gallegas, e huesas sobre calças, / ciento cavalleros devemos vencer aquellas mesnadas' *The Poem of the Cid* ed. Ian Michael [Manchester: MUP, 1975], ll. 992–5).
[3] 'Mourning and melancholia (1917)' in *Collected Papers*, IV (London, 1925), pp. 152–70.

Appendix I
The etymology of 'trobar' and 'amor hereos'

The purpose of this appendix is to discuss the etymology of two terms associated with Courtly Love: *trobar* and *amor hereos*. The much disputed origin of the Provençal word *trobar* is pertinent to the origins of the troubadour movement. The term *amor hereos*, which denoted a species of melancholia to which lovers were prone, elucidates certain aspects of Courtly Love, in particular the belief in the potentially destructive power of love.

1 'TROBAR'

According to *The Oxford Dictionary of English Etymology* (ed. C. T. Onions, revised edn. 1969), *s.v.* 'troubadour', the Provençal *trobar* and the Old French *trover* (whence *troveor*, nom. *trovere* or *trouvère*) meant 'compose' and later 'invent', 'find'. Corominas states that *trobar*, 'to find' or 'to compose verses', derives from the Low Latin *contropare*, 'to speak figuratively' or 'to make comparisons', from the Graeco-Latin *tropus*, 'a rhetorical figure' (*s.v.* 'trovar', *Diccionario crítico etimológico de la lengua castellana* [four vols, Madrid, 1954–57]). H. J. Chaytor writes that the Low Latin *tropus* denoted an 'air' or 'melody'; hence the *trobador* was, in the first instance, the composer of new melodies (*The Troubadours*, p. 10). Hans Spanke refers to *tropus* as a type of liturgical music, to which *tropatores* in north-east Germany set their music *c.*1070 (*AnMus*, I, 1946, 5–18).

Arabists have, on the other hand, proposed an alternative etymology. Ribera y Tarragó suggests in his *Disertaciones* (II, p. 141) that the word *trobador* may come from the Arabic *ṭarab*, 'music', 'song'. James T. Monroe notes an instance of the word *troba* in *La doncella Teodor*, a work translated from Arabic where the original text probably had *ṭarab*: 'e aprendí a tanner laúd e canón e las treynta e tres trobas'. Furthermore he observes the use of the term *taraví* in a poem in the *Cancionero general*, where it is clearly a synonym for *poeta*: the poet Juan Poeta is addressed as Juan Taraví (Monroe, 1970, pp. 166–7). Lemay (1966) derives *trobar* from the Arabic root *ḍaraba*, 'to strike', which was applied to the playing of string instruments, and from the suffix *ador*, 'doer' or 'maker'. Hussein (1971) suggests that *dour* could be the plural of *dar*, 'home', 'palace', 'castle'. H. A. R. Gibb remarked in *The Legacy of Islam* (ed. Arnold, 1936, p. 191 n.) that 'even if *trobar* is to be connected with *trouver*, it is interesting to note that the Arabic *wajada* "find" means also "feel the pangs of love or sorrow"'. Samuel M. Stern did not consider that the Arabic etymology of *trobar* warranted his serious attention (Stern, 1974, p. 226), but it is not impossible that the connotations of the Arabic *ṭarab* coalesced with those of *trouver.** 'Trobar', according to *Las flors del gay saber* (ed. Gatien-Arnoult, I, p. 3), 'es far noel dictat / En romanç, fi, be compassat'. Dante defines poetry as follows: 'fictio rethorica musicaque poita' (*De vulg. eloq.*, II, iv, 2).

2 'AMOR HEREOS'

The term *amor hereos* was used by Chaucer in the *Knight's Tale* (ll. 1373–4) and by Richard of Bury in *Philobiblon* (London, 1888, pp. 99–100). Its connotations are carried by the adjective *heroical*, employed by Robert Burton in his *Anatomy of Melancholy*. These passages were misunderstood by early commentators. A detailed study of the word was made by John Livingston Lowes: 'What we have, then, is the Greek *eros*, more or less technically used to start with, into which by a process of transfusion there have passed the exotic oriental associations of the Arabic *al-'ishq*; which has been still further modified by confusion with the Latin *herus* (quite certainly with *heros* too) . . . and which, after such vicissitudes, has slipped absolutely out of the memory of man' (Lowes, 1913–14, p. 524). Oribasius (b. A.D. 325), whose work was translated into Latin in the sixth century, was one of the first to discuss *eros* as a recognised cerebral malady. In the tenth-century translation (Laon MS No. 424) the title reads: 'Ad eos qui de amore contristantur, quos Greci *ton heroton* vocant' (*ibid.*, p. 519). This malady was mentioned in the medical treatises of Arnald of Villanova, Bernard Gordon, Valescus of Taranta and John of Tornamira, all of whom were connected with the medical school at Montpellier. These physicians relied on Rhazes and Avicenna.

Dino del Garbo, in the early fourteenth century, identified Cavalcanti's description of love with *amor hereos*: 'que passio est proprie circa actus venereos, in quibus actibus est furiositas et intemperentia . . . Et vocatur talis passio ereos ab auctoribus medicine' (cited in Nelson, *Renaissance Theory of Love*, p. 36). In the late fifteenth century Francisco López de Villalobos linked *amor hereos* with the troubadours: 'Amor hereos según nuestros autores / es una corrupta imaginación / por quien algún hombre se aquexa de amores, / y en éste qu'es *hito delos trovadores* / sin ser lisongero diré mi razón' (*El sumario de la medicina con un tratado de las pestíferas bubas*, Salamanca, 1498 [fol. 4v] [edited by María Teresa Herrera, Cuadernos de Historia de la Medicina Española, Monografías 25, Salamanca, 1973], p. 38). The term was also used by the philosopher El Tostado (Alfonso de Madrigal) in answer to a question on the meaning of Cupid: 'si no obedescamos al su movimiento [de Cupido] executando los carnales ayuntamientos, sigue crescimiento de ardor que consume las humedades tiernas, y el cuydado cerca de esto afflige e deseca y enmagresce, y síguense algunas vezes graves enfermedades, en especial si cae el amador enla passión llamada por los médicos amor hereos, ca trahe ésta alos hombres a

---

* 'There is no such thing as a false etymology.' (John Heath-Stubbs reports that this statement was once made by the scholar Hugh Gordon Porteus.)

punto de se perder' (*Tostado sobre Eusebio*, Salamanca, 1506–07, III, *El libro de las diez questiones vulgares*, fols. 36r–36v).

The poetic value of this distemper was heightened by the false etymology of *hereos* from 'heroic'. Thus Bernard Gordon wrote, 'Hereos dicitur quia hereosi et nobiles propter affluentiam delitiarum istam passionem consueverunt incurrere' (*Practica sive Lilium medicinae* [Venice, 1498] fol. 31v). Similarly, for Savonarola, 'hec passio a multis dicta est hereos, quia herois sive nobilibus plurimis contingit, nam hi ex aliis non impediti super alios procantur' (*Practica medicinae* [Venice, 1497] fol. 63v). Since it was believed that noble persons were particularly susceptible to this malady, its symptoms were not regarded as demeaning. These destructive and paradoxical effects of love were, on the contrary, an integral part of the Courtly Love tradition.

Appendix II
The affinity between love and hate and love's paradoxical virtues in European and Arabic literature

The purpose of this appendix is to cite various passages which illustrate the diffusion of certain ideas concerning the nature of love which would appear to have originated amongst the Arabs. These parallels are intended to suggest possible lines for further research.

1 AFFINITY BETWEEN LOVE AND HATE

'Opposites are of course likes, in reality; when things reach the limit o contrareity . . . they come to resemble one another. This is decreed by God's omnipotent power, in a manner which baffles entirely the human imagination. Thus, when ice is pressed a long time in the hand, it finally produces the same effect as fire. We find that extreme joy and extreme sorrow kill equally . . . Similarly with lovers: when they love each other with an equal ardour . . . they will turn against one another without any valid reason, each purposely contradicting the other in whatever he may say; they quarrel violently over the smallest things, each picking up every word that the other lets fall and wilfully misinterpreting it. All these devices are aimed at testing and proving what each is seeking in the other.' (Ibn Ḥazm [d. 1064], *The Ring of the Dove*, trans. Arberry, pp. 36–7.)

'Often bursts of anger arise between lovers in this state, often they start quarrels, and when true grounds of antagonism are not there they invent false ones, often not even probable. In this condition love often turns into hate, since nothing can satisfy their longing for each other . . . and in a wondrous, or rather in a wretched way, out of desire springs hate, and out of hate desire . . . Yet beyond measure, beyond nature even, fire gathers strength in water, in that the flame of love burns more fiercely through their opposition than it could through their being at peace.' (Richard of St Victor [d. 1173], *Tractatus de quatuor gradibus violentae charitatis*, quoted from Dronke, *Medieval Latin*, I, p. 65 n.)

'"Before the face of God rapt silence shouts". Look at other stations, and you will see the same [concord through opposition] there: when lovers fight in quarrels with each other, their peace of spirit grows through that war of words, love is spiced with hate. So too in metaphors: inwardly the words love each other, though on the outside there are enmities. Among the words themselves there is conflict, but the meaning calms all conflict in the words.' (Geoffrey de Vinsauf [writing between 1208 and 1213], *Poetria nova*, quoted from Dronke,

'Mediaeval rhetoric', in *The Mediaeval World*, ed. D. Daiches and A. Thorlby [London, 1973], pp. 334–5.)

'It is well if lovers pretend from time to time to be angry at each other, for if one lets the other see that he is angry and that something has made him indignant with his loved one, he can find out clearly how faithful she is. For a true lover is always in fear and trembling lest the anger of his beloved last for ever, and so, even if one lover does show at times that he is angry at the other without cause, this disturbance will last but a little while if they find that their feeling for each other is really love. You must not think that by quarrels of this kind the bonds of affection and love are weakened; it is only clearing away the rust.' (Andreas Capellanus [writing *c.* 1180], *De amore*, trans. Parry, pp. 158–9.)

> 'Pero donde yo me llego
> todo mal y pena quito;
> delos yelos saco fuego . . .
> No lo pruevo con milagro:
> cosa es sabida llana
> que se despierta la gana
> de comer con dulçe agro.
> Assí yo con galardón
> muchas vezes mezclo pena,
> que en la paz de dissensión
> entre amantes la quistión
> reyntegra la cadena.'

(Rodrigo Cota [writing *c.* 1490], 'Love's words', *Diálogo entre el Amor y un viejo*, in *Cancionero general*, facsimile of 1511 edition, ed. Antonio Rodríguez-Moñino [Madrid, 1958], fols. 73v and 74v.)

'Venus loves Mars, because Beauty, which we call Venus, cannot subsist without contrareity.' (Pico della Mirandola [d. 1494], *Commento sopra una canzone de amore composta da Girolamo Benivieni*, quoted from Edgar Wind, *The Pagan Mysteries in the Renaissance*, revised edn. [Harmondsworth, 1967], p. 89.) Pico defines beauty as 'an amicable enmity and a concordant discord', and admits his debt to the astrological works of Abenazra (Ibn-Ezra, d. 1167) and Moses (Maimonides, d. 1204), both Spanish Jews.

The coexistence of love and hate is also the subject of an interesting digression in Chrétien de Troyes' *Le Chevalier au Lion* [composed *c.* 1170–75], although here it is less psychological, since the combatants do not recognise each other:

> 'Mes ne s'antreconoissent mie
> Cil, qui conbatre se voloient,
> Qui mout antramer se soloient.
> Et or don ne s'antraimment il?

"Oïl" vos respong et "nenil".
Et l'un et l'autre proverai,
Si que reison i troverai.
Por voir, mes sire Gauvains aimme
Yvain et conpaignon le claimme,
Et Yvains lui, ou que il soit.
Neïs ci, s'il le conoissoit,
Feroit il ja de lui grant feste
Et si metroit por lui sa teste,
Et cil la soe aussi por lui,
Einçois qu'an li feïst enui.
N'est ce amors antiere et fine?
Oïl, certes. Et la haïne,
Don ne rest ele tote aperte?
Oïl; que ce est chose certe,
Que li uns a l'autre sanz dote
Voldroit avoir la teste rote,
Ou tant avoir fet li voldroit
De honte, que pis an vaudroit.
Par foi! c'est mervoille provee,
Qu'an a an un veissel trovee
Amor et Haïne mortel.
Des! meïsmes an un ostel
Comant puet estre li repeires
A deus choses, qui sont contreires?
An un ostel, si con moi sanble,
Ne pueent eles estre ansanble;
Que ne porroit pas remenoir
L'une avuec l'autre an un menoir,
Que noise et tançon n'i eüst,
Puis que l'une l'autre i seüst.
Mes an un chas a plusors manbres;
Que il a loges et chanbres.
Einsi puet bien estre la chose:
Espoir Amors s'estoit anclose
An aucune chanbre celee,
Et Haïne s'an iere alee
Es loges par devers la voie,
Por ce que viaut, que l'an la voie.'

('But those who were about to fight did not recognise each other, though their relations were wont to be very affectionate. Then do they not love each other now? I would answer you both "yes" and "no". And I shall prove that each answer is correct. In truth, my Gawain loves Yvain and regards him as his companion, and so does Yvain regard him, wherever he may be. Even here, if

he knew who he was, he would make much of him, and either one would lay
down his head for the other before he would allow any harm to come to him.
Is not that a perfect and lofty love? Yes, surely. But, on the other hand, is not
their hate equally manifest? Yes; for it is a certain thing that doubtless each
would be glad to have broken the other's head, and so to have injured him as
to cause his humiliation. Upon my word, it is a wondrous thing, that Love and
mortal Hate should dwell together. God! How can two things so opposed find
lodging in the same dwelling place? It seems to me they cannot live together;
for one could not dwell with the other, without giving rise to noise and
contention, as soon as each knew of the other's presence. But upon the ground
floor there may be several apartments: for there are halls and sleeping rooms.
It may be the same in this case: I think Love had esconced himself in some
hidden room, while Hate had betaken herself to the balconies looking on the
high road, because she wishes to be seen.') (Text from *Yvain*, ed. T. B. W. Reid
[Manchester: MUP, 1942], ll. 5998–6040, pp. 163–5; trans. W. W. Comfort,
Arthurian Romances, Everyman's Library 698 [London, 1914], pp. 258–9.)

2   LOVE'S PARADOXICAL VIRTUES

'A man in love will give prodigally to the limit of his capacity, in a way that
formerly he would have refused; as if he were the one receiving the donation,
he the one whose happiness is the object in view; all this in order that he may
show off his good points, and make himself desirable. How often has the miser
opened his purse strings, the scowler relaxed his frown, the coward leapt
heroically into the fray, the clod suddenly become sharp-witted, the boor
turned into the perfect gentleman, the stinker transformed himself into the
elegant dandy, the sloucher smartened up, the decrepit recaptured his lost
youth, the godly gone wild, the self-respecting kicked over the traces—all
because of love!' (Ibn Ḥazm, *The Ring of the Dove*, trans. Arberry, pp. 34–5.)

'Now it is the effect of love that a true lover cannot be degraded with any
avarice. Love causes a rough and uncouth man to be distinguished for his
handsomeness; it can endow a man even of the humblest birth with nobility of
character; it blesses the proud with humility; and the man in love becomes
accustomed to performing many services gracefully for everyone. O what a
wonderful thing is love, which makes a man shine with so many virtues and
teaches everyone, no matter who he is, so many good traits of character!'
(Andreas Capellanus, *De amore*, trans. Parry, p. 31.)

> 'Ancaras trob mais de ben en Amor,
> Qe.l vil fai car e.l nesci gen de parlan,
> E l'escars larc, e leial lo truan,
> E.l fol savi, e.l pec conoissedor;
> E l'orgoillos domesga et homelia;

E fai de dos cors un, tan ferm los lia.
Per c'om non deu ad Amor contradir,
Pois tant gen sap esmendar e fenir.'

('I also find more good in Love because he makes the wretched friendly, and
the silly man a clever talker, and the stingy generous, and the rogue trust-
worthy, and the madman wise, and the simpleton learned; and the proud he
tames and humbles; and of two hearts he makes one, so strongly does he bind
them. Therefore one should not oppose Love, since he knows how to correct
and to finish so nicely.') (Aimeric de Peguilhan [d. 1230], *The Poems*, ed.
William P. Shepard and Frank M. Chambers [Evanston, Ill.: Northwestern
University Press, 1950], No. 15, ll. 17–24, pp. 101 and 103.)

'Muchas noblezas ha en el que a dueñas sirve:
loçano, fablador, en ser franco se abive;
en servir a las dueñas el bueno non se esquive,
que si mucho trabaja, en mucho plazer bive.
   El amor faz'sotil al omne que es rudo;
fázele fablar fermoso al que antes es mudo;
al omne que es covarde fázelo muy atrevudo;
al perezoso faze ser presto e agudo.
   Al mancebo mantiene mucho en mancebez,
e al viejo faz'perder mucho la vejez;
faze blanco e fermoso del negro como pez:
lo que non vale una nuez amor le da gran prez.'

('There are many noble qualities in a man who serves the ladies: he is lively,
eloquent, he strives to be open-handed; a good man does not shirk serving the
ladies, for if he toils a great deal he lives in great pleasure.
   Love makes the uncouth man subtle; it makes him who was wordless speak
fair words; it makes bold the one who was craven; it makes the sluggard be
swift and keen.
   It preserves the young man for a long time in his youth, and makes the old
man lose his old age considerably; it turns white and handsome him who is
black as pitch: what is not worth a nut is given great value by love'.) (Juan
Ruiz [writing *c.* 1330], *Libro de Buen Amor*, ed. Raymond S. Willis [Princeton
University Press, 1972], sts 155–7, pp. 50–51.)

'Al rudo hago discreto,
al grossero muy polido,
desembuelto al encogido,
y al invirtuoso neto;
al covarde, esforçado,
escasso, al liberal,
bien regido, al destemplado,

muy cortés y mesurado
al que no suele ser tal.'

(Rodrigo Cota, *Diálogo entre el Amor y un viejo*, in *Cancionero general*, fol. 73ᵛ.)

'Aún podemos en otra manera dezir que las saetas que fazen amar sean de oro, por quanto, según los vulgares piensan, el amor mueve alos mancebos a alguna claridad de nobleza y de virtud humanal, aunque no divinal, ca son algunos mancebos, torpes, perezosos, no despiertos para actos de proeza, tristes en sí mismos, o no alegres, pesados, no curantes de sí mismos, agora sean apuestos, agora incompuestos, callados, no gastadores o destribuydores según alguna liberalidad; el amor les haze tomar todas las contrarias condiciones . . . todos los amadores curan andar alegres, y limpios, y apuestos, y conversan con las gentes, y distribuyen, y donan algo, como todo esto requiera el amor. Esto fará todo hombre que amare, aun que su natural condición sea melancólica, triste, pensosa y apartada, sin fabla, sin compostura, sin conversación, y escassa o avarienta, porque no es possible en otra manera amar y mostrarse amador.'
(El Tostado [d. 1455], *Libro de las diez questiones vulgares*, fol. 35ᵛ.)

'*Clau.* Que tan bien os parecen las mugeres?
Amin. Nascí d'ellas, y que donde ellas no andan ni hay alegría ni descanso ni perfeto gozo ni contentamiento, y por el contrario, el favor de la hembra da esfuerço al cobarde, y haze al [perezoso] despierto, y al tartamudo elocuente, y al nescio discreto, y al parlero templado. Y al grosero haze polido, y al bovo prudente, y del rudo avisado, y del descuidado torna diligente, y del liberal pródigo y del avaro liberal. Y al desabrido torna de dulce conversación, y del mudo torna parlero, y del cobarde haze esforçado, y del mal christiano torna y haze religioso, compeliendo all hombre a que ni pierda missa ni biésperas ni cumpletas.' (*La comedia Thebaida*, ed. G. D. Trotter and K. Whinnom [London: Tamesis, 1969], p. 180.)

'Iusto & ragione è (dicel Provenzale) ch'io cante de Amore, laudandomi con sue lodi di lui per Amore, cosa di tutti vitii netta: & che per amor cresce valor, senza valor non è honor, per amor virtù suo premio receve, & suo offitio exequisce cortesia: Amor olvida orgoglio da villania ne guarda, & pigritia discaccia, il vile fa animoso, el nescio eloquente, per costui lo scarso divene largo, liale il falso, lo pazo savio, aviva humiltà, & lo altiero domestica: De bei motti autore, virtù nutrisce, allegria adduce, & gaieza mantiene, solazo ne apporta, diversi cori coniunge, fermamente li unisce & liga: In doi un sol volere accoglie: Per ilche non si deve contradire ad Amore: Li piaceri delquale sono molte più che le noie, el ben più chel male . . .' (Mario Equicola [d. *c.* 1525], *Libro di natura de amore* [Venice, 1525], fol. 195ᵛ.)

A selected bibliography

Two bibliographies deal to some extent with the origins of Courtly Love: Käte Axhausen, *Die Theorien über den Ursprung der provenzalischen Lyrik* (1937), and Jean-Charles Payen, *Les Origines de la courtoisie dans la littérature française médiévale* (1966–67). Axhausen distinguishes between Arabic, folkloric, classical Latin, medieval Latin and liturgical theories of troubadour origins, which she traces from Dante onwards. Payen gives a more complete and up-to-date introduction to the subject in the form of lecture notes for students. An index of those troubadours who were cited by early scholars may be found in Eleonora Vicenti, *Bibliografia antica dei trovatori* (1963). Two other works may be consulted: Santorre Debenedetti, *Gli studi provenzali in Italia nel cinquecento* (1911), and Alfred Jeanroy, 'Les études provençales du XVIe siècle au milieu du XIXe siècle' (*AMid*, XLIII [1931], 129–59). Gerald Gillespie's review of research on the origins of Romance lyrics is brief but, on the whole, thorough (see below).

The Meaning of Courtly Love, ed. F. X. Newman (1968), contains one of the best general bibliographies. Rudolf Baehr, *Der provenzalische Minnesang* (1967), is extremely useful, but unreliable. François Pirot, *MA*, LXXIV (1968), 301–31, and Francis Lee Utley, *MH*, n.s., III (1972), 299–324, should be consulted for an account of the present state of scholarship. Some of the various approaches to Courtly Love have been discussed by Reto R. Bezzola, in *Les Origines . . . de la littérature courtoise en Occident*, II (1960), by Henri Davenson, in *Les Troubadours* (1961), and by Theodore Silverstein, in *The Meaning of Courtly Love* (pp. 77–90). On amatory literature and related topics, many of them far from courtly, there is the revised edition of Jules Gay, *Bibliographie des ouvrages relatifs à l'amour* (1893–99). Unfortunately it has no subject index.

There are a number of bibliographical works on the problem of Arabic influences: Ettore Li Gotti, *La 'tesi araba' sulle 'origini' della lirica romanza* (1955); Klaus Heger, *Die bisher veröffentlichten Ḫarǧas und ihre Deutungen* (1960); and Leo Pollmann, '*Trobar clus*'. *Bibelexegese und hispano-arabische Literatur* (1965). Further references are given in the first and second editions of *The Legacy of Islam*, 1st edn., ed. Thomas Arnold and Alfred Guillaume (Oxford, 1931), and 2nd edn., ed. Joseph Schacht and C. E. Bosworth (Oxford, 1974).

For Provençal literature Pierre-Louis Berthaud compiled a *Bibliographie occitane* for the years 1919–42 and, in collaboration with Jean Lesaffre, for the years 1943–56. It was continued by Lesaffre and Irénée-Marcel Cluzel for 1957–66. There is also A. Pillet and H. Carstens, *Bibliographie der Troubadours* (1933). For French there is R. Bossuat, *Manuel bibliographique de la littérature française du Moyen Âge* (Melun, 1951); *Suppléments* (Paris, 1955, 1961); for Spanish, José Simón Díaz, *Bibliografía de la literatura hispánica*, III (2nd edn.,

2 vols, Madrid, 1963–65) and Antonio Rodríguez Monino, *Manual de cancioneros y romanceros* (Madrid, 1973); for Italian, G. Contini, *Poeti del Duecento* (2 vols, Milan and Naples, 1960).

ACWORTH, EVELYN. *The New Matriarchy*. London: Victor Gollancz, 1965.

ADAMS, H. B. *Mont-Saint-Michel and Chartres*. London: Constable, 1950 (first edn. 1913).

AGUIRRE, J. M. *Calisto y Melibea, amantes cortesanos* (Colección de Ensayos Almenara, 1). Saragossa, 1962.

——. *Ensayo para un estudio del tema amoroso en la primitiva lírica castellana* (Publicaciones de la Revista *Universidad*, 11). Saragossa, 1965.

AGUIRRE, J. M. (ed.). Hernando del Castillo [compiler]. *Cancionero general. Antología temática del amor cortés*. Madrid: Anaya, 1971.

AHSMANN, H. P. J. M. *Le Culte de la Sainte Vierge et la littérature française profane du Moyen Âge*. Paris and Utrecht: A. Picard, 1929.

AKEHURST, F. R. P. 'Les étapes de l'amour chez Bernard de Ventadour', *CCMe*, XVI (1973), 133–47.

ALONSO, DÁMASO. 'Cancioncillas "de amigo" mozárabes (Primavera temprana de la lírica europea)', *RFE*, XXXIII (1949), 297–349.

ANDREAS CAPELLANUS. *The Art of Courtly Love* [*De amore*]. Trans. John Jay Parry. New York: Columbia University Press, 1941.

ANDRÉS, JUAN. *Dell'origine, progressi e stato attuale d'ogni letteratura*. 8 vols. Parma: Stamperia Reale, 1782–1822 (Spanish translation by Carlos Andrés. 6 vols. Madrid, 1784–93).

ANGLADE, JOSEPH. *Les Troubadours. Leurs vies, leurs œuvres, leur influence*. Paris: Armand Colin, 1908.

——. *Les Origines du Gai Savoir*. Paris: E. de Boccard, 1920.

ANITCHKOF, EUGÈNE. *Joachim de Flore et les milieux courtois*. Rome, 1931 (repr. Geneva: Slatkine, 1974).

AROUX, EUGÈNE. *Dante hérétique, révolutionnaire et socialiste. Révélations d'un catholique sur le moyen âge*. Paris: Jules Renouard, 1854.

——. *Les Mystères de la chevalerie et de l'amour platonique au Moyen Âge*. Paris: Jules Renouard, 1858.

ARTEAGA, STEFANO. *Della influenza delgi Arabi sull'origine della poesia moderna in Europa*. Rome: Pagliarini, 1791.

ASKEW, MELVIN W. 'Courtly Love: neurosis as institution', *PsR*, LII (1965), 19–29.

AUBRY, PIERRE. *Trouvères et troubadours* [on music]. Paris: F. Alcan, 1909 (rev. edn. 1919).

AUDIAU, JEAN. *Les Troubadours et l'Angleterre. Contribution à l'étude des poètes anglais de l'amour de 1250 à 1400*. Tulle, 1920 (rev. edn. Paris: J. Vrin, 1927).

AVICENNA (Ḥusain Ibn 'Abd Allāh, called Ibn Sīnā). ['*Risāla fi-'l-'Ishq*'] 'A Treatise on Love, by Ibn Sina', trans. Emil L. Fackenheim, *MedS*, VII (1945), 208–28.

AXHAUSEN, KÄTE. *Die Theorien über den Ursprung der provenzalischen Lyrik.* Marburg: G. H. Nolte, 1937.

BADESSA, RICHARD PAUL. 'Literary conventions of Courtly Love'. Unpubl. Ph.D. thesis. University of Indiana, 1967. (*DA*, XXVIII, 4114–A.)

BAEHR, RUDOLF. *Der provenzalische Minnesang.* Darmstadt: Wissenschaftliche Buchgesellschaft, 1967.

BAGLEY, C. P. 'Courtly love-songs in Galicia and Provence', *FMLS*, II (1966), 74–88.

BARBER, RICHARD. *The Knight and Chivalry.* London: Sphere Books, 1974.

BARBIERI, GIAMMARIA. *Dell'origine della poesia rimata.* Ed. Girolamo Tiraboschi. Modena, 1790 (written *c.* 1570).

BARET, EUGÈNE. *Espagne et Provence. Études sur la littérature du Midi de l'Europe . . . pour faire suite aux travaux de Raynouard et de Fauriel.* Paris: A. Durand, 1857.

BARRON, W. R. J. 'Luf-Daungere', in *Medieval Miscellany presented to Eugène Vinaver.* Manchester: MUP, 1965, pp. 1–18.

BASTERO, ANTONIO. *La crusca provenzale ovvero le voci, frasi, forme, e maniere di dire, che la gentilissima, e celebre lingua toscana ha preso dalla provenzale.* Rome: Antonio de'Rossi, 1724.

BEC, PIERRE. 'La douleur et son univers poétique chez Bernard de Ventadour', *CCMe*, XI (1968), 545–71; and XII (1969), 25–33.

—. 'Quelques réflexions sur la poésie lyrique médiévale. Problèmes et essai de caractérisation', in *Mélanges offerts à Rita Lejeune.* Gembloux: Éditions J. Duculot, 1969, II, pp. 1309–29.

—. 'L'antithèse poétique chez Bernard de Ventadour', in Irénée Cluzel and François Pirot (eds.), *Mélanges de philologie romane dédiés à la mémoire de Jean Boutière (1899–1967).* 2 vols. Liège: Éditions Soledi, 1971, I, pp. 107–37.

BÉDIER, JOSEPH. 'Les Fêtes de mai et les commencemens de la poésie lyrique au Moyen Âge', *RDM*, CXXXV (May 1896), 146–72.

BELPERRON, PIERRE. *La Joie d'amour. Contribution à l'étude des troubadours et de l'amour courtois.* Paris: Plon, 1948.

BEMBO, PIETRO. *Prose . . . nelle quali si ragiona della volgar lingua.* Venice: Giovan Tacuino, 1525.

BENTON, JOHN F. 'The court of Champagne as a literary center', *Sp*, XXXVI (1961), 551–91.

—. 'The evidence for Andreas Capellanus re-examined again', *SP*, LIX (1962), 471–8.

—. 'Clio and Venus. An historical view of medieval love', in *The Meaning of Courtly Love*, ed. F. X. Newman. Albany, N.Y., 1968, pp. 19–42.

BERTHAUD, PIERRE-LOUIS. *Bibliographie occitane, 1919–42.* Paris: Les Belles Lettres, 1946.

—, and LESAFFRE, JEAN. *Bibliographie occitane, 1943–1956.* Paris: Les Belles Lettres, 1958.

BERTONI, GIULIO. 'Alfonso X di Castiglia e il provenzalismo della prima lirica portoghese', *AR*, VII (1923), 171–5.

—. 'Le origini delle letterature romanze nel pensiero dei Romantici tedeschi', *AR*, XXIII (1939), 1–10.

BEYSTERVELDT, ANTONY VAN. *La poesía amorosa del siglo XV y el teatro profano de Juan del Encina.* Madrid: Insula, 1972.

BEZZOLA, RETO R. 'Guillaume IX et les origines de l'amour courtois', *R*, LXVI (1940), 145–237.

—. *Les Origines et la formation de la littérature courtoise en Occident (500–1200).* 3 vols. Paris: E. Champion, 1944–63.

BIZET, J.-A. *Suso et le minnesang; ou, la morale de l'amour courtois.* Paris: Aubier, 1948.

BOULTING, WILLIAM. *Woman in Italy, from the introduction of the chivalrous service of love to the appearance of the professional actress.* London: Methuen, 1910.

BOUTERWEK, FRIEDRICH. *Geschichte der Poesie und Beredsamkeit seit dem Ende des dreizehnten Jahrhunderts.* 12 vols. Göttingen, 1801–50.

—. *History of Spanish Literature.* Trans. Thomasina Ross. London: David Bogue, 1847.

BOWRA, SIR MAURICE. *Mediaeval Love-song.* London: Athlone, 1961.

BRIFFAULT, ROBERT S. *The Mothers. A study of the origins of sentiments and institutions.* 3 vols. London: Allen & Unwin, 1927 (abridged with introduction by G. R. Taylor, London, 1959).

—. *The Troubadours.* Trans. by author; ed. L. F. Koons. Bloomington: Indiana University Press, 1965 (French original, Paris, 1945).

BROADBENT, JOHN B. *Poetic Love.* London: Chatto & Windus, 1964.

BURCKHARDT, TITUS. 'Language and poetry' and 'Chivalric love', in *Moorish Culture in Spain,* trans. Alisa Jaffa. London: Allen & Unwin, 1972, pp. 81–109.

BURDACH, KONRAD. 'Über den Ursprung des mittelalterlichen Minnesangs, Liebesromans und Frauendienstes', *Sitzungsberichte des Preussischen Akademie der Wissenschaften* (1918), reprinted in *Vorspiel,* I (Halle: M. Niemeyer, 1925).

BURGESS, GLYN SHERIDAN. *Contribution à l'étude du vocabulaire pré-courtois* (PRF, 110). Geneva: Droz, 1970.

BURT, JOHN RICHARD. 'Courtly Love as ritual in early medieval Spanish poetry'. Unpubl. Ph.D. thesis. University of Minnesota, 1973. (*DA*, XXXIV, 719–A.)

CAILLOIS, ROGER. *Les Jeux et les hommes (Le masque et le vertige).* Paris: Gallimard, 1958. (English translation by Meyer Barash, New York, 1961.)

CAMPROUX, CHARLES. *Joy d'amor des troubadours (Jeu et joie d'amour).* Montpellier: Causse Castelnau, 1965.

CAPEFIGUE, J. B. H. R. *Les Cours d'amour, les comtesses, et châtelaines de Provence.* Paris: Amyot, 1863.

CASENEUVE, PIERRE DE. *L'Origine des Ieux-Fleureaux de Toulouse.* [Ed. F. Tornier.] Toulouse: R. Bosc, 1659.

CHABANEAU, CAMILLE. *Origine et établissement de l'Académie des Jeux Floraux.* Toulouse: É. Privat, 1885.

CHAILLEY, J. 'Les premiers troubadours et les versus de l'école d'Aquitaine', *R*, LXXVI (1955), 212–39.

—. 'Notes sur les troubadours, les versus et la question arabe', in *Mélanges I. Frank*, Saarbrücken, 1957, pp. 118–28.

CHAPELAIN, JEAN. *La Lecture des vieux romans* [written 1647]. See Huet, Pierre-Daniel.

CHAYTOR, H. J. *The Troubadours*. Cambridge: CUP, 1912.

—. *The Troubadours and England*. Cambridge: CUP, 1923.

CHEJNE, ANWAR G. 'Courtly Love', in *Muslim Spain. Its history and culture*. Minneapolis: University of Minnesota Press, 1974, pp. 247–62.

CINGRIA, CHARLES-ALBERT. 'Ieu oc tan', *Mes*, III (1937), No. 2, 123–43.

CLÉDAT, LÉON. 'Les troubadours et l'amour courtois en France aux XIIe et XIIIe siècles', *RPFP*, VII (1892), 81–128.

CLEUGH, JAMES. *Love Locked Out. A survey of love, licence, and restriction in the Middle Ages*. London: Anthony Blond, 1963.

CLOSS, HANNAH M. M. 'Courtly Love in literature and art', *S*, I (1947), 5–19.

CLUZEL, IRENÉE-MARCEL. 'Les *jarŷas* et l' "amour courtois"', *CN*, XX (1960), 233–50.

—. 'À propos des origines de la littérature courtoise en Occident', *R*, LXXXI (1960), 538–55.

—. 'Quelques réflexions à propos des origines de la poésie lyrique des troubadours', *CCMe*, IV (1961), 179–88.

—. 'L'état présent des études relatives à l'ancienne poésie provençale', in *Actes du Congrès Guillaume Budé*. 1966, pp. 435–45.

—, and PRESSOUYRE, LÉON. *Les Origines de la poésie lyrique d'oïl et les premiers trouvères. Textes*. Paris: A. G. Nizet, 1962 (revised edn., 1969.).

COHEN, GUSTAVE. 'Le problème des origines arabes de la poésie provençale médiévale', *BARB*, XXXII (1946), 266–78.

CONDREN, EDWARD I. 'The troubadour and his labor of love', *MedS*, XXXIV (1972), 174–95.

COPPIN, JOSEPH. *Amour et mariage dans la littérature française du Nord an Moyen Âge*. Paris: Librairie d'Argences, 1961.

CRANE, T. F. *Italian Social Customs in the Sixteenth Century* (Cornell Studies in English, 5). New Haven, Conn.: Yale University Press, 1920.

CREMONESI, CARLA. 'Problemi della lirica romanza', in Antonio Viscardi *et al.*, *Preistoria e storia degli studi romanzi*. Milan and Varese: Publ. della Cattedra di Fil. romanza dell'Università degli Studi di Milano, 1955.

CRESCIMBENI, GIOVANNI MARIO. *L'Istoria della volgar poesia*. Rome: Il Chracas, 1698 (rev. edn. 6 vols. Venice: Lorenzo Basegio, 1730–31).

CROSLAND, JESSIE. 'Ovid's contribution to the conception of love known as *L'amour courtois*', *MLR*, XLII (1947), 199–206.

CROSS, TOM PEETE, and NITZE, WILLIAM ALBERT. *Lancelot and Guenevere. A study on the origins of courtly love* (Modern Philology Monographs of the University of Chicago). Chicago, 1930.

CUMMINS, JOHN G. 'Methods and conventions in the fifteenth-century poetic debate', *HR*, XXI (1963), 307–23.

—. 'The survival in the Spanish *Cancioneros* of the form and themes of Provençal and Old French poetic debates', *BHS*, XLII (1965), 9–17.

CURTIUS, ERNST ROBERT. 'The medieval bases of Western thought', lecture delivered in 1949, appendix to *European Literature and the Latin Middle Ages*, trans. W. R. Trask. London: RKP, 1953.

DAHLBERG, CHARLES. 'Love and the *Roman de la Rose*', *Sp*, XLIV (1969), 568–84.

DANIEL, NORMAN. *The Arabs and Mediaeval Europe.* London and Beirut: Longman, 1975.

—. *The Cultural Barrier. Problems in the exchange of ideas.* Edinburgh University Press, 1975.

DANTE ALIGHIERI. *La vita nuova.* Ed. Daniele Mattalia. Turin: G. B. Paravia, 1951.

—. *De vulgari eloquentia.* Ed. Pier Vincenzo Mengaldo. Padua: Editrice Antenore, 1968.

D'ARCY, M. C. *The Mind and Heart of Love. Lion and unicorn: a study in Eros and Agape.* London: Faber & Faber, 1945.

DAVENSON, HENRI [H.-I. Marrou]. *Les Troubadours.* Paris: Éditions du Seuil, 1961.

DAWSON, CHRISTOPHER. 'The origins of the romantic tradition', in *Mediaeval Religion (the Forwood Lectures, 1934) and other Essays.* London: Sheed & Ward, 1935, pp. 121–54.

DEBENEDETTI, SANTORRE. *Gli studi provenzali in Italia nel cinquecento.* Turin: Ermanno Loescher, 1911.

DEFERRARI, HARRY AUSTIN. *The Sentimental Moor in Spanish Literature before 1600* (UPPRLL, 17). Philadelphia, 1927.

DELBOUILLE, MAURICE. 'À propos des origines de la lyrique romane: tradition "populaire" ou tradition "cléricale"', *MRo*, XX (1970), 13–27.

DELÉCLUZE, E. J. *Dante Alighieri, ou la Poésie amoureuse.* Paris: Amyot, 1848.

DEMATS, PAULE. 'D'*Amoenitas* à *Déduit*. André le Chapelain et Guillaume de Lorris' in *Mélanges Jean Frappier.* Geneva: Droz, 1970, I, pp. 217–33.

DENOMY, A. J. 'An inquiry into the origins of Courtly Love', *MedS*, VI (1944), 175–260.

—. '*Fin'Amors*. The pure love of the troubadours, its amorality, and possible source', *MedS*, VII (1945), 139–207.

—. 'The *De amore* of Andreas Capellanus and the condemnation of 1277', *MedS*, VIII (1946), 107–49.

—. *The Heresy of Courtly Love.* New York: MacMullen, 1947.

—. '*Jovens*. The notion of youth among the troubadours, its meaning and source', *MedS*, XI (1949), 1–22.

—. '*Jois* among the early Troubadours. Its meaning and possible source', *MedS*, XIII (1951), 177–217.

—. 'Concerning the accessibility of Arabic influence to the earliest trouba-dours', *MedS*, XV (1953), 147–58.

—. 'Courtly Love and courtliness', *Sp*, XXVIII (1953), 44–63.

DERMENGHEM, ÉMILE. 'Les grands thèmes de la poésie amoureuse chez les arabes précurseurs des poètes d'oc', *CS*, special issue, *Le Génie d'Oc*, Marseilles, 1943, 26–38.

DEROY, JEAN. 'Merce ou la quinta linea Veneris', in *Actes du VIème Congrès de langue et littérature d'Oc et d'études franco-provençales—Montpellier 1970*. Montpellier: Centre d'Estudis Occitans, 1971, II, pp. 309–28.

—. 'Thèmes et termes de la *fin'amor* dans les *Sermones super Cantica* de Bernard de Clairvaux', in *Actes du XIIème Congrès international de linguistique et philologie romanes, Quebec, 1971* (awaiting publication).

DIEZ, FRIEDRICH. *La Poésie des troubadours. Études traduites de l'Allemand et annotées par le baron Ferdinand de Roisin*. Paris: J. Labitte, 1845.

DINAUX, ARTHUR MARTIN. *Trouvères, jongleurs, et ménestrels du Nord de la France et du Midi de la Belgique*. 3 vols. Paris: Téchener, 1837–63.

DIVERRES, A. H. 'Chivalry and *fin'amor* in *Le Chevalier au Lion*', in *Studies in Medieval Literature and Languages in Memory of Frederick Whitehead*. Manchester: MUP, 1973, pp. 91–116.

DODD, WILLIAM G. *Courtly Love in Chaucer and Gower* (Harvard Studies in English, 1). Boston, Mass.: Ginn & Co., 1913.

DONALDSON, E. TALBOT. 'The myth of Courtly Love', in *Speaking of Chaucer*. London: Athlone, 1970, pp. 154–63. First publ. in *Ventures*, V [1965], 16–23.)

DOW, BLANCHE HINMAN. *The Varying Attitude towards Women in French Literature of the Fifteenth Century. The opening years*. New York: Institute of French Studies, 1936.

DRAGONETTI, ROGER. 'Trois motifs de la lyrique courtoise confrontés avec les *Arts d'aimer*', *RGand*, VII (1959), 5–48.

—. *La Technique poétique des trouvères dans la chanson courtoise. Contribution à l'étude de la rhétorique médiévale*. Bruges: De Tempel, 1960.

DRONKE, PETER. *Medieval Latin and the Rise of European Love Lyric*. 2 vols. Oxford: Clarendon, 1965–66.

—. 'Guillaume IX and Courtoisie', *RF*, LXXIII (1961), 327–38.

DUBY, GEORGES. 'Dans la France du Nord-Ouest, au XIIe siècle: les *jeunes* dans la société aristocratique', *AESC*, XIX (1964), 835–46.

DUMITRESCU, MARIA. 'Les premiers troubadours connus et les origines de la poésie provençale', *CCMe*, IX (1966), 345–54.

DUPIN, HENRI. *La Courtoisie au Moyen Âge (d'après les textes du XIIe et du XIIIe siècles)*. Paris: A. Picard, 1931.

DUTTON, BRIAN. '*Lelia doura, edoy lelia doura*, an Arabic refrain in a thirteenth-century Galician poem?', *BHS*, XLI (1964), 1–9.

—. 'Hurí y Midons: el amor cortés y el paraíso musulmán', *Fi*, XIII (1968–69), 151–64.

ECKER, LAWRENCE. *Arabischer, provenzalischer und deutscher Minnesang. Eine motivgeschichtliche Untersuchung.* Berne and Leipzig: Paul Haupt, 1934.

ECONOMOU, GEORGE D. *The Goddess Natura in Medieval Literature.* Cambridge, Mass.: Harvard University Press, 1972.

EQUICOLA, MARIO. *Libro de natura de amore.* Venice: Lorenzo da Portes, 1525.

ERCKMANN, RUDOLF. *Der Einfluss der arabisch-spanischen Kultur auf die Entwicklung des Minnesangs.* Darmstadt: G. L. Künzel, 1933.

ERRANTE, GUIDO. 'Old Provençal poetry. Latin and Arabic influences', *Th*, XX (1945), 305–30.

—. *Marcabru e le fonti sacre dell' antica lirica romanza.* Florence: G. C. Sansoni, 1948.

FABRE D'OLIVET, ANTOINE. *Le Troubadour. Poésies occitaniques du XIIIe siècle, traduites et publiées par Fabre d'Olivet.* 2 vols. Paris: Henrichs, 1803–04.

FARMER, H. G. A. *Historical Facts for the Arabian Musical Influence.* London: William Reeves, 1930.

FARNELL, IDA. *The Lives of the Troubadours, translated from the mediaeval Provençal.* London: David Nutt, 1896.

FAUCHET, CLAUDE. *Recueil de l'origine de la langue et poésie française, ryme et romans, plus les noms et sommaire des oeuvres de CXXVII poètes françois, vivans avant l'an M.CCC.* Paris: Mamert Patisson, 1581.

FAURIEL, CLAUDE. *Histoire de la poésie provençale. Cours fait à la faculté des lettres de Paris par M.F.* [ed. J. Mohl]. 3 vols. Paris: Jules Labitte, 1846.

FERNÁNDEZ PEREIRO, NYDIA G. B. DE. *Originalidad y sinceridad en la poesía de amor trovadoresca.* La Plata (Argentina): Inst. de Filología, 1968.

FERRANTE, JOAN M. *Woman as Image in Medieval Literature.* New York and London: Columbia University Press, 1975.

—. *The Conflict of Love and Honour.* The Hague: Mouton, 1973.

FERRANTE, J. M., G. D. ECONOMOU et al. *In Pursuit of Perfection. Courtly love in medieval literature.* Port Washington, N.Y.: Kennikat Press, 1975.

FERRARESI, ALICIA ROSA C. DE. '*Religio Amoris* en la poesía castellana de la edad media'. Unpubl. Ph.D. thesis. Stanford University, 1973. (*DA*, XXXIV, 5961–A.)

FEUERLICHT, Ignaz. 'Vom Ursprung der Minne', *AR*, XXIII (1939), 140–77.

FIORE, SILVESTRO. *Ueber die Beziehungen zwischen der arabischen und der früh-italienischen Lyrik* (Kölner Romanistische Arbeiten, 8). Cologne, 1956.

—. 'La Tenson en Espagne et en Babylonie. Évolution ou polygenèse?', in *Actes du IVe Congrès international de littérature comparée.* The Hague, 1965, pp. 982–92.

FISHER, JOHN H. 'Tristan and courtly adultery', *CL*, IX (1957), 150–64.

FLACELIÈRE, ROBERT. *Love in Ancient Greece.* Trans. James Cleugh. London: Frederick Muller, 1962.

FLETCHER, JEFFERSON BUTLER. *The Religion of Beauty in Woman, and other essays on platonic love in poetry and society.* New York: Macmillan, 1911.

FOSTER, DAMON S. 'Marie de France: psychologist of Courtly Love', *PMLA*, XLIV (1929), 968–96.

FOSTER, KENELM. *Courtly Love and Christianity* (Aquinas Paper, 39). London: Aquin, 1963.

FORSTER, LEONARD. *The Icy Fire. Five studies in European Petrarchism.* Cambridge: CUP, 1969.

FRANK, DONALD K. 'On the troubadour *fin'amors*', *RoN*, VII (1965–66), 209–17.

—. 'On the troubadour sense of merit', *RoN*, VIII (1966–67), 289–96.

FRANK, GRACE. 'The distant love of Jaufre Rudel', *MLN*, LVII (1942), 528–34.

FRANK, ISTVÁN. 'Poésie romane et Minnesang autour de Frédéric II', *BCSS*, III (1955), 51–83.

—. 'Les débuts de la poésie courtoise en Catalogne et le problème des origines lyriques', in *Actas y Memorias del VII° Congreso internacional de lingüística románica*. University of Barcelona, 1955, I, pp. 181–7.

FRAPPIER, JEAN. 'Vues sur les conceptions courtoises dans les littératures d'oc et d'oïl au XIIe siècle', *CCMe*, II (1959), 135–56.

—. ' "D'amors", "par amors" ', *R*, LXXXVIII (1967), 443–74.

—. 'Sur un procès fait à l'amour courtois' [rev. art. on *The Meaning of Courtly Love*, ed. F. X. Newman], *R*, XCIII (1972), 145–93.

—. *Amour courtois et table ronde* (PRF, 126). Geneva: Droz, 1973.

—. 'Notes lexicologiques: I. *Gole*. II. *Amour courtois*', in *Mélanges Jean Boutière*. Liège: Éditions Soledi, 1971, I, pp. 233–52.

FRIEDMAN, LIONEL J. 'Gradus amoris', *RPh*, XIX (1965–66), 167–77.

FRINGS, THEODOR. *Minnesinger und Troubadours* (Deutsche Akademie der Wissenschaften zu Berlin Vorträge und Schriften, 34). Berlin, 1949.

—. *Die Anfänge der europäischen Liebes-Dichtung im 11. und 12. Jahrhundert.* Munich: Bayerischen Akademie der Wissenschaften, 1960.

GABRIELI, FRANCESCO. 'La poesia araba e le letterature occidentali', *Bel*, IX (1954), 377–86; 510–20.

—. 'Islam in the Mediterranean world', in *The Legacy of Islam*, ed. Joseph Schacht and C. E. Bosworth. Oxford: Clarendon, 1974, pp. 63–104.

GALPIN, S. L. *Cortois and Vilain. A study of the distinctions made between them by the French and Provençal poets of the twelfth, thirteenth and fourteenth centuries.* New Haven, Conn.: Ryder's Printing House, 1905.

GALVANI, GIOVANNI. *Osservazioni sulla poesia de'trovatori e sulle principali maniere e forme di essa confrontate brevemente colle antiche Italiane.* Modena: Eredi Soliani, 1829.

GANZ, P. F. 'The *cancionerillo mozárabe* and the origin of the Middle High German *Frauenlied*', *MLR*, XLVIII (1953), 301–9.

GARCÍA GÓMEZ, EMILIO. 'La lírica hispanoárabe y la aparición de la lírica románica', *And*, XXI (1956), 303–38. (French translation in *Arab*, V [1958], 113–44.)

GASELEE, SIR STEPHEN. 'The soul in the kiss', *Criterion*, II (1923–24), 349–59.

—. *The Transition from the Late Latin Love Lyric to the Medieval Love Poem. Being the substance of three lectures delivered at the University of Cambridge on the J. H. Gray Foundation.* Cambridge: Bowes & Bowes, 1931.

GAY, JULES. *Bibliographie des ouvrages relatifs à l'amour, aux femmes, au mariage* . . . 4th edn., rev. by J. Lemonnyer. 4 vols, Paris: Lemonnyer, 1894–1900.

GAY-CROSIER, RAYMOND. *Religious Elements in the Secular Lyrics of the Troubadours* (UNCSRLL, 111). Chapel Hill, N.C., 1971.

GÉGOU, FABIENNE. 'Un "arthurien" convaincu: Jean Chapelain', in *Mélanges Jean Frappier*. Geneva: Droz, 1970, I, pp. 329–35.

GÉLIS, FRANÇOIS DE. *Histoire critique de l'Académie des Jeux Floraux depuis leur origine jusqu'à leur transformation en Académie (1323–1694)* (Bibliothèque Méridionale, 2nd series, 15). Toulouse University, 1912.

GETTY, AGNES K. 'Chaucer's changing conceptions of the humble lover', *PMLA*, XLIV (1929), 202–16.

GIBB, H. A. R. 'Literature', in *The Legacy of Islam*, ed. Sir Thomas Arnold and Alfred Guillaume. Oxford: Clarendon, 1931, pp. 180–209.

—. 'The influence of Islamic culture on medieval Europe', *BJRL*, XXXVIII (1955–56), 82–98.

GIBSON, M. CARL. 'Background to the theory of Arabic origins', *BYUS*, IV (1962), 219–34.

GIFFEN, LOIS ANITA. *Theory of Profane Love among the Arabs. The development of the genre* (New York University Studies in Near Eastern Civilization, 3). New York University Press, 1971; University of London Press, 1972.

GILLESPIE, GERALD. 'Origins of Romance lyrics. A review of research', *YCGL*, XVI (1967), 16–32.

GILSON, ÉTIENNE. 'Saint Bernard and Courtly Love', Appendix IV in *The Mystical Theology of Saint Bernard*, trans. A. H. C. Downes. London and New York: Sheed & Ward, 1940 (French original, Paris, 1934).

GINGUENÉ, PIERRE LOUIS. *Histoire littéraire d'Italie*. 14 vols. Revised edn., Paris: L. G. Michaud, 1824–35.

GIST, MARGARET ADLUM. *Love and War in the Middle English Romances*. Philadelphia: University of Pennsylvania Press; London: OUP, 1947.

GOLDIN, FREDERICK. *The Mirror of Narcissus in the Courtly Love Lyric*. Ithaca, N.Y.: Cornell University Press, 1967.

GOLDSCHMIDT, LOTHAR. *Die Doktrin der Liebe bei den italiänischen Lyrikern der 13. Jahrhunderts. Inaugural Dissertation*. Breslau: Wilhelm Koebner, 1889.

GOMBRICH, E. H. 'Huizinga and *Homo Ludens*', *TLS*, 4 October, 1974, 1083–9.

GONZÁLEZ PALENCIA, ÁNGEL. 'El amor platónico en la corte de los califas', *Boletín de la Real Academia de Ciencias, Bellas Letras y Nobles Artes de Córdoba*, 1929, 1–25.

—. *Influencia de la civilización árabe. Discursos leídos ante la Academia de la Historia*. Madrid, 1931 (repr. as *El Islam y Occidente*, Madrid [Tip. de Archivos], 1931).

—. 'Posición de Arteaga en la polémica sobre música y poesía arábigas', *And*, XI (1946), 241–5.

— and EUGENIO MELE. *La Maya. Notas para su estudio en España* (Biblioteca de Tradiciones Populares, 7). Madrid, 1944.

GORCY, G. '"Courtois" et "courtoisie" d'après quelques textes du Moyen Français', *BJR*, IV (1961), 15–25.

GORDON, IDA L. *The Double Sorrow of Troilus. A study of ambiguities in 'Troilus and Criseyde'*. Oxford: Clarendon, 1970.

GORRA, EGIDIO. *Fra drammi e poemi. Saggi e ricerche*. Milan: U. Hoepli, 1900.

—. 'Origini, spiriti e forme della poesia amorosa di Provenza', *RIL*, II, xliii, 14; xlv, 3 (1910–12).

GORTON, T. J. 'Arabic influence on the troubadours. Documents and directions', *JAL*, V (1974), 11–16.

GOUGENHEIM, GEORGES. 'Poésie arabe et poésie occidentale au Moyen Âge', *Crit*, XIII (1957), No. 218, 213–20.

GOURMONT, RÉMY DE. *Dante, Béatrice et la poésie amoureuse. Essai sur l'idéal féminin en Italie à la fin du XIIIe siècle*. Paris: Société du Mercure de France, 1908. (First publ. *RML*, VI [1885], 451 ff.)

GRAVES, ROBERT. 'The word "romantic"', in *Poetic Craft and Principle*. London: Cassell, 1967, pp. 183–95.

—. *The White Goddess. A historical grammar of poetic myth*. London: Faber & Faber, 1961.

GREEN, OTIS H. 'Courtly Love in the Spanish *Cancioneros*', *PMLA*, LXIV (1949), 247–301, or in *The Literary Mind of Medieval and Renaissance Spain*. Lexington: University of Kentucky Press, 1970.

—. *Courtly Love in Quevedo* (University of Colorado Studies. Series in Language and Literature, 3). Boulder, Col., 1952.

GRIMM, CHARLES. 'Chrestien de Troyes's attitude towards woman', *RR*, XVI (1925), 236–43.

GRISAY, A., LAVIS, G., and DUBOIS-STASSE, M. *Les Dénominations de la femme dans les anciens textes littéraires français*. Gembloux: J. Duculot, 1969.

GRUNEBAUM, GUSTAVE E. VON. 'Avicenna's *Risâla fi'l-'išq* and Courtly Love', *JNES*, XI (1952), 233–8.

—. '"Lírica romanica" before the Arab conquest', *And*, XXI (1956), 403–5.

GUIETTE, ROBERT. 'D'une poésie formelle en France au Moyen Âge', *RGand*, VIII (1960), 9–32.

GUIRAUD, PIERRE. 'Les structures étymologiques du *trobar*', *P*, II (1971), 417–26.

GUNN, A. M. F. *The Mirror of Love. A reinterpretation of 'The Romance of the Rose'*. Lubbock: Texas Tech. Press, 1952.

HACKETT, W. M. 'Le problème de *midons*', in *Mélanges Jean Boutière*. Liège: Éditions Soledi, 1971, pp. 285–94.

HAMMER-PÜRGSTALL, J. VON. 'Sur la chevalerie des arabes antérieure à celle d'Europe, sur l'influence de la première à la seconde', *JA*, IV (1849), 1–14.

—. 'Sur les passages relatifs à la chevalerie chez les historiens arabes', *JA*, V (1855), 282–90.

HANNING, ROBERT W. 'The social significance of twelfth-century chivalric romance', *MH*, n.s., III (1972), 3–29.

HARDEN, A. ROBERT. 'The element of love in the *Chansons de geste*', *AnMed*, V (1964), 65–80.

HATTO, ARTHUR T. (ed.). *Eos. An enquiry into the theme of lovers' meetings and partings at dawn in poetry*. The Hague: Mouton, 1965.

HEER, FRIEDRICH. 'Courtly Love and courtly literature', in *The Medieval World. Europe, 1100–1350*, trans. Janet Sondheimer. London: Sphere Books, 1974, pp. 153–92 (first edn. 1962).

HEERS, JACQUES. *Fêtes, jeux, et joutes*. Montreal: Institut des Études Médiévales, 1971.

HEGER, KLAUS. *Die bisher veröffentlichten Ḥarǧas und ihre Deutungen* (BZRP, 101). Tübingen, 1960.

HENRIOT, JACQUES. *Le Jeu*. Paris: PUF, 1969.

HOEPFFNER, ERNEST. *Les Troubadours dans leur vie et dans leurs œuvres*. Paris: A. Colin, 1955.

HOLMAN, C. HUGH. 'Courtly Love in the Merchant's and Franklin's Tales', *ELH*, XVIII (1951), 241–52.

HOLZKNECHT, KARL JULIUS. *Literary Patronage in the Middle Ages*. London: Frank Cass, 1966 (first publ. 1923).

HOUDOY, JULES. *La Beauté des femmes dans la littérature et dans l'art du XIIe au XVIe siècle. Analyse du livre de A. Niphus 'Du Beau et de l'Amour'*. Paris: A. Aubry, 1876.

HOWARD, DONALD R. *The Three Temptations. Medieval man in search of the world*. Princeton University Press, 1966.

HUEFFER, FRANCIS. *The Troubadours. A history of Provençal life and literature in the Middle Ages*. London: Chatto & Windus, 1878.

HUET, PIERRE-DANIEL. *Lettre-traité de Pierre-Daniel Huet sur l'origine des romans. Édition du tricentenaire, 1669–1969. Suivie de la Lecture des vieux romans par Jean Chapelain*. Ed. Fabienne Gégou. Paris: A.-G. Nizet, 1971 ('De l'origine des romains', prefixed to Reynauld de Segrais, *Zayde. Histoire espagnol*, 1671).

HUIZINGA, JOHAN. *The Waning of the Middle Ages. A study of the forms of life, thought and art in France and the Netherlands in the fourteenth and fifteenth centuries*. Trans. F. Hopman. Harmondsworth: Penguin, 1955 (first edn. 1924).

——. *Homo Ludens. A study of the play element in culture*. Trans. George Steiner. London: Paladin, 1970 (prepared from German edition of 1944).

——. *Men and Ideas. History, the Middle Ages, the Renaissance*. Trans. James S. Holmes and Hans van Marle. New York and London: Harper & Row, 1970.

HUSSEIN, HASSAN SOLEIMAN. 'The Koran and Courtly Love. A study of the Koran and its influence on the development of divine and courtly love'. Unpubl. Ph.D. thesis. University of Southern California, 1971. (*DA*, XXXII, 3254-A.)

IBN DĀWŪD AL-IṢFAHĀNĪ, MUḤAMMAD. *Kitāb al-Zahra*. Ed. A. R. Nykl and Ibrāhīm Tūqān (Studies in Ancient Oriental Civilization, 6). Chicago: University of Chicago Press, 1932.

IBN ḤAZM ('Ali Ibn Aḥmad). *The Ring of the Dove. A treatise on the art and practice of Arab love*. Trans. A. J. Arberry. London: Luzac, 1953.

—. *El collar de la paloma*. *Tratado sobre el amor y los amantes*. Trans. Emilio García Gómez; prologue by José Ortega y Gasset. Madrid: Rivadeneyra, 1952.

IGLY, FRANCE. *Troubadours et trouvères* (Collection Melior). Paris: Seghers, 1960.

IMBS, PAUL J. 'De la *fin'amor*', *CCMe*, XII (1969), 265–85.

IVENTOSCH, HERMAN. 'Cervantes and Courtly Love. The Grisóstomo–Marcela episode of *Don Quixote*', *PMLA*, LXXXIX (1974), 64–76.

JACKSON, W. T. H. 'The *De amore* of Andreas Capellanus and the practice of love at court', *RR*, XLIX (1958), 243–51.

—. *The Literature of the Middle Ages*. New York: Columbia University Press, 1960.

—. 'Faith Unfaithful. The German reaction to Courtly Love', in *The Meaning of Courtly Love*, ed. F. X. Newman, Albany, N.Y., 1968, pp. 55–76.

—. *The Anatomy of Love. The Tristan of Gottfried von Strassburg*. New York: Columbia University Press, 1971.

JEANROY, ALFRED. *Les Origines de la poésie lyrique en France au Moyen Âge*. Paris: Hachette, 1889.

—. 'Les études provençales du XVIe siècle au milieu du XIXe siècle', *AMid*, XLIII (1931), 129–59.

—. *La Poésie lyrique des troubadours*. 2 vols. Toulouse and Paris: Édouard Privat, 1934.

JODOGNE, OMER. 'Encore sur l'origine arabe de la poésie provençale', *LR*, IV (1950), 237–8.

JONES, DAVID J. *La Tenson provençale*. Paris: Droz, 1934.

JONES, ROSEMARIE. *The Theme of Love in the 'Romans d'Antiquité'* (Modern Humanities Research Association Dissertation Series, 5). London, 1972.

JONES, R. O. 'Isabel la Católica y el amor cortés', *RLit*, XXI (1962), 55–64.

KELLY, AMY. 'Eleanor of Aquitaine and her courts of love', *Sp*, XII (1937), 3–19.

—. *Eleanor of Aquitaine and the Four Kings*. London: Cassell, 1952.

KELLY, DOUGLAS. 'Courtly Love in perspective. The hierarchy of love in Andreas Capellanus', *Trad*, XXIV (1968), 119–48.

KELLY, HENRY ANSGAR. *Love and Marriage in the Age of Chaucer*. Ithaca, N.Y., and London: Cornell University Press, 1975.

KELSO, RUTH. *Doctrine for the Lady of the Renaissance*. Urbana: University of Illinois Press, 1956.

KILGOUR, R. L. *The Decline of Chivalry, as shown in the French Literature of the Late Middle Ages* (HSRL, 12). Cambridge, Mass., 1937 (see pp. 108–94).

KIRBY, THOMAS A. *Chaucer's Troilus. A study in courtly love* (Louisiana State University Studies, 39). Baton Rouge, La., 1940.

KOENIGSBERG, RICHARD A. 'Culture and unconscious fantasy. Observations on Courtly Love', *PsR*, LIV (1967), 36–50.

KÖHLER, ERICH. *Trobadorlyrik und höfischer Roman. Aufsätze zur französischen und provenzalischen Literatur des Mittelalters* (NBL, 15). Berlin, 1962.

—. 'Observations historiques et sociologiques sur la poésie des troubadours', *CCMe*, VII (1964), 27–51.

—. 'Sens et fonction du terme *jeunesse* dans la poésie des troubadours', in *Mélanges René Crozet*. Poitiers: Société d'Études Médiévales, 1966, I, pp. 569–83.

—. 'Lés troubadours et la jalousie', in *Mélanges Jean Frappier*. Geneva: Droz, 1970, I, pp. 543–59.

KOLB, HERBERT. *Der Begriff der Minne und das Entstehen der höfischen Lyrik* (Her, n.s., 4). Tübingen: Niemeyer, 1958.

KRÁSA, JOSEF. *Die Handschriften König Wenzels IV*. Prague: Odeon, 1971.

LAFITTE-HOUSSAT, JACQUES. *Troubadours et Cours d'amour* ('Que sais-je?'). Paris: PUF, 1950.

LAMPILLAS, XAVIER. *Saggio storico-apologetico della letteratura spagnuola contro le pregiudicate opinioni di alcuni moderni scrittori italiani*. 6 vols. Genoa: Presso F. Repetto, 1778–81 (Spanish translation by Doña Josefa Amar y Borbón, 7 vols, Madrid, 1789).

LAPESA, RAFAEL. '¿Amor cortés o parodia? A propósito de la primitiva lírica de Castilla', *EstRom*, IX (1962), 11–14.

LAURIE, HELEN C. R. '*Eneas* and the doctrine of Courtly Love', *MLR*, LXIV (1969), 283–94.

LAVIS, GEORGES. *L'Expression de l'affectivité dans la poésie lyrique française du Moyen Âge (XIIe–XIIIe siècles). Étude sémantique et stylistique du réseau lexical 'joie-dolor'* (Bibliothèque de la Faculté de Philosophie et Lettres de l'Université de Liège, 200). Paris: Les Belles Lettres, 1972.

LAWLOR, JOHN (ed.). *Patterns of Love and Courtesy. Essays in memory of C. S. Lewis*. London: Arnold, 1966.

LAWNER, LYNNE. 'Marcabrun and the origins of *Trobar clus*', in *The Mediaeval World*, ed. David Daiches and Anthony Thorlby. London: Aldus, 1973, pp. 485–523.

LAZAR, MOSHÉ. *Amour courtois et 'fin'amors' dans la littérature du XIIe siècle*. Paris: Klincksieck, 1964.

LE GENTIL, PIERRE. *La Poésie lyrique espagnole et portugaise à la fin du Moyen Âge*. 2 vols. Rennes: Plihon, 1949–52.

—. *Le Virelai et le villancico. Le problème des origines arabes* (Collection Portugaise, 9). Paris: Les Belles Lettres, 1954.

—. 'La strophe zadjalesque, les khardjas, et le problème des origines du lyrisme roman', *R*, LXXXIV (1963), 1–27; 209–50.

LEGGE, M. DOMINICA. 'The lyric and its background', in *Anglo-Norman Literature and its Background*. Oxford: Clarendon, 1963, pp. 332–61.

LEGRAND D'AUSSY, P. J. B. *Observations sur les troubadours*. Paris: E. Onfroy, 1781.

LEHMANN, ANDRÉE. *Le Rôle de la femme dans l'histoire de France au Moyen Âge*. Paris: Berger-Levrault, 1952.

LEJEUNE, RITA. 'Rôle littéraire d'Aliénor d'Aquitaine et de sa famille', *CN*, XIV (1954), 5–57.

LEMAY, RICHARD. 'A propos de l'origine arabe de l'art des troubadours', *AESC*, XXI (1966), 990–1011.

LESAFFRE, JEAN and CLUZEL, IRÉNÉE MARCEL. *Bibliographie occitane, 1957–66.* Paris: Les Belles Lettres, 1969.

LEUBE-FEY, CHRISTIANE. *Bild und Funktion der 'dompna' in der Lyrik der Trobadors* (Studia Romanica, 21). Heidelberg: Carl Winter, 1971.

LÉVI-PROVENÇAL, ÉVARISTE. 'Poésie arabe d'Espagne et poésie d'Europe médiévale', in *Islam d'Occident. Études d'histoire médiévale* (Islam d'hier et d'aujourd'hui, 7). Paris: G. P. Maisonneuve, 1948, pp. 283–304.

—. 'Les vers arabes de la chanson V de Guillaume IX d'Aquitaine', *Arab*, I (1954), 208–11.

LEWIS, CHARLES BERTRAM. 'A ritual formula in troubadour poetry', *ZRP*, L (1930), 595–8.

—. 'The *Aguilaneuf* and *Trimazo* begging songs and their origin', in *A Miscellany of Studies in Romance Languages and Literatures, presented to Leon E. Kastner*, ed. Mary Williams and James A. de Rothschild. Cambridge: W. Heffer & Sons, 1932, pp. 308–41.

—. 'Survivals of a pagan cult. The loved one far away', *The Proceedings of the Scottish Anthropological Society*, I (1934), 7–32.

LEWIS, C. S. *The Allegory of Love. A study in medieval tradition.* Oxford: Clarendon, 1936.

LIDA DE MALKIEL, MARÍA ROSA. 'La dama como obra maestra de Dios', *RPh*, XXVIII (1974–75), 267–324.

LI GOTTI, ETTORE. *La 'tesi araba' sulle 'origini' della lirica romanza.* Palermo: Sansoni Antiquariato, 1955.

LOLLIS, CESARE DE. *Poesie provenzali sulla genesi d'amore* (Biblioteca Neolatina, 5). Rome: Libreria di scienze e lettere, 1927.

LOMBA FUENTES, JOAQUÍN. 'La beauté objective chez Ibn Ḥazm', *CCMe*, VII (1964), 1–18; 161–78.

LOT-BORODINE, MYRRHA. 'Sur les origines et les fins du *service d'amour*', in *Mélanges Alfred Jeanroy*. Paris: Droz, 1928, pp. 223–42.

—. *De l'amour profane à l'amour sacré.* Paris: Nizet, 1961.

LOWES, JOHN LIVINGSTON. 'The Loveres Maladye of Hereos', *MP*, XI (1913–14), 491–546.

LÜDERITZ, ANNA. *Die Liebestheorie der Provençalen bei den Minnesingern der Stauferzeit. Eine literarhistorische Untersuchung* (Literarhistorische Forschungen, 29). Berlin and Leipzig: Emil Felber, 1904.

MACKAIL, J. W. *Lectures on Poetry.* New York, Bombay and Calcutta: Longmans Green & Co., 1914.

MANNING, STEPHEN. 'Game and earnest in the Middle English and Provençal love lyrics', *CL*, XVIII (1966), 225–41.

MARCUSE, HERBERT. *Eros and Civilization. A philosophical inquiry into Freud* (Humanitas: Beacon Studies in Humanities). Boston, Mass.: Beacon Press, 1955.

MARGONI, IVOS. *Fin'amors, mezura e cortezia. Saggio sulla lirica provenzale del XII secolo*. Milan and Varese: Istituto Editoriale Cisalpino, 1965.

MARKALE, JEAN. *Women of the Celts*. Trans. A. Mygind, C. Hauch and P. Henry. London: Gordon Cremonesi, 1975 (French original, Paris: Payot, 1972).

MARROU, H.-I. 'Au dossier de l'amour courtois', *RMAL*, III (1947), 81–9.

MARTIN, JUNE HALL. *Love's Fools. Aucassin, Troilus, Calisto and the Parody of the Courtly Lover*. London: Tamesis, 1972.

MATHEW, GERVASE. 'Marriage and *amour courtois* in late fourteenth-century England', in *Essays Presented to Charles Williams*. London, New York and Toronto: OUP, 1947, pp. 128–35.

MEADER, WILLIAM G. *Courtship in Shakespeare. Its relation to the tradition of courtly love*. New York: King's Crown Press, 1954.

MÉNARD, PHILIPPE. *Le Rire et le sourire dans le roman courtois en France au Moyen Âge, 1150–1250* (PRF, 105). Geneva: Droz, 1969.

MENÉNDEZ PIDAL, RAMÓN. *Poesía árabe y poesía europea*. Madrid: Austral, 1941.

—. 'La primitiva lírica europea. Estado actual del problema', *RFE*, XLIII (1960), 279–354.

MÉRAY, ANTONY. *La Vie au temps des Cours d'Amour. Croyances, usages, et mœurs intimes des XIe, XIIe & XIIIe siècles*. Paris: A. Claudin, 1876.

MERRILL, RODNEY HARPSTER. 'Formal elements in the late medieval Courtly Love lyric'. Unpubl. Ph.D. thesis. Stanford University, 1970. (See section on Courtly Love as game, pp. 222–397; *DA*, XXXI, 4172–A.)

MEYER, PAUL. 'De l'influence des troubadours sur la poésie des peuples romans', *R*, V (1876), 257–68.

—. 'Des rapports de la poésie des trouvères avec celle des troubadours', *R*, XIX (1890), 1–62.

MILLÁS VALLICROSA, J. M. 'Influencia de la poesía popular hispanomusulmana en la poesía italiana', *RABM*, XLI (1920), 550–64; and XLII (1921), 37–59.

MILLER, DAVID L. *God and Games. Towards a theology of play*. New York: World Publishing Co., 1970.

MOLLER, HERBERT. 'The social causation of the Courtly Love complex', *CSSH*, I (1958–59), 137–63.

—. 'The meaning of Courtly Love', *JAF*, LXXIII (1960), 39–52.

MOLTMANN, JÜRGEN. *Theology of Play*. Trans. Reinhard Ulrich. New York, San Fransisco and London: Harper & Row, 1972.

MONROE, JAMES T. 'The muwashshaḥāt', in *Collected Studies in Honour of Américo Castro's Eightieth Year*. Oxford: Lincombe Lodge, 1965, pp. 335–71.

—. *Islam and the Arabs in Spanish Scholarship* (*Sixteenth Century to the Present*). Leiden: Brill, 1970.

—. 'Formulaic diction and the common origins of Romance lyric traditions', *HR*, XLIII (1975), 341–50.

MOORE, JOHN C. 'Love in twelfth-century France. A failure in synthesis', *Trad*, XXIV (1968), 429–43.

MOORE, O. H. 'Jaufré Rudel and the Lady of dreams', *PMLA*, XXIX (1914), 543–54.

156   *The Origin and Meaning of Courtly Love*

MOORMAN, CHARLES. 'Courtly Love in Chaucer', *ELH*, XXVII (1960), 163–73.

MORÈRE, M. 'Les données historiques de l'influence de la poésie andalouse sur la poésie lyrique des troubadours', in *Annales de l'Institut d'Études Occitanes*. Toulouse, 1951, pp. 48–60.

MOREWEDGE, ROSMARIE THEE (ed.) *The Role of Woman in the Middle Ages*. Albany: State University of New York Press, 1975.

MORRALL, JOHN B. 'Lords, ladies, land and people', in *The Medieval Imprint. The founding of the Western European tradition*. London: A. C. Watts, 1967, pp. 86–120.

MOTT, LEWIS FREEMAN. *The System of Courtly Love studied as an introduction to the Vita Nuova of Dante*. Boston and London: Ginn & Co., 1896.

MUÑOZ SENDINO, JOSÉ. *La escala de Mahoma. Traducción del árabe al castellano, latín y francés, ordenada por Alfonso X el sabio*. Madrid: Ministerio de Asuntos Exteriores, 1949.

MUSCATINE, CHARLES. *Chaucer and the French Tradition. A study in style and meaning*. Berkeley, Los Angeles and London: University of California Press, 1957.

NARDI, BRUNO. 'Filosofia dell'amore nei rimatori italiani del Duecento e in Dante', in *Dante e la cultura medievale* (Biblioteca di cultura moderna, 368). Bari: Laterza, 1949, pp. 1–92.

—. 'L'amore e i medici medievali', in *Studi in onore di Angelo Monteverdi*. Modena: Società tip. editrice modenese, 1959, II, pp. 517–42.

NAVARRO GONZÁLEZ, ALBERTO. *El amor en la literatura medieval castellana*. Santa Cruz de Tenerife, 1962.

NEILSON, WILLIAM ALLAN. *The Origins and Sources of the Court of Love* (HUSNPL, 6). Boston, Mass.: Ginn & Co., 1899.

—. 'The purgatory of cruel beauties', *R*, XXIX (1900), 85–93.

NELLI, RENÉ. *De l'amour provençal*. Toulouse: Editions I.E.O., 1951.

—. *L'Amour et les mythes du cœur*. Paris: Hachette, 1952.

—. 'L'amour et la poésie' and 'Amour courtois, amour chevaleresque', in *Les Troubadours. Le trésor poétique de l'Occitanie*. Bruges: Desclée de Brouwer, 1960–66, II, pp. 9–27; 337–56.

—. *L'Érotique des troubadours* (Bibliothèque Méridionale, 2nd series, 38). Toulouse: É. Privat, 1963.

NELSON, JOHN CHARLES. *Renaissance Theory of Love. The context of Giordano Bruno's 'Eroici furori'*. New York: Colombia University Press, 1958.

NEUMEISTER, SEBASTIAN. *Das Spiel mit der höfischen Liebe. Das altprovenzalische Partimen* (Beihefte zur *Poetica*, 5). Munich: Fink, 1969.

NEWMAN, F. X. (ed.). *The Meaning of Courtly Love*. Albany: State University of New York Press, 1968 [reviewed by: C. Muscatine, *Sp*, XLVI (1971), 749–50; J. M. Ferrante, *RR*, LXIII (1972), 42–3; J. Frappier, *R*, XCIII (1972), 145–93].

NICHOLS, STEPHEN G., Jr. 'Towards an aesthetic of the Provençal *Canso*', in *The Disciplines of Criticism. Essays in literary theory, interpretation and history honoring René Wellek*, ed. P. Demetz, T. M. Greene and L. Nelson, Jr. New Haven, Conn., and London: Yale University Press, 1968, pp. 349–74.

——. 'The medieval lyric and its public', *MH*, III (1972), 133–53.

NOSTREDAME, JEAN DE. *Les Vies des plus célèbres et anciens poètes provençaux*. Ed. Camille Chabaneau; introd. Joseph Anglade. Paris: H. Champion, 1913 (first edn., Lyons: A. Marsilii, 1575).

NYKL, A. R. 'L'influence arabe-andalouse sur les troubadours', *BH*, XLI (1939), 305–15.

——. *Troubadour Studies. A critical survey of recent books published in this field*. Cambridge, Mass., 1944.

——. *Hispano-Arabic Poetry and its Relations with the Old Provençal Troubadours*. Baltimore, Md.: publ. by author, 1946.

OMER HALEBY ABOU OTHMAN. *El ktab des lois secrètes de l'amour d'après le khôdja d'O. H. Abou O*. Trans. and ed. by Paul de Régla. Paris: G. Carré, 1893.

ORTEGA Y GASSET, JOSÉ. *On Love . . . aspects of a single theme*. Trans. Toby Talbot. London: Jonathan Cape, 1967 (first edn. 1941).

OWEN, D. D. R. *Noble Lovers*. London: Phaidon, 1975.

PAGÈS, AMÉDÉE. 'Le thème de la tristesse amoureuse en France et en Espagne du XIVe au XVe siècle', *R*, LVIII (1932), 29–43.

PAGET, VIOLET [Vernon Lee]. 'Mediaeval love', in *Euphorion, being Studies of the Antique and the Mediaeval in the Renaissance*. 2 vols. London: T. Fisher Unwin, 1884, II, pp. 123–217.

PAINTER, SIDNEY. *French Chivalry. Chivalric ideas and practices in mediaeval France*. Baltimore, Md.: Johns Hopkins University Press, 1940.

PALERMO, J. 'La poésie provençale à la cour de Frédéric II de Sicile', *RLR*, LXXVIII (1969), 71–82.

PARIS, GASTON. 'Lancelot du Lac, II. *Le Conte de la Charrette*', *R*, XII (1883), 459–534.

——. 'Les origines de la poésie lyrique en France', *JS*, November–December 1891, 674–88 and 729–42; March–July 1892, 155–67 and 407–30. (Repr. in G. Paris, *Mélanges de littérature française du Moyen Âge*, ed. Mario Roques. Paris: H. Champion, 1912, pp. 539–615.)

PARMISANO, STANLEY ANTHONY. 'A study of the relationship between the attitudes toward love and marriage in late fourteenth- and early fifteenth-century English poetry and contemporary ecclesiastical teaching on these topics'. Unpubl. Ph.D. thesis. Cambridge University, 1969–70.

PATERSON, LINDA M. *Troubadours and Eloquence*. Oxford: Clarendon, 1975.

PAYEN, JEAN-CHARLES. *Les Origines de la courtoisie dans la littérature française médiévale* (Centre de Documentation Universitaire). 2 parts, Paris, 1966–67.

PEARSON, LU EMILY. *Elizabethan Love Conventions*. Berkeley, Cal.: University of California Press, 1933.

PELLEGRINI, SILVIO. *Studi su trove e trovatori della prima lirica ispano-portoghese*. Turin: Giuseppe Gambino, 1937 (revised edn., Bari: Adriatica, 1959).

—. 'Intorno al vassallaggio d'amore nei primi trovatori', *CN*, IV–V (1944–45), 21–36.

PERELLA, NICOLAS J. *The Kiss Sacred and Profane. An interpretative history of kiss symbolism and related religio-erotic themes*. Berkeley and Los Angeles: University of California Press, 1969.

PÉRÈS, HENRI. *La Poésie andalouse en arabe classique au XIe siècle* (Publications de l'Institut des études orientales, Faculté des Lettres d'Alger, 5). Paris, 1937.

—. 'La poésie arabe d'Andalousie et ses relations possibles avec la poésie des troubadours', *CS*, special issue, *L'Islam et L'Occident*, Marseilles, 1947, pp. 107–30.

PIAGET, ARTHUR. 'La Cour amoureuse dite de Charles VI', *R*, XX (1891), 417–54.

—. 'Un manuscrit de la Cour amoureuse de Charles VI', *R*, XXXI (1902), 597–602.

PICCOLO, FRANCESCO. *Arte e poesia dei trovatori*. Naples: R. Ricciardi, 1938.

PIERREFEU, N. DE. 'À propos des "Fidèles d'amour"', *CEC*, VIII, 31 (1957), 142–9.

PILLET, A., and CARSTENS, H. *Bibliographie der Troubadours*. Halle: Max Niemeyer Verlag, 1933.

PIROT, F. 'L'"Ideologie" des troubadours. Examen de travaux récents', *MA*, LXXIV (1968), 301–31.

PITANGUE, F. *Les Troubadours furent-ils les missionnaires de l'Albigéisme?* Toulouse, 1946.

POIRION, DANIEL. *Le Poète et le prince. L'évolution du lyrisme courtois de Guillaume de Machaut à Charles d'Orléans* (Université de Grenoble. Publications de la Faculté des Lettres et Sciences Humaines, 35). Paris, 1965.

POLLMANN, LEO. 'Trobar clus'. *Bibelexegese und hispano-arabische literatur* (Forschungen zur Romanischen Philologie, 16). Münster, 1965.

—. *Die Liebe in der hochmittelalterlichen Literatur Frankreichs. Versuch einer historischen Phänomenologie* (Analecta Romanica, 18). Frankfurt: Klostermann, 1966.

PONSAN, GUILLAUME DE. *Histoire de l'Académie des Jeux Floraux dans laquelle on examine tout ce que contient d'historique l'antique Registre de la Compagnie des Sept Trobadors ou Poètes de Toulouse*. Toulouse, 1764–69.

POOLE, ROBERT HAWKINS. 'Women in early Spanish literature, with special emphasis on the women in the medieval Spanish ballads'. Unpubl. Ph.D. thesis. Stanford University, 1949. (Vestiges of a primitive matriarchy; see *Stanford Abstracts*, 1949–50, 235–8.)

POUND, EZRA. 'Psychology and the troubadours', in *The Spirit of Romance*. Rev. edn., London: Peter Owen, 1952, pp. 87–100.

POWER, EILEEN. 'The position of women', in *The Legacy of the Middle Ages*, ed. C. G. Crump and E. F. Jacob. Oxford: Clarendon, 1926, pp. 401–33 (repr. 1962).

—. *Medieval Women*. Ed. M. M. Postan. Cambridge University Press, 1975.

PRESS, A. R. 'La strophe printanière chez les troubadours et les poètes latins du Moyen Âge', *RLLO*, XII–XIII (1962–63), 70–8.

—. 'The adulterous nature of *fin'amors*. A re-examination of the theory', *FMLS*, VI (1970), 327–41.

—. 'Amour courtois, amour adultère?', in *Actes du VIème Congrès International de Langue et Littérature d'Oc et d'Études franco-provençales, Montpellier 1970*. Montpellier: Centre d'Estudis Occitans, 1971, II, pp. 435–42.

PRESTAGE, EDGAR (ed.). *Chivalry. A series of studies to illustrate its historical significance and civilizing influence*. London: Kegan Paul, 1928.

PRESTON, HARRIET W. *Troubadours and Trouvères*. Boston, Mass.: Roberts Brothers, 1876.

QUADRIO, FRANCESCO SAVERIO. *Della storia e della ragione d'ogni poesia*. 5 vols. Bologna and Milan: F. Pisarri, 1739–52.

RAHN, OTTO. *Kreuzzug gegen den Gral. Die Tragödie des Katharismus*. Freiburg, 1933.

RAHNER, HUGO. *Man at Play, or, did you ever practise eutrapelia?* (Compass Books, 8). Trans. Brian Battershaw and Edward Quinn. London: Burns & Oates, 1965.

RAJNA, PIO. *Le Corti d'Amore*. Milan: U. Hoepli, 1890.

RAYNOUARD, FRANÇOIS. *Choix des poésies originales des Troubadours*. 6 vols. Paris: Impr. de Didot, 1816–21.

RECKZEH, ERICH. *Beiträge zur Entwicklungsgeschichte der Frauenideals in der französischen Literatur am Ausgang des Mittelalters. Inaugural-Dissertation*. Greifswald: Emil Hartmann, 1912.

REGAN, MARIANN S. '*Amador* and *Chantador*. The lover and the poet in the *Cansos* of Bernart de Ventadorn', *PQ*, LIII (1974), 10–28.

REMY, PAUL. 'Les "Cours d'amour". Légende et réalité', *RUB*, VII (1954–55), 179–97.

RIBERA Y TARRAGÓ, JULIÁN. *La música de las Cantigas*. Madrid, 1922 (trans. and abridged by Eleanor Hague and Marion Leffinghall, *Music in Ancient Arabia and Spain*. Stanford University Press, 1929).

—. *La música andaluza medieval en las canciones de trovadores, troveros y minnesinger*. 3 vols. Madrid: Tip. de la Revista de Archivos, 1923.

—. *Disertaciones y opúsculos*. Introd. Miguel Asín Palacios. 2 vols. Madrid: Impr. de E. Maestre, 1928.

RICHARDSON, LULA MCDOWELL. *The Forerunners of Feminism in French Literature of the Renaissance from Christine de Pisan to Marie de Gournay* (Johns Hopkins Studies in Romance Literatures and Languages, 12). Baltimore, Md.: Johns Hopkins University Press; Paris: PUF, 1929.

RICKETTS, PETER T. 'The Hispanic tradition of the *Breviari d'amor* by Matfré Ermengaud of Béziers', in *Hispanic Studies in Honour of Joseph Manson*. Oxford: Dolphin, 1972, pp. 227–53.

RICOLFI, ALFONSO. *Studi sui 'Fedeli d'Amore'* (Biblioteca della Nuova Revista Storica, 11 and 14). 2 vols, Rome, 1933–40.

RIQUER, MARTÍN DE. 'La littérature provençale à la cour d'Alphonse II d'Aragon', *CCMe*, II (1959), 177–210.

—. *Los trovadores. Historia literaria y textos*. 3 vols, Barcelona: Planeta, 1975.

RIVERS, ELIAS L. 'Certain formal characteristics of the primitive love sonnet', *Sp*, XXXIII (1958), 42–55.

ROBERTSON, D. W., JR. 'The doctrine of charity in medieval literary gardens. A topical approach through symbolism and allegory', *Sp*, XXVI (1951), 24–49.

—. 'Amors de terra lonhdana', *SP*, XLIX (1952), 566–82.

—. 'The subject of the *De Amore* of Andreas Capellanus', *MP*, L (1952–53), 145–61.

—. 'Some medieval doctrines of love', in *A Preface to Chaucer. Studies in medieval perspectives*. Princeton University Press, 1962, pp. 391–503.

—. 'The concept of Courtly Love as an impediment to the understanding of medieval texts', in *The Meaning of Courtly Love*, ed. F. X. Newman. Albany, N.Y., 1968, pp. 1–18.

RODRIGUES LAPA, MANUEL. *Lições de literatura portuguesa. Época medieval.* Lisbon: Centro de Estudios Filológicos, 1934 (seventh edn., revised, Coimbra Editora, 1970).

ROLAND-MANUEL [Roland Alexis Manuel Lévy]. 'La musique et l'amour courtois', *TR*, XCVII (1956), 82–3.

ROLLAND D'ERCEVILLE, BARTHÉLEMY GABRIEL. *Recherches sur les prérogatives des dames chez les Gaulois, sur les cours d'amour.* . . . Paris: Nyon l'aîné, 1787.

ROMEO, LUIGI. 'A sociolinguistic view of medieval Romance erotic poetry', *ForIt*, VII–VIII (1973–74), 81–97.

RONCAGLIA, AURELIO. 'Di una tradizione pretrovatoresca in lingua volgare', *CN*, XI (1951), 213–49.

—. '*Trobar clus*. Discussione aperta', *CN*, XXIX (1969), 5–55.

ROSENBERG, M. V. *Eleanor of Aquitaine, Queen of the Troubadours and of the Courts of Love.* London: Hamish Hamilton, 1937.

ROSENTHAL, FRANZ. 'Literature', in *The Legacy of Islam*, ed. J. Schacht and C. E. Bosworth. Oxford: Clarendon, 1974, pp. 321–49.

ROSSETTI, GABRIELE P. G. *Disquisitions on the Antipapal Spirit which Produced the Reformation.* Trans. Miss C. Ward. 2 vols. London: Smith, Elder & Co., 1834 (Italian original, London, 1832).

—. *Il misterio dell'amor platonico del medio evo derivato da'misteri antichi.* 5 vols. London: R. & G. E. Taylor, 1940.

ROUGEMONT, DENIS DE. *L'Amour et l'Occident.* Paris: Plon, 1939. Trans. Montgomery Belgion, *Passion and Society.* London: Faber & Faber, 1940 (rev. edn., 1956).

—. 'Tableau du phénomène courtois', *TR*, XCVII (1956), 16–27.

—. *Les Mythes de l'amour.* Paris: Gallimard, 1961. Trans. R. Howard, *The Myths of Love.* London: Faber & Faber, 1964.

ROUSSELOT, PIERRE. *Pour l'histoire du problème de l'amour au Moyen Âge* (BGPTM, 6). Münster, 1908.

ROWBOTHAM, JOHN FREDERICK. *The Troubadours and Courts of Love* (Social England series). London: Swan Sonnenschein; New York: Macmillan, 1895.

RUGGERIO, MICHAEL J. *The Evolution of the Go-between in Spanish Literature through the Sixteenth Century* (UCPMP, 78). Berkeley and Los Angeles, 1966.

RUHE, DORIS. *Le Dieu d'Amours avec son paradis. Untersuchungen zur Mythenbildung um Amor in Spätantike und Mittelalter* (Beiträge zur romanische Philologie des Mittelalters, 6). Munich: Wilhelm Fink, 1974.

RUIZ DE CONDE, JUSTINA. *El amor y el matrimonio secreto en los libros de caballerías.* Madrid: Aguilar, 1948.

RUIZ MORALES, J. M. 'Relaciones culturales entre España y el mundo árabe', *Revista del Instituto Egipcio de Estudios Islámicos*, Madrid, 1959–60, 1–40.

RUSSELL, JEFFREY B. 'Courtly Love as religious dissent', *CHR*, LI (1965–66), 31–44.

RUTHERFORD, JOHN. *The Troubadours. Their loves and their lyrics; with remarks on their influence, social and literary.* London: Smith, Elder & Co., 1873.

RYMER, THOMAS. *A Short View of Tragedy. Its original excellency and corruption.* London: Richard Baldwin, 1693.

SAINTE-PALAYE, J. B. DE LA CURNE DE. *Histoire littéraire des troubadours, contenant leurs vies, les extraits de leurs pièces et plusieurs particularités sur les moeurs, les usages et l'histoire du douzième et du treizième siècles.* Ed. C. F. X. Millot. 3 vols. Paris: Durand neveu, 1774.

——. *Mémoires sur l'ancienne chevalerie.* Ed. Nodier. 2 vols. Paris: Girard, 1826 (trans. Mrs S. Dobson, London: J. Dodsley, 1784).

SALLEFRANQUE, C. 'Périples de l'amour en Orient et en Occident (Les origines arabes de l'amour courtois)', *CS*, special issue, *L'Islam et l'Occident*, Marseilles, 1947, 92–106.

SALTER, ELIZABETH. 'Courts and Courtly Love' and 'The mediaeval lyric', in *The Mediaeval World*, ed. D. Daiches and A. Thorlby. London: Aldus, 1973, pp. 407–84.

SALVERDA DE GRAVE, JEAN-JACQUES. 'Quelques observations sur les origines de la poésie des troubadours', *N*, III (1918), 247–52.

SÁNCHEZ-ALBORNOZ, CLAUDIO. 'El Islam de España y el Occidente', in *L'Occidente e l'Islam nell'alto medioevo* (Settimane di Studio del Centro Italiano di Studi sull'alto medioevo). Spoleto, 1965, I, pp. 149–308.

SANTANGELO, SALVATORE. *Le origini della lirica provenzaleggiante in Sicilia.* Catania: Gianotta, 1949.

SARMIENTO, MARTÍN. *Memorias para la historia de la poesía y poetas españoles.* Madrid: J. Ibarra, impresor de la cámera de S.M., 1775.

SARRASIN, JEAN FRANÇOIS. 'S'il faut qu'un jeune homme soit amoureux', in *Les Oeuvres de Monsieur Sarrasin.* Ed. G. Ménage. 2 vols. Paris: Augustin Courbé, 1656, I, pp. 137–257.

SAVILLE, JONATHAN. *The Medieval Erotic 'Alba'. Structure as meaning.* New York and London: Columbia University Press, 1972.

SCAGLIONE, ALDO D. *Nature and Love in the Late Middle Ages.* Berkeley: University of California Press, 1963.

SCARLATA, G. P. 'Dante et les "Fidèles d'amour"', *CEC*, VIII, 29 (1957), 142–9.

SCHACK, ADOLF FRIEDRICH VON. *Poesía y arte de los árabes en España y Sicilia.* Trans. Juan Valera. 3 vols. Madrid: Rivadeneyra, 1867–71 (German original, Berlin, 1865).

SCHELUDKO, DIMITRI. 'Beiträge zur Entstehungsgeschichte der altprovenzalischen Lyrik', *AR*, XI (1927), 273–312; XII (1928), 30–127; XV (1931), 132–206.

—. 'Ovid und die Trobadors', *ZRP*, LIV (1934), 128–74.

—. 'Über die Theorien der Liebe bei der Trobadors', *ZRP*, LX (1940), 191–234.

SCHLAUCH, MARGARET. *English Medieval Literature and its Social Foundations.* Warsaw: Państwowe Wydawnictwo Naukowe, 1956.

SCHLEGEL, AUGUST WILHELM VON. *Observations sur la langue et la littérature provençales.* Paris: Librairie Grecque–Latine–Allemande, 1818.

SCHLÖSSER, FELIX. *Andreas Capellanus. Seine Minnelehre und das christliche Weltbild des 12. Jahrhunderts* (AKML, 15). Bonn: H. Bouvier, 1960.

SCHLUMBOHM, CHRISTA. *Jocus und Amor. Liebesdiskussionem vom mittelalterlichen 'joc partit'.* Hamburg: Romanisches Seminar der Universität Hamburg, 1974.

SCHNEIDER, M. 'A propósito del influjo árabe en España, ensayo de etnografía musical', *AnMus*, I (1946), 31–41.

SCHOECK, R. J. 'Andreas Capellanus and St Bernard of Clairvaux. The twelve rules of love and the twelve steps of humility', *MLN*, LXVI (1951), 295–300.

SCHRÖDER, F. R. 'Die Tristansage und das persische Epos *Wīs und Rāmīn*', *GRM*, XLII (1961), 1–44.

SCHRÖTTER, WILIBALD. *Ovid und die Troubadours.* Halle: Niemeyer, 1908.

SCHUTZ, A. H. 'La tradición cortesana en dos coplas de Juan Ruiz', *NRFH*, VIII (1954), 63–71.

SEIGNOBOS, CHARLES. *The Rise of European Civilization.* London: Jonathan Cape, 1939.

SHAH, IDRIES. *The Sufis.* Introd. Robert Graves. London: Jonathan Cape, 1969.

SHAPIRO, NORMAN R. *The Comedy of Eros. Medieval French guides to the art of love.* Chicago: Illinois Press, 1971.

SHAW, J. E. *Guido Cavalcanti's Theory of Love. The 'Canzone d'amore' and other related problems* (University of Toronto Romance Series, 1). Toronto, 1949.

SHEDD, GORDON MICHAEL. 'Amor dethroned. The Ovidian tradition in courtly love poetry'. Unpubl. Ph.D. thesis. State University of Pennsylvania, 1965. (*DA*, LXV, 14785–A.)

SHIRT, DAVID J., 'Chrétien de Troyes and the cart', in W. Rothwell, *et al.* (eds.), *Studies . . . in Memory of Frederick Whitehead.* Manchester: MUP, 1973, pp. 279–301.

SHOTA RUSTAVELI. *The Knight in the Tiger's Skin.* Trans. M. S. Wardrop; rev. E. Orbelyani and S. Jordanishvili. Moscow: Co-operative Publishing Society of Foreign Workers in the USSR, 1938.

SICILIANO, ITALO. *François Villon et les thèmes poétiques du Moyen Âge.* Paris: A. Colin, 1934.

SILVERSTEIN, THEODORE. 'Andreas, Plato and the Arabs. Remarks on some recent accounts of Courtly Love', *MP*, XLVII (1949–50), 117–26.

—. 'Guenevere, or the uses of Courtly Love', in *The Meaning of Courtly Love*, ed. F. X. Newman. Albany, N.Y., 1968, pp. 77–90.

SINGER, IRVING. *The Nature of Love. Plato to Luther.* New York: Random House, 1966.

SINGER, SAMUEL. 'Arabische und europäische Poesie im Mittelalter', *Abhandlungen der Preussischen Akademie der Wissenschaften, Phil.-Hist. Klasse*, XIII (1918).

SINGLETON, CHARLES S. 'Dante. Within Courtly Love and beyond', in *The Meaning of Courtly Love*, ed. F. X. Newman. Albany, N.Y., 1968, pp. 43–54.

SISMONDI, J. C. L. SIMONDE DE. *Histoire de la littérature du Midi de l'Europe.* 4 vols. Paris and Strasbourg, 1813 (trans. Thomas Roscoe, *Historical View of the Literature of the South of Europe.* 2 vols. London: Henry Colburn, 1823).

SLAUGHTER, EUGENE. *Virtue according to Love in Chaucer.* New York: Bookman, 1957.

SMITH, JUSTIN H. *The Troubadours at Home. Their lives and personalities, their songs and their world.* 2 vols. New York and London: G. P. Putman's Sons, 1899.

SPANKE, HANS. 'La teoría árabe sobre el origen de la lírica románica a la luz de las últimas investigaciones', *AnMus*, I (1946), 5–18.

SPITZER, LEO. 'The Mozarabic lyric and Theodor Frings' theories', *CL*, IV (1952), 1–22.

—. *L'Amour lointain de Jaufré Rudel et le sens de la poésie des troubadours* (UNCSRLL, 5). Chapel Hill, N.C., 1944.

STAËL-HOLSTEIN, MADAME DE. *De l'Allemagne.* Paris: H. Nicolle, 1810 (repr. London, 1813).

—. *De la Littérature considérée dans ses rapports avec les institutions sociales.* 2 vols. Geneva: Droz, 1959 (first edn. 1812).

STEADMAN, JOHN M. '"Courtly Love" as a problem of style', in *Chaucer und seine Zeit. Symposion für Walter F. Schirmer.* Tübingen: Max Niemeyer Verlag, 1968, pp. 1–33.

STENDHAL [Marie Henri Beyle]. *De l'amour.* Introd. Étienne Rey. Paris: H. Champion, 1926 (first edn. 1853).

STERN, SAMUEL M. 'Les vers finaux en espagnol dans les *muwaššaḥ* hispano-hébraïques. Une contribution à l'histoire du *muswaššaḥ* et à l'étude du vieux dialecte espagnole', *And*, XIII (1948), 299–346.

—. 'Esistono dei rapporti letterari tra il mondo islamico e l'Europa occidentale nell'alto medioevo?' in *L'Occidente e l'Islam nell'alto medioevo.* Spoleto, 1965, pp. 639–66. (Trans. in *Hispano-Arabic Strophic Poetry.* Oxford: Clarendon, 1974.)

STEVENS, JOHN. *Music and Poetry in the Early Tudor Court.* London: Methuen, 1961.

—. *Medieval Romance. Themes and approaches.* London: Hutchinson, 1973.

STRONSKI, S. *La Poésie et la réalité au temps des troubadours. The Taylorian Lecture 1943.* Oxford: Clarendon, 1943.

SUSSKIND, NORMAN. 'Love and laughter in the *romans courtois*', FR, XXXVII (1963–64), 651–7.

SUTHERLAND, D. R. 'The language of the troubadours and the problem of origins', *FS*, X (1956), 199–215.

——. 'The love meditation in courtly literature', in *Studies in Medieval French Literature presented to Alfred Ewert in Honour of his Seventieth Birthday*. Oxford, Clarendon, 1961, pp. 165–93.

SYMONDS, JOHN ADDINGTON. *A Problem in Greek Ethics*. London, published privately, 1883.

TAYLOR, G. RATTRAY. *Sex in History*. London: Thames & Hudson, 1953.

TERÉS SÁDABA, ELÍAS. 'Préstamos poéticos en al-Andalus', *And*, XXI (1956), 415–19.

TERRASSE, HENRI. *Islam d'Espagne. Une rencontre de l'Orient et de l'Occident*. Paris: Plon, 1958.

TERRY, P. *Lays of Courtly Love in verse translation*. New York: Anchor Books, 1963.

THOMAS, ANTOINE. *Francesco da Barberino et la littérature provençale en Italie au Moyen Âge* (Bibliothèque des Écoles Françaises d'Athènes et de Rome, 35). Paris, 1883.

TILDEN, JILL HELEN. 'The moral and religious implications of early Italian courtly love poetry'. Unpubl. M.Litt. thesis. Cambridge University, 1969–70.

TOBIN, FRANK. '*Concupiscentia* and Courtly Love', *RoN*, XIV (1972–73), 387–93.

TONELLI, LUIGI. *L'amore nella poesia e nel pensiero del Rinascimiento*. Florence: G. C. Sansoni, 1933.

TOPSFIELD, L. T. 'Raimon de Miraval and the art of Courtly Love', *MLR*, LI (1956), 33–48.

——. 'Three levels of love in the poetry of the early troubadours, Guilhem IX, Marcabru and Jaufre Rudel', in *Mélanges Boutière*. Liège, 1971, pp. 571–87.

——. *Troubadours and Love*. Cambridge: CUP, 1975.

TORRACA, FRANCESCO. 'Federico secondo e la poesia provenzale', in *Studi su la lirica italiana del Duecento*. Bologna: Ditta N. Zanchielli, 1902, pp. 235–341.

UITTI, KARL D. 'Remarks on Old French narrative. Courtly Love and poetic form', *RPh*, XXVI (1972–73), 77–93.

UTLEY, FRANCIS LEE. *The Crooked Rib. An analytical index to the argument about women in English and Scots literature to the end of the year 1568* (Ohio State University Contributions in Languages and Literature, 10). Columbus, O., 1944.

——. 'Must we abandon the concept of Courtly Love?', *MH*, n.s., III (1972), 299–324.

VADET, JEAN-CLAUDE. *L'Esprit courtois en Orient dans les cinq premiers siècles de l'Hégire*. Paris: G. P. Maisonneuve & Larose, 1968.

VALENCY, MAURICE. *In Praise of Love. An introduction to the love poetry of the Renaissance*. New York: Macmillan, 1958.

VANCE, EUGÈNE. 'La Combat érotique chez Chrétien de Troyes. De la figure à la forme', *P*, III (1972), 544–71.

VAN DE VOORT, DONNELL. *Love and Marriage in the English Medieval Romance.* Nashville, Tenn.: Vanderbilt University Press, 1938.

VAN DER WERF, H. *The Chansons of the Troubadours and Trouvères. A study of their melodies and their relation to the poems.* Utrecht: Oosthock, 1972.

VELÁZQUEZ DE VELASCO, LUIS JOSÉ. *Orígenes de la poesía castellana.* Málaga: Martínez de Aguilar, 1754.

VINAVER, EUGÈNE. *À la recherche d'une poétique médiévale.* Paris: A.-J. Nizet, 1970.

VINAY, GUSTAVO. 'Il *De Amore* di Andrea Capellano nel quadro della letteratura amorosa e della rinascita del secolo XII', *SM*, n.s., XVII (1951), 203–76.

VINCENTI, ELEONORA. *Bibliografia antica dei trovatori* (Documenti di Filologia, 6). Milan and Naples: Riccardo Ricciardi, 1963.

VISCARDI, ANTONIO. 'Scoperta dei rapporti fra la tradizione letteraria latina e medio-latina e le nuove letterature volgari', in *Storia letteraria d'Italia. Le origini* (rev. edn.). Milan: Francesco Vallardi, 1973.

—. 'Le origini della letteratura cortese', *ZRP*, LXXVIII (1962), 269–91. (Mainly a review of Bezzola, *Les Origines.*)

VISSER, MARIE SOPHIE. *Der figuur van der vrouw in der troubadourslyriek. Eine studie van der hoofse liefde* [with summaries in English and French; doctoral dissertation submitted to Univ. of Leyden]. The Hague: Uitgeverij Excelsior, 1950.

VOSSLER, KARL. *Mediaeval Culture. An introduction to Dante and his times.* Trans. W. C. Lawton. 2 vols. London: Constable, 1929.

WAIS, K. 'Chevalerie et courtoisie en tant que créateurs de rapports sociaux dans la littérature du Moyen Âge', in *Actes du VIème Congrès de l'Association Internationale de Littérature Comparée.* Stuttgart: Erich Bieber, 1975, pp. 297–302.

WALSH, PATRICK GERARD. *Courtly Love in the 'Carmina Burana'* (University of Edinburgh Inaugural Lecture, 47). Edinburgh University Press, 1972.

WARREN, F. M. 'The Romance lyric from the standpoint of antecedent Latin documents', *PMLA*, XXVI (1911), 280–314.

WARTON, THOMAS. 'On the origin of Romantic fiction in Europe', prefix to *The History of English Poetry from the Close of the Eleventh to the Commencement of the Eighteenth Century.* 3 vols. London: J. Dodsley, 1775–81.

WASIF BUTRUS GHĀLI. *La Tradition chevaleresque des arabes.* Paris: Plon, 1919.

WATT, W. MONTGOMERY. *The Influence of Islam on Medieval Europe* (Islamic Surveys, 9). Edinburgh University Press, 1972.

WECHSSLER, EDUARD. *Das Kulturproblem des Minnesangs. Studien zur Vorgeschichte der Renaissance.* Halle: Max Niemeyer, 1909.

WEIGAND, HERMANN J. *Three Chapters on Courtly Love in Arthurian France and Germany* (UNCSGLL, 17). Chapel Hill, N.C., 1956.

WEST, CONSTANCE B. *Courtoisie in Anglo-Norman Literature* (MAeM, 3). Oxford: Basil Blackwell, 1938.

WETHERBEE, WINTHROP. *Platonism and Poetry in the Twelfth Century. The literary influence of the School of Chartres*. Princeton University Press, 1972.

WETTSTEIN, JACQUES. '*Mezura*'. *L'Idéal des troubadours: son essence et ses aspects*. Zurich: Impr. Leemann frères, 1945.

WHINNOM, KEITH. 'Hacia una interpretación y apreciación de las canciones del *Cancionero general* de 1511', *Fi*, XIII (1968–69), 361–81.

—. 'Introducción crítica', in *Obras completas de Diego de San Pedro*, II. Madrid: Clásicos Castalia, 1971.

WHITBOURN, CHRISTINE J. *The 'Arcipreste de Talavera' and the Literature of Love* (Occasional Papers in Modern Languages, 7). University of Hull, 1970.

WILCOX, JOHN. 'Defining Courtly Love', *Michigan Academy of Science, Arts and Letters*, XII (1930), 313–25.

WILHELM, JAMES J. *The Cruelest Month. Spring, nature and love in classical and medieval lyrics*. New Haven, Conn., and London: Yale University Press, 1965.

WIMSATT, JAMES. *Chaucer and the French Love Poets. The literary background of the Book of the Duchess* (UNCSCL, 43). Chapel Hill, N.C., 1968.

WIND, BARTINA. 'Ce jeu subtil, l'amour courtois', in *Mélanges Rita Lejeune*, Gembloux: J. Duculot, 1969, II, pp. 1257–61.

ZADDY, Z. P. '*Le Chevalier de la Charrete* and the *De amore* of Andreas Capellanus', in *Studies . . . in Memory of Frederick Whitehead*. Manchester, 1973, pp. 363–99.

ZORZI, DIEGO. *Valori religiosi nella litteratura provenzale: la spiritualità trinitaria* (Pubblicazioni dell'Università Cattolica del Sacro Cuore, n.s., 44). Milan, 1954.

ZUMTHOR, PAUL. 'Au berceau du lyrisme européen', *CS*, XL, No. 326 (1954), 3–29.

—. *Langue et techniques poétiques à l'époque romane (XIe-XIIIe siècles)*. Paris: Klincksieck, 1963.

—. *Essai de poétique médiévale*. Paris: Éditions du Seuil, 1972.

—. 'Du nouveau sur la poésie des troubadours et trouvères', *RR*, LXVI (1975), 85–92.

Index